FULFILLING THE 21ST CENTURY LAND-GRANT MISSION

FULFILLING THE 21ST CENTURY LAND-GRANT MISSION

Essays in Honor of The Ohio State University's Sesquicentennial Commemoration

EDITED BY STEPHEN M. GAVAZZI
AND DAVID J. STALEY

TRILLIUM, AN IMPRINT OF
THE OHIO STATE UNIVERSITY PRESS
COLUMBUS

Trillium, an imprint of The Ohio State University Press.

Library of Congress Cataloging-in-Publication Data
Names: Gavazzi, Stephen M., editor. | Staley, David J., 1963– editor.
Title: Fulfilling the 21st century land-grant mission : essays in honor of the Ohio State University's sesquicentennial commemoration / edited by Stephen M. Gavazzi, David J. Staley.
Other titles: Fulfilling the twenty-first century land-grant mission
Description: Columbus : Trillium, an imprint of The Ohio State University Press, 2020. | Includes bibliographical references. | Summary: "A collection of essays by current and former leaders of The Ohio State University about the contributions that OSU continues to make as part of its century land-grant mission"—Provided by publisher.
Identifiers: LCCN 2020003834 | ISBN 9780814214442 (cloth) | ISBN 9780814278130 (ebook)
Subjects: LCSH: Ohio State University. | Education, Higher—Aims and objectives—Ohio.
Classification: LCC LD4228 .F85 2020 | DDC 378.771/57—dc23
LC record available at https://lccn.loc.gov/2020003834

Cover design by Laurence J. Nozik
Text design by Juliet Williams
Type set in Adobe Garamond Pro

♾ The paper used in this publication meets the minimum requirements of the American National Standard for Information Sciences—Permanence of Paper for Printed Library Materials. ANSI Z39.48-1992.

Contents

Manifestation of the Mission

The Student Experience

Insider Observations

Outsider Observations

Conclusion

Illustrations

Editorial Preamble

1

The Prominence and Preeminence of The Ohio State University

Stephen M. Gavazzi and David J. Staley

This preamble sets the stage for all the essays contained in this volume. As this volume's coeditors, we begin by asserting the prominence and preeminence of The Ohio State University, defined in terms of the highly visible activities of faculty, staff, and students that place this institution at the very forefront of higher education today. The instructions that were given to authors are detailed, with specific attention paid to three main issues: the difference between A and A+, the context of the land-grant mission, and the need to attend to innovation.

Our introduction to this collection of essays begins with a brief historical note about how the two of us came together to help guide and shape this book. In 2017, each of us was writing a book on higher education, two scholarly efforts that we will mention in a bit more detail below (as well as in our own essay contributions). We don't quite remember how we found each other that year, but we had enjoyed meeting for lunch on occasion to discuss the topics of our respective books. The next year, we were thrilled to discover that both of our books were going to published by Johns Hopkins University Press. It made us kindred spirits, of a fashion.

Serendipitously, while putting the finishing touches on these books in 2018, we both were asked to provide some different kinds of assistance associated with Ohio State's upcoming sesquicentennial celebration in 2020. Gavazzi was asked to be on the planning committees of three interrelated events that together would highlight Ohio State's important contributions to university teaching, research, and engagement efforts. Staley was tapped to teach a massive open online course (MOOC) detailing the history and future of The Ohio State University that would be available to the public at large. As longtime faculty members who recognized the importance of faculty involvement in the managerial side of university life, we both were thrilled to involve ourselves in this sort of service.

At the same time, we soon began to wonder if there might be some sort of scholarship that could be produced for this celebratory event as well. Given the fact that we both were completing our present manuscripts, our thoughts quickly turned to the possibility of writing (or in this case, coediting and contributing to) another book on higher education. This time, however, we wanted to center attention on all the remarkable things that the people associated with our university were doing to make this institution of higher learning such a special place. And to do this, we decided to create a platform that would serve to highlight the prominence and preeminence of work done by Ohio State's faculty, staff, students, and stakeholders.

Prominence and Preeminence

Let us briefly define our terms here. By *prominence,* we assert that there are people and activities that create the conditions where Ohio State noticeably stands apart from other universities. Simply put, our presence in higher education circles is particularly visible. And by *preeminence,* we mean to say that the unique contributions of these people and their activities have placed The Ohio State University at the very forefront of institutions of higher learning. This combination of terms—*prominence* and *preeminence*—was the framework we wished to provide to our colleagues as we began to assemble the outline of this edited book. So, we asked them to respond directly to our primary objective: Help us to tell the story of how our university demonstrates critical leadership in observable and significant ways on an everyday basis.

We were confident that we were not alone in the belief that Ohio State was both a prominent and preeminent institution of higher learning. In fact, we needed to look no farther than the words of our university's president, Michael V. Drake, who has his own special way of communicating this line of thinking in his public speaking engagements. To President Drake, it is all about the difference between A and A+ activities. Take as but one example what he says about this sort of comparison in his 2014 university address:

> As you know, our world is more competitive than it has ever been. We compete for the very best students, the very best faculty, and the very best jobs. When I talk to our philanthropic community, I focus on their role in helping us move in that space between A and A+. One of my mentors, Professor Lloyd H. Smith, once said to me with a hand on my shoulder, "The difference between A and A+ is huge." And he would know; he's truly an A+. The difference between A and A+ is the difference between doing a good job and being your best self. That's why at a modern land-grant university, we must do our very best to compete on a global scale and have meaningful impact in society—we must be our best selves.

In this light, we wished to challenge our contributing authors to think about the difference between A and A+ when it came to the activities they were writing about in their essays. We also seized upon Dr. Drake's use of the term *modern land-grant university* to provide some further food for thought to the essayists. This afforded us the opportunity to pose two additional questions for consideration: (1) What does it mean to be a "land-grant" university in the twenty-first century? and (2) How does the idea of being "modern" shape our understanding of how our university must innovate to remain relevant?

The Context of the Land-Grant Mission

Let us pick up on the circumstance that we are a land-grant university. The term *land-grant* refers to the fact that in 1862, through what was known as the Morrill Act, the US Congress *granted* 30,000 acres of federally owned *land* to each state in the union for use in financially supporting the development of the US's first public universities. No longer was a college degree only to be within the reach of those individuals who were wealthy or otherwise socially connected enough to be admitted to a private college. The land-grant universities were designed to be the "people's universities," thus allowing the offspring of working-class families to gain access to an affordable college degree. Subsequent governmental actions—including the Morrill Act of 1890—eventually created at least one land-grant institution in every state in the US and in each of the US territories, including the seventeen additional land-grant institutions known now as historically black colleges and universities (HBCUs) that were specifically designed to educate African American students as part of the "separate but equal" doctrine of the times. At present, there are 110 institutions of higher learning that have land-grant status.

Two additional congressional acts helped define the comprehensive mission of the land-grant university: the Hatch Act of 1887 and the Smith-Lever Act of 1914. The Hatch Act designated federal funds for the development of experiment stations that were to be attached to each land-grant institution. Although initially focused on agricultural issues, over time the expansion of empirical activities into other disciplinary fields contributed directly to the elevation of research as a primary objective of the modern land-grant university. In turn, the Smith-Lever Act established what is known today as the Cooperative Extension Services system. This federal legislation created the wherewithal for land-grant institutions to take important findings from the research experiment stations and apply them directly to the benefit of farms, fields, family homes, and other community assets.

Taken together, this meant that our essays needed to highlight the fact that Ohio State has a tripartite mission of teaching, research, and engagement, which elements, in combination, are supposed to directly meet the most pressing needs of our communities. But what exactly does that mission look like in 2020 and beyond? That was the exact line of questioning raised by the book Gavazzi (along with West Virginia University president E. Gordon Gee) had just finished writing on land-grant universities. One specific quote from the beginning of that book seemed especially germane here:

> We are passionate—nay, zealous—about public higher education. And we are radical adherents to the idea that land-grant universities—based as they are on the ideals put forward by Senator Justin Morrill, President Abraham Lincoln, and the other social and political giants of their time—continue to set the bar for performance excellence in the realm of public higher education. We are, you might say, fiercely land-grant in our orientation. (Gavazzi and Gee 2018, 1)

Hence, we were determined to encourage our essayists to become more "land-grant fierce" in their writing as they pondered how our teaching, research, and engagement activities served the direct needs of various stakeholders from the communities our university was designed to provide. In so doing, we believed that these authors would produce essays that would center attention on precisely those issues that placed Ohio State in the forefront of defining the twenty-first century mission of the land-grant university.

Innovation in Higher Education

This provides the perfect segue to President Drake's more specific use of the term *modern* in his depiction of Ohio State's activities as a land-grant institution. Here, we believed that we needed our authors to think about not only where we were as a university in 2020 but also where we were headed in terms of our future as an institution of higher learning. Again, we were fortunate to have expertise immediately on hand to further define this sort of futuristic speculation. Staley's latest book was written as a thought experiment that considered ten different models for how we might organize the mission and purpose of the university of the future as responses to the trends and grand challenges facing higher education today (Staley 2019).

This writing centers important attention on innovation in higher education, with references made to visionaries such as John Andrew Rice, the founder of Black Mountain College; Wilhelm von Humboldt, founder of the University of Berlin and of the idea of the research university; and, of course, Justin Morrill, the chief architect of the land-grant university. A historical context for innovation in higher education is established, thus challenging the canard—often stated by critics of higher education—that US universities are lumbering dinosaurs, unable or unwilling to change and innovate. We believe that history suggests otherwise. The land-grant university in particular is an excellent example of an innovation, a response to a particular set of nineteenth-century grand challenges: industrialization, an emerging national economy, a need for a technically trained workforce, and, especially, the need for greater access to and affordability of higher learning.

It is axiomatic to state that higher education today also faces a variety of grand challenges. Jon McGee, author of *Breakpoint: The Changing Marketplace for Higher Education,* has identified five such challenges: accessibility, affordability, accountability, sustainability, and differentiation. There are others we could add to this list, including increasing managerialism, widespread "adjunctification" of university faculty, declining support for public higher education, and indeed greater skepticism about the value of higher education itself. Therefore, we wished to have our essayists ponder such questions as: How will the twenty-first century land-grant university respond to these grand challenges? And how has Ohio State more specifically responded through innovative ideas and practices?

The Contents of This Book

In addition to the challenges provided to the authors as described above—defining the difference between an A and A+, attending to the context of the land-grant mission, and pondering the innovation that is required to remain relevant as institutions of higher learning—we also specified two basic parameters surrounding the writing of these essays. First, we implored authors to refrain from using academic jargon so that the essays were reader-friendly to the widest possible audience. Second, we asked contributors to keep their remarks to no more than 3,000 words so that the essays would offer coherent yet brief glimpses inside the many and varied activities occurring throughout the university.

Taken together, we are proud to present this collection of essays as a body of accumulated evidence regarding the prominence and preeminence of The Ohio State University. As editors, we took pains to organize the contributions into five meaningful sections of readings: setting the stage, the tripartite mission, manifestation of the mission, the student experience, and insider and outsider observations. That said, our sincere hope is that readers will be able to read these essays in any order they wish. Peruse the table of contents, select whatever topics seem most interesting at the time, and enjoy!

References

Drake, Michael V. 2014. "The Heart of Innovation: Our 21st-Century Land-Grant Mission." University address, October 30, 2014. https://president.osu.edu/21st-century-land-grant-mission.

Gavazzi, Stephen M., and E. Gordon Gee. 2018. *Land-Grant Universities for the Future: Higher Education for the Common Good.* Baltimore: Johns Hopkins University Press.

McGee, Jon. 2015. *Breakpoint: The Changing Marketplace for Higher Education,* Baltimore: Johns Hopkins University Press.

Staley, David J. 2019. *Alternative Universities: Speculative Design for Innovation in Higher Education.* Baltimore: Johns Hopkins University Press.

Setting the Stage

2

Defining the Modern Land-Grant University

Michael V. Drake

For those of us who have served in higher education for many years, the inspiration behind the Morrill Act of 1862 speaks to our highest calling and why we are here. When The Ohio State University was founded in 1870 as the Ohio Agricultural and Mechanical College, our land-grant purpose was to bring a college education within the reach of all people, including the sons and daughters of farmers and the working class—that is, "the sons of toil" (Parker 1924). As early board member Joseph Sullivant described Ohio State's land-grant purpose, depicted on its original university seal in 1871: "Above and crowning all, we place the Lamp of Knowledge, by which we intend to signify that the [Ohio] Agricultural and Mechanical College is a light on a high place; to illuminate all that comes within its sphere (Ohio State Board Proceedings 1871)."

Today, despite time and change across our university and around the world, the central purpose of our land-grant mission remains clear and relevant: We are here to illuminate a pathway to learning and discovery that changes lives and uplifts society. Even so, the ways in which we teach, conduct research, live, and enjoy life are always evolving. Our historic university must evolve continuously, planning not just for the foreseeable future, but for those things that will define our work twenty, thirty, and even fifty years from now. As we celebrate Ohio State's sesquicentennial in

2020, we must reenvision our land-grant role in the modern light of the twenty-first century.

To chart a course forward, we must understand our origins in the summer of 1862, during the presidency of Abraham Lincoln. The Civil War had dragged into its second year and hopes for a quick ending and mending of the frayed union had been dashed. The Battle of Shiloh had happened only a few months previously, a calamity whose 23,000 casualties were a grim harbinger of what was to come. This was more than a moral and military crisis—Lincoln and the Union faced a genuine existential crisis as the country's fate hung in the balance.

During the worst of the war, we nevertheless saw major advancements: The Morrill Act of 1862, the National Academy of Sciences, and the Emancipation Proclamation became reality. Despite the incredible pressures of the day, Lincoln and other leaders resolved to create a brighter future. These three extraordinary policies were brought into being over a six-month period, creating a pathway to help move our country forward. The ramifications of these acts—on higher education, in the science community, on human rights—are routinely prominent in national and international affairs, even today. It is fitting that on Ohio State's Columbus campus, the two tallest towers—the ones that rise above Ohio Stadium and the Olentangy River—are named Morrill and Lincoln Towers.

In the beginning, the knowledge transmitted in our classrooms was primarily agricultural and mechanical—agriculture being the centerpiece of the nineteenth-century economy and mechanical sciences associated with the important railroads and technology of the time. The Morrill Act was later expanded to support the more diversified economies of communities and included more modern disciplines, such as math, sciences, and the arts. The transfer of knowledge also expanded beyond the universities to touch the regions around the state through the Hatch and Smith-Lever Acts. Together, this legislation created a constellation of higher education institutions centered on educating the sons and daughters of the region for the purpose of uplifting society.

As noble as these measures were, they reflected the times in which they were created. The first Morrill Act was limited to states that were *not* in rebellion against the Union. It took more than two decades to bring the former Confederate states under the land-grant umbrella through the second Morrill Act in 1890. Within "Morrill II," there is language stating that "no money shall be paid for the support and maintenance of a college where a distinction of race or color is made in the admission of students." However, in the next breath, it says, "But the establishment and maintenance of such colleges separately for white and colored students shall be held to be in compliance with the provisions of this act." Essentially, the Morrill Act of 1890 worked to institutionalize segregation even before *Plessy v. Ferguson,* in which the Supreme Court codified the "separate but equal" doctrine of Jim Crow. As a result, the second Morrill Act sets up a dual system in several states, which is the reason that there are seventy-two land-grant universities.

The nation's land-grant institutions were founded upon profound public ideals; foremost among them was to extend higher education to everyone, regardless of social standing. As a starting point for an institution, this value is among our most noble, and it must remain central to our work. Our universities—of all places—must welcome and celebrate all individuals. In line with this ideal, Ohio State is committed to providing broad access to people from a variety of walks of life and points of view. We do all we can to enable more and more individuals from diverse backgrounds to cross the bridge of higher education to the middle class.

We often can look in our own families to somebody who crossed that bridge from poverty to the middle class, and that crossing usually involved getting an education. Through a college education, many people have moved out of poverty and into prosperity. The land-grant legacy is critical to so many young people and to the future of Ohio and our country. Because the legacy of the Morrill Act is intertwined with the idea of broad access, it clearly speaks to the issue of affordability. The challenge for Ohio State and for higher education overall is to provide access to an outstanding, affordable education during a time of funding constraints and rising costs.

As educational costs continue to escalate, many communities and families are seriously affected. Far too many talented high school students do not attend college because of financial hurdles. Yet the value of a college degree has never been more clear. Research shows that college graduates earn on average roughly $1 million more than their high school counterparts over the course of their careers (Carnevale, Cheah, and Hanson 2015). College graduates are more likely to be employed than those without degrees. Studies also indicate that people with college degrees have higher levels of happiness and engagement, better health, and longer lives. If living a longer, healthier, and happier life is a good thing, then, yes, college is worth the investment.

Balancing affordability and excellence is complicated but critical. Affordability is not simply about tuition. It involves decreasing time to graduation, identifying ways to help more students succeed, increasing scholarships and aid, and being ever more effective and efficient in our operations. Since 2015, Ohio State's expanded programs focused on access and affordability have committed an additional $200 million to students and families from Ohio. One such initiative is our Land-Grant Opportunity Scholarship, which covers the full cost of attendance for two students who demonstrate academic merit and financial need from each of Ohio's eighty-eight counties.

Over the past several years, our university also has had a significant impact in leading national coalitions in higher education—particularly in increasing access to a college degree for all students. Ohio State is a founding member of the American Talent Initiative, a collaboration with Bloomberg Philanthropies to enroll an additional 50,000 low- and moderate-income students at top colleges and universities by 2025. Ohio State is also a founding member of the University Innovation Alliance, a partnership of eleven public research institutions working to increase the number and diversity of college graduates.

Once students arrive on our campuses, we are committed to providing them with the best possible curricular and extracurricular experiences. We know that students do better with great teaching. Studies indicate this is especially true with students who are more vulnerable, such as those who are the first in their families to attend college. As we increase the quality of our teaching—and the innovative ways we provide it to our students—more Buckeyes should succeed in the classroom and graduate on time.

To modernize our teaching, the university recently completed a significant overhaul of its undergraduate general education requirements—the first of its kind in three decades. Our new approach will include a focus on citizenship, with sustainability as a primary pillar. We embarked on an exciting collaboration with Apple to incorporate more learning technologies into classrooms and to provide app development and coding opportunities to the university community. To respond to emerging trends in the innovative job market, we have created new multidisciplinary majors.

Of course, one of the most important things we do is to prepare students for the innovative jobs of the future. Of the eighty-four in-demand jobs requiring a bachelor's degree identified by the state of Ohio, our spring 2019 graduates accepted employment in eighty-two (97.6 percent) of those areas. Ohio State works with countless businesses, organizations, and government partners to further research and create career opportunities for our students and the community. Along with access to education, our founding land-grant mission is also about creating and extending new knowledge throughout society. Our collaboration with the people and communities we serve sets us apart—allowing us to transform knowledge into progress and prosperity by working alongside those who will benefit the most.

As it turned out, the noble US experiment of the land-grant universities was extraordinarily successful, and by the middle of the twentieth century, the US had become the world leader in the exalted field of higher education. Our public universities became tireless research engines for the state and the nation, expanding the boundaries of discovery from the atom to the stars. After the Second World War, the research mission of our public land-grant universities became as prominent as our educational charge. Other countries also had a chance to see the impact of our institutions on the US's position in the world—economically and militarily. It became apparent in the 1960s, '70s, and '80s, particularly among developing countries that had been decimated in World War II, that investing in science, technology, engineering, and math education drove economic development decades into the future.

Our universities are, in many ways, the backbone of our democracy, the backbone of our economy, and the backbone of our culture. For our country to stay ahead of the innovation curve, we have to look at what worked for the last 150 years and continue to innovate and invest in research and discovery. In addition to preparing tomorrow's teachers, scientists, artists, and social workers—many of whom will graduate and live and work in Ohio—our universities are sharing knowledge around the world; building partnerships in manufacturing, technology, and business; and uplifting communities in myriad ways. As Ohio's land-grant university, we are committed to all corners and regions of the state. Ohio State has six campuses around Ohio—in Columbus, Lima, Mansfield, Marion, Newark, and Wooster—and we have extension offices in all eighty-eight counties to share the scholarship of our research.

Every day, scholars and scientists at Ohio State are hard at work partnering with local and global communities to combat disease, enhance our culture, and make important contributions to engineering, health care, and other disciplines. We are committed to making measurable progress on the most pressing issues of our time, both locally and globally, including food security, water quality, infant mortality, and opioid addiction. An Ohio State scientist recently received the 2019 Japan Prize, one of the most prestigious worldwide awards in science and technology, for his research on sustainable soil management. Considering there are 600 million farms of varying sizes around the world, this type of research to improve global food security and mitigate climate change will have an enduring impact and improve the future prospects of humankind. We recently announced that Ohio State was selected as the lead institution for a $65.9 million federal research grant to significantly reduce opioid deaths in nineteen Ohio counties. We will lead a consortium of universities and community organizations in alignment with RecoveryOhio, the statewide effort to address substance abuse prevention, treatment, and recovery.

Broadly, our medical enterprise continues to drive breakthrough health care solutions to improve people's lives. The demand in our community for the exceptional care and service provided by the medical center is surging—and we are looking to meet that challenge for individuals and families throughout our city, state, and region. It really is a distillation of our larger land-grant mission—so we are proud that our excellence is serving so many throughout our communities. Building on this excellence, and guided by our mission and values, the university launched a new strategic plan in 2017 to become a more forward-looking land-grant university. We will continue to do the great things that have brought us to this point, but we must also take the next steps in our journey to grow our impact and continue elevating people and communities across Ohio and around the world.

We unveiled a long-term physical plan to create the campus of the future. Over the coming decades, we plan to create an innovation district where scientists, entrepreneurs, small business owners, and industry leaders converge to advance technology and innovation. One project is the Energy Advancement and Innovation Center, part of a tech commercialization partnership to manage our energy systems and reduce our energy consumption by 25 percent over the next decade. This partnership marks the single largest-ever investment in our academic mission—just one example of how we are thinking outside the box to innovate and generate revenue.

Historically, our higher education institutions have played an important role in creating the knowledge and scientific ideas that have kept our country at the forefront of discovery and ingenuity. At our core, that is what we do and how we make a difference. While universities and human society continue to change and evolve, we must continue to define and refine our land-grant mission for a modern world.

As land-grant universities, we are on this noble quest together, a quest founded on the principle that education transforms lives. We have an obligation to continue to steer a path forward as we create an environment that inspires discovery and knowledge, values and celebrates diverse opinions, and is welcoming to all—now and for generations to follow. Together, we will ensure that the Lamp of Knowledge shines brightly, illuminating a path to the American Dream for all who wish to pursue it.

References

Carnevale, Anthony P., Ban Cheah, and Andrew R. Hanson. 2015. "*The Economic Value of College Majors.*" https://cew.georgetown.edu/wp-content/uploads/Exec-Summary-web-B.pdf.

Morrill Act of 1862, 37th Congress, 2nd session, 2 July 1862, chap. 130.

Parker, William Belmont. 1924. *The Life and Public Services of Justin Smith Morrill.* New York City: Houghton-Mifflin.

Record of Proceedings of the Board of Trustees of the Ohio Agricultural and Mechanical College and The Ohio State University. 1871.

3

Prima Inter Pares

Ohio State's Position as the First among Equals within the US Public and Land-Grant University System

STEPHEN M. GAVAZZI

Primus inter pares is a Latin phrase that translates best as "first among equals." This expression classically has been used as an honorary title for those individuals who officially are the equal of other members of a group, and yet are accorded additional stature or respect in some unofficial capacity. Perhaps most often employed in government circles, this notion has been used to describe such positions as the chief justice of the US Supreme Court and the chair of the Federal Reserve, for example.

In this essay, I contend that The Ohio State University is the first among equals in the US public and land-grant system of higher education. In large part, I make this claim as part of an interpretation of data generated from recent interviews I conducted with university presidents and chancellors across the nation. At the beginning of this essay, I will describe the original research project containing these interviews and some of the main findings that already have been presented in published literature. Next, I will make the case for the *prima inter pares* position of The Ohio State University, based in part on the further exploration of the qualitative data stemming from the interviews of these senior academic leaders. Finally, I will conclude with some thoughts about the significant responsibilities that accompany such a prominent status among land-grant universities.

A small note about terminology before proceeding. The term *primus* technically connotes a male figure in the Latin language. My preference, however, is to think of universities in more feminine terms. After all, the phrase *alma mater* translates almost verbatim as "nourishing mother." Hence, I will use the term *prima inter pares* instead of *primus inter pares* throughout this essay.

The Land-Grant University Project

In 2018, I published—along with former Ohio State president and current West Virginia University president E. Gordon Gee—a book entitled *Land-Grant Universities for the Future: Higher Education for the Public Good.* This book was based largely on a set of interviews that I conducted with twenty-seven presidents and chancellors of land-grant institutions across the US. The project itself was structured around a SWOT analysis—that is, an examination of the strengths (S), weaknesses (W), opportunities (O), and threats (T) facing these institutions of higher learning, especially in terms of meeting the needs of the communities these universities were designed to serve.

While each of the senior leaders who participated in these interviews shared some very idiosyncratic viewpoints with me about the potencies and challenges confronting land-grant institutions at this moment in our country's history, certain common topics and conversational threads emerged as well. President Gee and I presented seven specific themes we had derived from the interview data in our *Land-Grant Universities for the Future* book as a series of dialectical statements that we thought best illustrated some of the dynamic tensions we witnessed inside the comments made by the presidents and chancellors:

1. Concerns about funding declines from state government versus the need to create more efficient business practices within the university
2. Focusing on research prowess versus the promotion of teaching and service excellence
3. Using science to generate knowledge for knowledge's sake versus a more applied focus
4. The focus on national rankings versus an emphasis on access and affordability
5. Meeting the needs of rural communities versus the needs of a more urbanized US
6. Global reach versus the closer-to-home impact of university activities
7. The overall benefits of higher education versus the devaluation of a college diploma

In our book, President Gee and I asserted that it was possible to address both sides of each dialectical statement. Taking the first theme as an example, we stated that a university could deal directly with issues surrounding funding declines from the state *and* simultaneously tackle the challenges associated with reducing administrative costs within the university. Keeping tuition costs at the lowest level possible would be keeping true to the original mission assigned to land-grant universities, we argued, because that mission demanded a heavy emphasis on access to an affordable education (forming an immediate connection to the fourth theme noted above and discussed below).

President Gee and I expressed similar opinions about the remaining thematic statements. We contended that outstanding teaching and meritorious service to various community stakeholders should be at least as important as research excellence at a land-grant university, for instance. Likewise, while both basic research (knowledge for knowledge's sake) and applied research efforts were to be valued, we argued that adherence to the land-grant mission would tilt the scales decidedly toward those empirical activities that could display immediate and direct value to the people of the state who were paying for those pursuits.

Access to higher education was combined with affordability in the fourth theme we presented, a place where we provided a cautionary note about the pursuit of national rankings at the expense of not allowing fully prepared and yet non-elite (and often less well-resourced) individuals to enroll as incoming students. After all, land-grant universities originally were designed to educate the sons (and eventually daughters) of those working-class parents whose children heretofore had not been able to gain access to a college diploma because of its exorbitant cost.

Our *Land-Grant Universities for the Future* book also paid a great deal of attention to meeting the needs—and representing the values—of both rural and urban communities. Thinking about some of the more disconcerting political divides facing our country today, we argued that land-grant universities could not afford to be viewed as slanted toward either side of the rural-urban continuum (nor, we asserted in related fashion, should they be viewed as "liberal" or "conservative" in their orientation). In turn, our discussion of the sixth theme generated from our analysis of the interview data could be summed up through the adage "think globally, act locally." Institutions of higher learning may well have international aspirations and responsibilities, we noted, yet the citizens of the state whose tax dollars provide funding for land-grant universities deserve to understand how those resources are making an immediate difference in their own lives.

Last but certainly not least, we asserted that the theme highlighting the dynamic tension between the benefits of higher education versus the devaluation of a college diploma was resolved best through the work we described in the first six themes. That is, we stated unequivocally that those land-grant universities that are more affordable, that remain accessible to all qualified state residents, that equally value excellence in teaching, research, and service, that display ample evidence of products and services of immediate benefit to the state's citizens and businesses, and that objectively serve and personify the values of their rural and urban peoples will be thought of as the richest and therefore most valued sector of our economy.

First among Equals

So, what does all of this tell us about the place of The Ohio State University among its land-grant university peers? Readers who have gotten this far through the essay now know a lot more about what university presidents *think* about land-grant institutions in general, but what does this say about Ohio State more specifically, especially regarding the idea that it holds sway as a first among equals? Here is where we need to further explore additional information generated from the interviews I conducted with the land-grant presidents and chancellors.

It is important to note from the outset that I had no idea my affiliation with The Ohio State University would matter in the least bit to these university presidents and chancellors. That is, until I conducted my first interview. In reply to a question I posed about the present strengths of land-grant universities, the university president I was speaking to had used an example from his own university—in this case, an emerging economic development initiative that was being jointly run by the campus and the local chamber of commerce. After a brief pause, he then quipped, "But we aren't Ohio State." I wasn't at all sure what to make of that statement, so I simply proceeded to ask the next question in the research protocol. And so, a somewhat awkward moment passed.

The same thing happened in my next interview, however. Again, the university president offered up an example from her own institution in answer to the strengths question I had posed; in this instance, the president pointed to a long-standing partnership surrounding an urban-based agriculture program her university had initiated. In a similar fashion to the first president I had interviewed, she ended her reply by saying, "But of course, we aren't Ohio State." I was intrigued this time, and so I asked her what she meant by that statement. Her response was illuminating. She pointed out that her university was situated in a rather remote rural location of her state, whereas the Columbus campus of Ohio State was located within a major metropolitan area. Therefore, she said, trying to make urban connections had to be so much easier for Ohio State faculty, staff, and students.

And, of course, this is true. Whereas other land-grant university personnel must deal with travel and other long-distance logistics, Ohio State faculty, staff, and students simply need to walk outside their offices. Columbus, Ohio, is the fourteenth largest city in the US, and it does give Ohio State a distinct location advantage from the standpoint of involvement in urban-based activities. In fact, there is only one other land-grant institution that is set in an urban area: the University of Minnesota in Minneapolis. Yet as the forty-sixth largest city, Minneapolis is approximately half the size of Columbus.

More statements from land-grant university presidents and chancellors made to me in these interviews revealed other distinct advantages enjoyed by The Ohio State University. For example, one president was lamenting the fact that his university did not have a medical school. While this created the opportunity for a unique collaboration between that institution's school of public health and its Cooperative Extension Services, it was not viewed as having quite the same distinction as a hospital system at the level of The Ohio State University Wexner Medical Center. Others spoke longingly about having an athletics program as successful as Ohio State's team sports. For all the occasional troubles yielded by compliance with NCAA regulations, they noted, the vast amount of national exposure created by Ohio State's top-ranked teams and athletes was publicity that was invaluable. Being a regular champion in a variety of sports contained within the Big 10 athletics conference, as well as fielding teams that annually compete for national championships among other Power 5 athletic conferences, raises the profile of Ohio State in inestimable ways.

One final advantage identified through the interviews I conducted that bears notation here is the sheer size of Ohio State. A few of the presidents and chancellors spoke longingly about the large scope and wide reach of Ohio State's teaching, research, and outreach and engagement activities due to its employment of over 6,000 faculty members and 30,000 administrative employees. Others were enamored by the large numbers of undergraduate (52,500) and graduate and professional students (14,000) who were living and studying on all six of Ohio State's campuses. And at least one senior leader mentioned the envy she felt about Ohio State having over 500,000 living alumni. Size really does matter, it would seem, especially regarding the overall impact of the land-grant mission and its related activities of teaching, research, and engagement.

With Great Stature Comes Great Responsibilities

The interview data lead me to conclude that there is no other land-grant institution quite like The Ohio State University. Strikingly, its vision statement captures this uniqueness well: "The Ohio State University is the model 21st-century public, land-grant, research, urban, community engaged institution." As I have documented in this brief essay, the viewpoints of other senior administrators across the nation speak to the unique combination of its urban location, medical center complex, involvement in a Power 5 athletics conference, and great size, among other distinct advantages enjoyed by the faculty, staff, and students of Ohio State. Taken together, I believe these remarks underscore the *prima inter pares* status of The Ohio State University among its peer universities.

With this great stature comes great responsibilities, however. Just as current chief justice John Roberts provides leadership for his US Supreme Court colleagues, and just as the present chair of the Federal Reserve, Jerome Powell, serves as the active executive officer of the Board of Governors, so too must Ohio State provide guidance and direction to its sister land-grant institutions and other aspirational peers. At the personal level, Ohio State's fifteenth and current president, Michael V. Drake, MD, certainly has been doing his part since taking the helm of this extraordinary university. From the time he assumed the presidency in 2014, Dr. Drake has provided his service as chair of the Association of American Universities, chair-elect of the Association of Public and Land-grant Universities, and vice-chair of the Big Ten Conference, to name but a few of the many leadership positions he has taken on during his tenure as president.

More significant than those individual contributions, however, are the numerous actions that have been taken as the result of the *Time and Change* strategic plan launched by President Drake and The Ohio State

University's board of trustees in 2017. Critically, many of these activities speak directly to the themes reported in the *Land-Grant Universities for the Future* book that were discussed at the beginning of this essay. Two examples shall suffice here. First, Dr. Drake initially directed the university to identify $400 million in operational efficiencies to lower costs and improve value for students and families. This speaks directly to the theme of concerns about funding declines versus the need to create efficiencies; in fact, over $1.5 billion has been identified and redirected to date. Second, the President's Affordability Grant Program has committed more than $100 million in additional needs-based aid to middle-income and lower-income students since 2015, while the Buckeye Opportunity Program covers the cost of tuition and fees for over 4,000 students on all six of Ohio State's campuses. These latter two actions straightforwardly address the need to emphasize access and affordability and, because these programs affect students from across the entire state, also directly impact the theme of meeting the needs of urban *and* rural communities.

While Dr. Drake is an exceptional leader, however, and although he spearheads a very capable senior administrative team dedicated to the fulfillment of his executive vision, the workhorses of The Ohio State University are its faculty and staff members. In consequence, the prominence and preeminence of this institution of higher learning have been built and maintained by the everyday greatness of its employees. In that light, the contents of the section of this book entitled "Manifestation of the Mission" provide copious evidence that Ohio State's faculty and staff members are defining the twenty-first-century land-grant mission. Reading any of these contributions as a stand-alone document will leave the distinct impression of leadership. When viewed as a collection, however, the reader indisputably will gain a true sense of Ohio State as the *prima inter pares* of the land-grant realm.

References

Gavazzi, Stephen M., and E. Gordon Gee. 2018. *Land-Grant Universities for the Future: Higher Education for the Common Good.* Baltimore: Johns Hopkins University Press.

4

The History and Future of The Ohio State University

David J. Staley

In 2013, I was invited to take over the leadership of a course titled "The Ohio State University: Its History and World," a course I am pleased to team teach with Tamar Chute, the university archivist. This affords us the opportunity to teach the history of Ohio State by introducing students to its primary documents. An important feature of the class is that we invite university leadership to deliver guest lectures. President Drake makes an annual visit to the class (as did President Gee before him). The provost, a college dean, a member of the board of trustees, and a department chair each describe to the students their particular roles within the university, with the overall goal of explaining "how this university is run." The class is as much a sociology of the university as it is a history of the institution.

We begin the course by situating the founding of the Ohio Agricultural and Mechanical College in a wider historical context. We begin with an examination of "the university as an idea" created during the European Middle Ages. We look in particular at the formation of the Universities of Oxford and Cambridge in England. The colleges that collectively made up those universities were the model for the first colonial colleges; we note that before 1776 there were only a handful of colleges, one in each colony, in fact. After the American Revolution, the number of small Oxbridge-inspired colleges proliferated, nowhere more evidently than in Ohio. These denominationally based colleges sprung up across the state. These early colleges, even Harvard, the first college established in the colonies, were surprisingly small to our modern sensibilities. A college might have only a few dozen students and have just a handful of faculty members. They were frequently underfunded, and in the course of the nineteenth century several of these colleges shuttered their doors. It is important to emphasize that although the number of colleges proliferated, college attendance in the US in the nineteenth century was the exception, not the rule. Only those training for the ministry or civic leadership usually attended college. Indeed, it is not an exaggeration to say that hardly anybody attended college in the nineteenth century.

Into this context came the land-grant university. Vermont senator Justin Morrill proposed that the federal government identify and grant to each of the states an amount of land that could be then sold, the proceeds of which would allow for

> the endowment, support, and maintenance of at least one college where the leading object shall be, without excluding other scientific and classical studies, and including military tactics, to teach such branches of learning as are related to agriculture and the mechanic arts, in such manner as the legislatures of the States may respectively prescribe, in order to promote the liberal and practical education of the industrial classes in the several pursuits and professions in life. (Transcript of Morrill Act)

Our history of Ohio State class spends a class period examining the consequences of the Morrill Act of 1862 for the history of higher education in the US. The land-grant university was differentiated from the denominational college in a number of ways.

1. Unlike other countries, the US never developed a national university, which, among other things, left the financing of higher education as a local matter. The Morrill Act was the first significant instance of federal intervention in US higher education. If there would not be a federal national university, there would at least be a federally funded university in each of the states.
2. Although not explicitly stated in the Morrill Act, land-grant colleges in general, and the Ohio Agricultural and Mechanical College in particular, were not tied to a particular religious denomination, as was practically every other college in the US. That is not to suggest that religious instruction was not to be found at land-grants—chapel was a regular feature of life at Ohio State even into the early twentieth century—but they were not tied to a specific Christian denomina-

tion. Indeed, by the turn of the century, with the rise of the research university as a catalyst, colleges and universities shed their religious focus and moved toward a secular, scientific orientation. Land-grants were at the vanguard of this transformation.

3. Land-grant universities were to be financially accessible and have a practical orientation. They were to be open to all and to teach skills and subjects appropriate to the needs of an industrializing society. Morrill said:

> This bill proposes to establish at least one college in every State upon a sure and perpetual foundation, accessible to all, but especially to the sons of toil, where all of needful science for the practical avocations of life shall be taught, where neither the higher graces of classical studies nor that military drill our country now so greatly appreciates will be entirely ignored, and where agriculture, the foundation of all present and future prosperity, may look for troops of earnest friends, studying its familiar and recondite economies, and at last elevating it to that higher level where it may fearlessly invoke comparison with the most advanced standards of the world. (New York (State) Legislature Assembly)

We sometimes forget that the land-grant university was a new kind of institution of higher learning. To be sure, it retained the symbols of the medieval university and its curriculum was still influenced by the traditional classical curriculum. But land-grants featured courses in engineering and agriculture, fields that were hitherto not considered academic subjects. We would today call such an institution of higher learning "innovative."

Indeed, in our history of Ohio State course, we present the early history of Ohio A&M as a "start-up." We have the students examine some of the early documents of the university (such as trustees' reports and minutes of faculty meetings), which allows them to see firsthand the challenges the university faced at its foundation: The main building was not complete when classes first opened in 1873, with only twenty-four students and seven faculty. (Again, such a small size was not uncommon.) We also explore the controversies in the founding of the university. Some wondered why Ohio needed yet another college. Ohio University and Miami University both claimed that the land-grant should be given to them rather than creating a new institution (some states gave the land-grant to a preexisting college). Today, looking at the thriving university Ohio State has become, it is important for students to see that there was nothing inevitable or preordained about Ohio State's rise to prominence.

Because it is also a course on how the modern university operates, "OSU and Its World" affords us the opportunity to explore Ohio's land-grant university today, and to contemplate the future of the land-grant university. Interestingly, the issues we currently face regarding higher education are similar to those Morrill was confronting a century and a half ago: access and affordability. Ohio State saw steady enrollment growth throughout the twentieth century. In 1900, there were around 1,100 students; twenty-five years later, that number was over 10,000. After the Second World War—and fueled by both the GI Bill and the arrival of the demographically enormous baby boom generation—enrollments approached 50,000. In the 1960s and early 1970s, the strategic plan was preparing for a Columbus campus of 100,000 students. There were to be six dormitory towers planned (instead of the two that were actually built). West Campus was imagined as a heavily populated mini campus. The Drake Union was built to provide a second student union to serve the students that would be bursting on the west side of campus. Building such a mega-university would certainly have made for greater access to all who wanted to attend Ohio State.

After Ohio State decided to pursue selective admissions, this consequently limited who could attend the university. In the "OSU and Its World" course, students examine documents surrounding President Jennings's controversial decision in the 1980s to pursue selective admissions. Prior to this moment, Ohio State accepted any student who had graduated from an Ohio high school on a first-come, first-served basis. President Jennings estimated that perhaps a quarter of incoming students did not stay beyond their first year, and so wondered whether being more selective at the beginning of the acceptance process might result in fewer students dropping out. One result of selective admissions is that it is much harder to be admitted to Ohio State today than it was prior to 1985. This decision continues to rankle alumni, as it has had an effect on who and how many have access to an Ohio State education.

At the same time, the cost to attend Ohio State has been inching upward. State support of higher education has been reduced steadily since the 1980s. The cost of educating a student has not increased as dramatically, but the price a student must pay has been rising, the result in part of the diminished state subsidy. We eagerly await a recommitment from the state of Ohio to help make tuition more affordable.

Until that happens, we look for alternatives that might make an Ohio State education affordable and more accessible. Digital delivery of courses offers one such option. To help celebrate the sesquicentennial, we were invited to develop a MOOC—a massive open online course—on the history of Ohio State. This course is not intended to be credit-bearing, and thus is not a part of the regular undergraduate curriculum. Instead, it will be made freely available online for anyone to take, which we see as a service to the citizens of Ohio. To be clear, a MOOC or other kind of online course is a very different experience than a face-to-face class. It is the difference between attending a football game in person at the Shoe versus watching the game on a high-definition television. Yet online courses have proven to be effective at delivering certain types of classes, and some populations—working adults and others who wish to have some flexibility as to the time they take their classes—are especially drawn to online courses. Indeed, MOOCs have been held up as a potential model for the delivery of college classes that is both accessible and (at least in theory) affordable.

Imagine an entire curriculum of MOOCs that were a regular part of the undergraduate curriculum. Could we then imagine a "digital regional campus" that would open up an Ohio State education to a wider audience, at a potentially lower cost? Online courses represent a different set of overhead costs than face-to-face courses; they are not free to produce, and so providing courses like our history of Ohio State MOOC for free across an entire curriculum is simply not feasible.

With that said, a "digital regional campus" could theoretically be scaled in size to help accommodate 100,000 students, as was imagined in the 1960s. Ohio State already offers online courses in a wide variety of subjects, and indeed some programs (like nursing) have fully online programs. What I am envisioning would be an entity formally organized to offer the same range of courses available at any regional campus. The "digital regional campus," like its physical counterparts at Marion, Lima, Newark, and Mansfield, would have its own faculty, and would be led by a campus dean. Like the physical regional campuses, the digital regional campus would be tethered to the main campus: After a period of successfully navigating curricula there, students would be eligible to transfer to the main campus. In this scenario, the main campus remains governed by selective admissions, and does not grow beyond the numbers that are there today. If the regional campuses serve as feeders to the main campus, then the digital regional campus would take its place within this structure.

Students at the digital regional campus need not be eighteen- to twenty-two-year-old "traditional" students. Online courses, where successful, often attract working adults, military personal, and other so-called nontraditional students. Online universities such as Southern New Hampshire University and Western Governor's University and the master's degree program in computer science at Georgia Tech demonstrate that this mode can work successfully. Is the future of the land-grant university—with its commitment to accessibility and affordability—the "virtual land-grant"?

The regional campuses—built in the 1960s as a way to provide educational opportunities to people around the state—altered their missions after selective admissions. In addition to providing local access to an Ohio State experience, the regionals are now an entry point for those not directly admitted to main campus. In the future, we could see the regional campuses each grow in size beyond the 1,500 to 2,000 students currently at each. Perhaps the regionals will grow to as high as 5,000 students each, opening up access to an Ohio State education. If we were to expand the capacity of the regional campuses, clearly this would mean a capital investment in new buildings, especially dormitories (the regionals are already transforming from commuter campuses into residential campuses, and in this scenario that trend accelerates). At present, it is difficult for a student to remain at a regional campus for four years since there are a limited number of degrees that can be earned there; most students need to transfer to the Columbus campus to finish most programs. In the future, the regionals might offer a broader range of majors and degree programs, such that more students are able to matriculate from a regional campus.

If accessibility means a larger number of students, and if the current regionals can only expand up to a certain point, it is possible to imagine Ohio State founding a new regional campus, its first in many decades. Perhaps a new campus will be built in Marysville, for example. With a robust and expanding number of regional campuses, both virtual and physical, Ohio State might develop a system of campuses across the state, something like the Pennsylvania state system or the SUNY system in New York. As smaller colleges struggle, I can even envision a scenario where Ohio State acquires these schools as new regional campuses, serving many of the same students and with a commitment to the undergraduate education these small liberal arts colleges are known for. If history is any guide, the land-grant university of the future will strive to be accessible and affordable, and it will pioneer new forms of knowledge that respond to the needs of the twenty-first-century society.

References

New York (State) Legislature Assembly, Documents of the Assembly of the State of New York, Eighty-Sixth Session 9, nos. 233–34. Albany: Comstock and Cassidy, 1863. 123.

Transcript of Morrill Act (1862). https://www.ourdocuments.gov/doc.php?flash=false&doc=33&page=transcript.

The Tripartite Mission

5

Teaching Excellence in the Twenty-First Century

Meeting the Mission, Extending the Vision

Kay Halasek

> Ohio State will be an exemplar of the best teaching, demonstrating leadership by adopting innovative, at-scale approaches to teaching and learning to improve student outcomes.
>
> —Time and Change Strategic Plan

Among the grand challenges facing Ohio State and the twenty-first-century land-grant university—and, indeed, all of higher education—is, as our editors note, responding efficaciously to a host of issues. These include those noted by Jon McGee in *Breakpoint: The Changing Marketplace for Higher Education* (2015)—"accessibility, affordability, accountability, sustainability, and differentiation"—as well as increasing managerialism, widespread "adjunctification" of university faculty, declining support for public higher education, and indeed greater skepticism about the value of higher education itself" (see chapter 1 of this volume). Each of these issues, while certainly impacting the land-grant university as a whole, also has direct and significant impact on teaching and learning. Moreover, those who teach at the university (and who therefore *themselves* have direct and significant impact on student outcomes and achievement) are fully aware (sometimes personally and painfully so) of the shifting demands on the university, the fiscal and political challenges it faces, and the implications of these issues for the university as it strives to meet its land-grant mission.

I wish to thank Dr. Tamar Chute, Dr. Robert Griffiths, Dr. Andrew Heckler, and Dr. Judy Ridgway for their time and support as I drafted this chapter.

On any given day, faculty[1] at The Ohio State University have ready access to news related to higher education. Daily eNewsletters or digests from *The Chronicle of Higher Education* and *Inside Higher Ed* offer insights into the current state of the university and the events, people, and politics that impact its work. On November 1, 2018, for example, three pieces came across my screen from *The Chronicle* alone that piqued my attention because of their direct relationship to teaching and learning: "New Book Renews Debate about Donor Influence," "Big Data, AI Prompt Major Expansions at UC Berkeley and MIT," and "Virtual Reality, Other 3-D Tools Enhance Classroom Experiences as Institutions Navigate Experimentation."[2] Throughout the past several months as I've been drafting this chapter, I have collected dozens of such *Chronicle* and *Inside Higher Ed* pieces: "Historians Need to Measure What Their Students Learn," "How One Email from You Could Help Students Succeed," "How One University Tries to Make Its Teaching Training Stick," "At U. of Maryland, an Effort to Make Introductory Courses Extraordinary," "Teaching Is a Private Act. How Can Professors Open Up about It?," just to name a few.[3] Each one speaks to the depth and breadth of the conversations around *and concern* about the quality of teaching and its impact on learning in higher education. The challenges facing higher education are certainly numerous and complex and sometimes seem overwhelming (even apocalyptic), but I see, nevertheless, a collective and affirmative shift in the conversation cross the country—and Ohio State has responded with a vision for and investment in elevating teaching and learning. In the pages that follow, I turn my attention not to engaging challenges and issues themselves but to the ways that the university, through its vision for and investment in teaching and learning, is creating the foundation from which it can realize its goal of becoming the "exemplar of the best teaching, demonstrating leadership by adopting innovative, at-scale approaches to teaching and learning to improve student outcomes."

---

1. Although I refer above to "those who teach" at Ohio State, I have elected in the remainder of this chapter to use *faculty* as the term to identify "those who teach at the university." I use that term to stand in for any person in a compensated, teaching capacity through which they instruct students.

2. These three articles, by Marjorie Valbrun, Greg Toppo, and Mark Lieberman, respectively, all appeared in the online edition of *Inside Higher Ed* on November 2, 2018. They may be accessed through a search at www.InsideHigherEd.com.

3. See Wineburg et al. 2018; Supiano 2018; McMurtrie and Supiano 2018; Berrett 2012, 2017.

Cultivating a Culture That Engages, Impacts, and Transforms

> I was drawn to the institute because I embrace its mission to bring together faculty of all ranks and categories from across the university with the expressed [sic] purpose of enhancing teaching and learning. . . . Through thoughtful and creative discussion, innovative pedagogies and collaborative research, the institute is poised to contribute meaningfully to faculty engagement in teaching and, by extension, students' learning experiences.
>
> —Kay Halasek (*Ohio State News*)

I don't know that I've ever quoted myself so explicitly or extensively in any other piece I've written, but the quotation above, from an interview about the University Institute for Teaching and Learning (UITL), struck me as capturing both my enthusiasm and the institutional vision for the institute. UITL, as a "campus-wide institute," was "designed to help instructors share successful teaching techniques and lead to increased adoption of modern methods that enhance student learning"; it seeks to "enhance support for excellent teaching, expand teaching and learning scholarship, and apply student-centered analytics to improve learning outcomes."[4] In short, we take as the charge in UITL to inspire all members of the university community in their pursuit of teaching and learning achievement by promoting and supporting a culture of teaching excellence.

It's important for me to note that UITL did not step onto an empty landscape. Teaching and learning—and support for teaching and learning—have been critical and defining features of the OSU faculty experience since the inception of the university. The institute both is lifted up by and lifts up these predecessors, many of whom remain among its most valued partners.

Support for teaching and learning—in the form of an office exclusively dedicated to supporting teaching and learning, independent from a given college or department—has a nearly forty-year history at Ohio State. The former University Center for the Advancement of Teaching (UCAT), now a part of UITL, was established in 1980 as the Instructional Development and Evaluation unit of the Office of Learning Resources. Later named Faculty and TA Development and situated in the Center

4. UITL, before its merger with the University Center for the Advancement of Teaching in January 2019, included a staff of four faculty fellows, Dr. Maria Pruchnicki (pharmacy), Dr. Mary Jo Fresch (emerita, teaching and learning), Dr. Andrew Heckler (physics), and Dr. Jonathan Baker (statistics). Associate director Dr. Melinda Rhodes-DiSalvo joined the institute in 2018.

for Teaching Excellence (in 1987), the unit was renamed the University Center for the Advancement of Teaching in 2009. UCAT merged in January 2019 with UITL, creating one of the nation's most unique teaching and learning institutes. The Office of Distance Education and eLearning (ODEE), another primary partner of UITL, was formed in 2012 with the goal of integrating and centralizing extended continuing and distance education with learning technologies in the office of the CIO. In just six years, ODEE has led Ohio State to national prominence in online learning: The online bachelor's program was ranked #1 by *US News and World Report.*

Colleges, departments, and programs across the university—in Veterinary Medicine; the College of Medicine; the College of Nursing; the College of Education and Human Ecology; the Department of Engineering Education; and the Department of Agricultural Communication, Education, and Leadership, to name just a few—also stand as models of engagement, impact, and transformation in teaching and learning. One program in particular, however, has served as a point of inspiration and vision for UITL: the Center for Life Sciences Education (CLSE), which was established in 2006. An interdisciplinary and interdepartmental program within the College of Arts and Sciences, CLSE offers professional development programming and courses for graduate teaching associates in the life sciences and conducts research on and pursues grants related to biology education. Since 2015, CLSE has also held the National Academies Summer Institute (NASI) at Ohio State, week-long seminars during which "faculty and staff participants . . . develop and peer-review teaching materials and learn how to implement scientific teaching in the classroom, [and] tak[e] a research-based approach to biology teaching" (Rutkowski). The director, Dr. Caroline Breitenberger, noted in a 2015 interview, "The primary goal is to facilitate institutional reform of STEM education, focusing initially on biology courses" (Rutkowski). As the program grows and matures, Breitenberger anticipates extending to other disciplines, across regional campuses, and to other institutions in Ohio. These programs—continuing professional learning for graduate teaching associates and a summer institute for faculty—stand as testament to faculty and institutional commitment to teaching in CLSE, a commitment that UITL took as the basis from which to build its own enterprise-wide programming.

Taking the CLSE professional development programming as models, UITL—in deep and ongoing collaboration with its partners in UCAT, ODEE, and university libraries—has conceived, developed, and launched three initiatives intended to not only "meet faculty where they are" but also extend and enrich their understanding and learning, with the goal of impacting student learning. The first program developed, in 2016, was a yearlong FIT (foundation, impact, transformation) *new faculty program,* a "set of coordinated learning experiences" designed to help faculty new to the university familiarize themselves with the resources at the university, engage evidence-based practices in their teaching, "build community, and encourage reflection and sharing [of] what we know about excellent teaching" (UITL 2019a). UITL launched its second program, the *teaching endorsements* initiative, in 2017. As credentials sponsored by UITL, endorsements recognize those individuals who participate in extended, certified, in-depth professional learning programs, nearly all of which are collaboratively developed and offered by UITL partners. Topics range from affordable learning to inclusive teaching, teaching with technology, online teaching, and teaching through writing. Collectively, endorsements address two of the four "top issues" identified by Beach et al. (2016) as integral to faculty development efforts in higher education (teaching in online and distance environments and multiculturalism and diversity related to teaching).

The third of UITL initiatives, the *Teaching Support Program,* was announced in September 2018 as an extended opportunity to engage faculty in a range of discrete but related activities: the Teaching Practices Inventory; Teaching@OhioState; focused reading in the areas of designing for learning, supporting instruction, and considering course impact; and instructional (re)design. The first three elements launched in September 2018, and the fourth, the instructional redesign program, launched in January 2019.

The *Teaching Practices Inventory* (TPI) is a survey instrument designed to identify which evidence-based practices faculty currently use in their teaching. A validated instrument developed by Wieman and Gilbert (2014), the inventory was initially created to capture data in mathematics and science but has since been revised to include the social sciences. To date, over 2,800 faculty have completed the TPI at Ohio State, creating a rich and deep view of the kinds of teaching practices that inform instruction.

Teaching@OhioState is a "self-directed online experience" that introduces faculty "to key topics about teaching at The Ohio State University, including cross-disciplinary faculty perspectives and an introduction to evidence-based teaching practices" (UITL 2018c). A five-module course, Teaching@OhioState leads faculty through such topics as the principles of course design and evidence-based practice, assessment, course content and organization, effective teaching methods, and shaping inclusive and positive learning environments. The course closes by articulating the value of peer feedback on and personal reflection about teaching. What is perhaps most compelling about Teaching@OhioState is the way its modules are framed. Each begins with an "In Practice" roundtable featuring OSU faculty discussing their teaching. That roundtable is then followed by "Strategy and Theory" units that introduce the evidence-based practices and principles that guide instruction that leads to improved student outcomes. Each module then introduces "Other Perspectives," adding the voices and strategies of other OSU faculty to the conversation.

The UITL *Reading List* is a curated list of scholarly books and articles on designing for learning, supporting instruction, and considering course impact. Created to complement and extend the content of Teaching@OhioState, the reading list offers faculty over two dozen books and nearly three dozen articles from which to continue their inquiry into more effective teaching.

Instructional Redesign, a program that launched in 2019, creates opportunities for faculty to design or redesign a course using the principles and strategies articulated throughout the Teaching Support Program. As a method of course and curriculum reform, the instructional redesign program engages faculty in yet another "top issue" in faculty development. This UITL program in particular utilizes many of the top approaches to faculty development: learning communities, asynchronous online programs, web-based resources, institutes, department/discipline-specific workshops, peer observation of teaching with feedback, individual consultation, and seminars.

UITL, by aligning its work with the strategic plan and institutional goals, creates the spaces from which "second-order transformations—nonreversible, systemic changes that broaden the framework for faculty development"—can occur. It is just the "deep learning process" of integrative learning Rossing and Lavitt (2016) call for that informs the work of UITL. We know from research on faculty continuing learning that training, time, and incentives are critical foundational features for successful programs. Seeking to affect change through discrete, short-term engagements, Brownell and Tanner write "seems incongruent with the notion that pedagogical change for any instructor is an iterative and ongoing process" (2012, 340). Moreover, "training alone is likely insufficient by itself to achieve lasting pedagogical change" (Brownell and Tanner 2012, 340). Institutions must recognize that asking faculty to shift their teaching to include evidence-based practices demands faculty attention and time—attention and time that has, traditionally, been rewarded when focused on research and scholarship, but not teaching. Ample time alone, Brownell and Tanner argue, is not enough. Lasting pedagogical change of the sort Brownell and Tanner envision—and that UITL embraces and seeks to achieve for faculty at the university—is certainly elusive, but not impossible to achieve. Programming, together with a focused research engagement, institutional financial support, and faculty incentives, provide the bases for success.

Faculty: The Neglected Learners

> Current practices and structures in higher education neglect faculty as learners and . . . the ambitions of liberal education at engaged universities can only be actualized if integrative learning for faculty becomes foundational.
>
> —Jonathan P. Rossing and Melissa R. Lavitt (2016, 36)

I take the metaphor of faculty as the "neglected learner" from Rossing and Lavitt, who identify "integrated learning and engaged work" as "foundational" for faculty success. Their call and vision inform the approaches UITL has used and will continue to use as it seeks to create a meaningful and sustainable impact on teaching and, by extension, student learning.

We will ultimately judge UITL efforts and evaluate success by assessing the impact on teachers and students. To realize both change and impact, however, faculty participation in continued professional learning must be recognized through the university reward structure of appointment, reappointment, promotion, and tenure. In creating the programs I outline above, we in UITL turned our primary attention to identifying and reshaping existing professional learning opportunities and designing new programs to meet the needs of faculty. Through the various engagements available for faculty through UITL and its partners, we seek first to encourage faculty to attend more fully and intentionally with their teaching by providing opportunities for, recognizing, and incentivizing growth and reflection. We also seek to encourage faculty to extend that engagement by supporting research and promoting scholarly productivity in the scholarship of teaching and learning (SoTL) and discipline-based education research (DBER), especially research that leads to and reports on assessment of student learning outcomes, identified by Beach et al.

(2016) as a "top issue" in faculty development. Even with the programs already in place, UITL—and the university as a whole—has a great deal more to contribute. Creating lasting and meaningful partnerships across the university and among all professionals bound by a common goal of student success requires years of planning, and trial and error. It also takes investment—financial investment and incentives. And, in 2018, the university became the first land-grant institution to provide across-the-board base-salary increases for all faculty completing a course of continued professional learning related to teaching. The base salary increase of $1,600 is roughly equivalent to a 1.5 percent increase in the average salary of full professors.[5]

These initiatives and incentives, together with the continued partnerships that have informed the work of UITL in its first three years, are the first steps toward elevating teaching and learning as a core mission of the university. In many ways, the work of the institute specifically and the university more broadly understands teaching in a decidedly land-grant fashion. The land-grant mission is one that recognizes that the "body of knowledge constantly changes through research and experimentation and is disseminated to the public"—something true of the body of knowledge around teaching (Texas A&M n.d.). Just as "new knowledge [generated by scientific and humanistic research] brings new ideas and expanded opportunities," so, too, does new knowledge generated by the scholarship of teaching and learning and discipline-based education research "bring[ ] new ideas and expanded opportunities" to the faculty and students of The Ohio State University (Texas A&M n.d.).

Conclusion

The questions posed by our editors to those of us contributing to this volume echo those asked by William H. Scott, third president of The Ohio State University (1883–1895), at his inaugural address, delivered at the eleventh commencement of the university, on June 18, 1884: "The paramount question is, what shall the future be? On what principles shall it be founded? By what policy shall it be guided? To what ends shall it be directed?" In this chapter, I have attempted to answer both Gavazzi and Staley and Scott. By describing the current landscape of teaching and

5. Part-time lecturers, those on teaching appointments less than 75 percent full-time equivalent (FTE), will realize a one-time $1,600 cash incentive.

learning at the university, I have articulated the principles and policies that guide the University Institute for Teaching and Learning and the end (student success) to which our work is directed.

UITL—with its new faculty FIT program and mentoring, endorsements, Teaching Support Program, research in higher education teaching and learning, and policy and government relations emphases—has propelled Ohio State well on its way to achieving its many goals. UITL and its partners have moved in the past three years toward creating a more robust and inclusive teaching culture at Ohio State—but much more work remains. Meaningful continued professional learning for faculty incentivized by the university and rewarded through reappointment, promotion, and tenure are just some of the initiatives the university might offer. Sustaining and growing a culture of teaching also entails changing policies and practices within the university and across higher education. The university might, for example, consider demonstrated teaching effectiveness in our hiring processes or focus more attention on developing the teaching preparedness of our own graduate students. UITL programs, in addition to engaging the "top issues" of and "top approaches" to faculty development, recognize that "sustained and intensive professional development for teaching is related to student achievement gains"; "effective professional development is intensive, ongoing, and connected to practice"; and "teachers typically need substantial professional development in a given area (close to 50 hours) to improve their skills and their students' learning" (Darling-Hammond et al. 2009, 5). Our goal, to again borrow a finding from Darling-Hammond et al., is to offer faculty what they have not typically had the opportunity to do: engage in "extended learning opportunities and productive collaborative communities" (6) in an effort to align faculty development with increased student outcomes (Guskey and Yoon 2009; Yoon et al. 2007).

Jon McGee, in *Breakpoint: The Changing Marketplace for Higher Education* (2015), reminds us that we face a "new and complicated environment," one that includes "new students with new needs and demands, scarce family and institutional resources, heightened competition, rising expectations for better performance and management. No college or university," McGee continues,

> will have the luxury of wholly avoiding the demographic, economic, and cultural forces reshaping the marketplace today. And yet, there is a something-old-something-new quality to it all. This is not the first disruptive period for higher education nor will it be the last. We have

> faced these kinds of challenges—sometimes expressed in similar ways, sometimes not—many times before over the last century. Our history as institutions and as an industry has been characterized by an ability to innovate, adapt, and subsequently thrive in response to change. But that can happen only after we wrap our minds around the demands of a new operating environment and then acted [sic] assertively in response. (100)

We live in an exciting but also vexing time for higher education, with emerging advances in teaching and learning based on empirical research that promise a very bright future for our students. But this is also a time during which the university must become more explicitly and systematically engaged in research and development of higher education teaching and learning. For a large university to make a collective difference in teaching and learning—and for a unit like the University Institute for Teaching and Learning to contribute meaningfully to that effort—it must develop and enact a comprehensive plan, long-range strategic goals, and institutional policies and practices that ensure that faculty actively working to improve their teaching and student outcomes, engaging in the scholarship of teaching and learning, and conducting research to contribute to the body of knowledge in learning sciences and higher education are supported, acknowledged, and rewarded for their efforts.

References

Beach, Andrea L., Mary Deane Scorcinelli, Ann E. Austin, and Jaclyn K. Rivard. 2016. *Faculty Development in the Age of Evidence: Current Practices, Future Imperatives.* Sterling, VA: Stylus Publishing.

Berrett, Dan. 2012. "At U. of Maryland, an Effort to Make Introductory Courses Extraordinary." *The Chronicle of Higher Education,* December 17, 2012. https://www.chronicle.com/article/At-U-of-Maryland-an-Effort/136317.

———. 2017. "Teaching Is a Private Act. How Can Professors Open Up about It?" *The Chronicle of Higher Education,* December 7, 2017. https://www.chronicle.com/article/Teaching-Is-a-Private-Act-How/241998?cid=at&utm_source=at&utm_medium=en&elqTrackId=25da6d3daca94602ac55dfae5c9c2%E2%80%A6.

Brownell, Sara E., and Kimberly D. Tanner. 2012. "Barriers to Faculty Pedagogical Change: Lack of Training, Time, Incentives, and . . . Tensions with Professional Identity?" *CBE—Life Sciences Education* 11, no. 4 (December): 339–46. https://doi.org/10.1187/cbe.12-09-0163.

Center for Life Sciences Education, The Ohio State University. 2018. "Summer Institutes." https://clse.osu.edu/summer-institutes.

Darling-Hammond, Linda, Ruth Chung Wei, Althea Andree, Nikole Richardson, and Stelios Orphanos. 2009. *Professional Learning in the Learning Profession: A Status Report on Teacher Development in the United States and Abroad.* Oxford, OH: National Staff Development Council.

Guskey, Thomas R., and Kwang Suk Yoon. 2009. "What Works in Professional Development?" *Phi Delta Kappan* 90, no. 7 (March): 495–500. https://doi.org/10.1177/003172170909000709.

Lieberman, Mark. "Virtual Reality, Other 3-D Tools Enhance Classroom Experiences as Institutions Navigate Experimentation." *Inside Higher Ed,* November 2, 2018. https://www.insidehighered.com/digital-learning/article/2018/11/02/virtual-reality-other-3-d-tools-enhance-classroom-experiences?utm_source=Inside+Higher+Ed&u%E2%80%A6.

McGee, Jon. 2015. *Breakpoint: The Changing Marketplace for Higher Education.* Baltimore: Johns Hopkins University Press.

McMurtrie, Beth, and Becky Supiano. 2018. "How One University Tries to Make Its Teaching Training Stick." *The Chronicle of Higher Education,* August 16, 2018. https://www.chronicle.com/article/How-One-University-Tries-to/244286/#.W3bieoY8Xog.email.

Office of Academic Affairs, The Ohio State University. 2012. "Expanding Distance Education Opportunities." December 1, 2012. http://web.archive.org/web/20130327225422/https:/www.oaa.osu.edu/distanceed.

Office of Distance Education and eLearning, The Ohio State University. 2018. "Distance Education." https://odee.osu.edu/distance-education.

Office of the President, The Ohio State University. 2018. "William Henry Scott." https://president.osu.edu/presidents/william-scott.html.

Ohio State News. 2016. "Ohio State Names Inaugural Director of Institute for Teaching and Learning." July 28, 2016. https://news.osu.edu/ohio-state-names-inaugural-director-of-institute-for-teaching-and-learning/.

Ridgway, Judith S., Isaac Y. Ligocki, Jonathan D. Horn, Erica Szeyller, and Caroline A. Breitenberger. 2017. "Perceptions of Ongoing, Personalized TA Professional Development: Initial Lessons and Plans for the Future." *Journal of College Science Teaching* 46, no. 5 (May): 73–83.

Rossing, Jonathan P., and Melissa R. Lavitt. 2016. "The Neglected Learner: A Call to Support Integrative Learning for Faculty." *Liberal Education* 102, no. 2 (Spring): 34–41. https://www.aacu.org/liberaleducation/2016/spring/rossing.

Rutkowski, Sandi. 2015. "Teaching Ohio State's Largest Major Gets a Makeover: CLSE Holds Ohio State's First National Academies Summer Institute June 8–12." College News, College of Arts and Sciences, The Ohio State University, June 5, 2015. https://

artsandsciences.osu.edu/news/teaching-ohio-state-s-largest-major-gets-makeover-clse-holds-ohio-states-first-national.

Scott, William Henry. 1884. "Inaugural Address of President Wm. H. Scott." Delivered at the eleventh commencement of The Ohio State University, June 18, 1884. University Archives, The Ohio State University. https://kb.osu.edu/bitstream/handle/1811/53832/ARV_Commencement_1884_Spring_Scott.pdf?sequence=1&isAllowed=y.

Supiano, Becky. 2018. "How One Email from You Could Help Students Succeed." *The Chronicle of Higher Education,* August 9, 2018. https://www.chronicle.com/article/How-One-Email-From-You-Could/244223?cid=at&utm_source=at&utm_medium=en&elqTrackId=b18c8c471bc341b3b0ba5d8c6%E2%80%A6.

Texas A&M AgriLife Extension Service, Texas A&M University. n.d. "Land-Grant Impacts." https://landgrantimpacts.org/we-are-teaching/.

Toppo, Greg. "Big Data, AI Prompt Major Expansions at UC Berkeley and MIT." *Inside Higher Ed,* November 2, 2018. https://www.insidehighered.com/print/news/2018/11/02/big-data-ai-prompt-major-expansions-uc-berkeley-and-mit?width=775&height=500&iframe=true.

University Center for the Advancement of Teaching, The Ohio State University. 2018. "About." https://ucat.osu.edu/about/.

University Institute for Teaching and Learning, The Ohio State University. 2018a. "FIT Mentoring Program."

———. 2018b. "New Faculty FIT Program."

———. 2018c. "Teaching@OhioState."

———. 2018d. "Teaching Practices Inventory."

———. 2019a. "New Faculty Program." https://uitl.osu.edu/professional-learning/faculty-fit-program.

———. 2019b. "Teaching Endorsements." https://uitl.osu.edu/instructors/teaching-endorsements.

U.S. News and World Report. 2018. "Best Online Bachelor's Programs." https://www.usnews.com/education/online-education/bachelors/rankings.

Valbrun, Marjorie. 2018. "New Book Renews Debate about Donor Influence." *Inside Higher Ed,* November 2, 2018. https://www.insidehighered.com/news/2018/11/02/new-book-renews-debate-about-donor-influence?utm_source=Inside+Higher+Ed&utm_campaign=5ff5b903a9-DN%E2%80%A6.

Wieman, Carl, and Sarah Gilbert. 2014. "The Teaching Practices Inventory: A Tool for Characterizing College and University Teaching in Mathematics and Science." *CBE—Life Sciences Education* 13, no. 3 (October): 552–69. https://www.lifescied.org/doi/10.1187/cbe.14-02-0023.

Wineburg, Sam, Joel Breakstone, and Mark Smith. 2018. "Do We Know What History Students Learn?" *Inside Higher Ed,* April 3, 2018. https://www.insidehighered.com/

views/2018/04/03/historians-need-measure-what-their-students-learn-opinion?width=775&height=500&iframe=true.

Yoon, Kwang Suk, Teresa Duncan, Silvia Wen-Yu Lee, Beth Scarloss, and Kathy L. Shapley. 2007. *Reviewing the Evidence on How Teacher Professional Development Affects Student Achievement.* Issues & Answers Report, REL 2007-No. 033. US Department of Education, Institute of Education Sciences, National Center for Educational Evaluation and Regional Assistance, Regional Educational Laboratory Southwest. https://ies.ed.gov/ncee/edlabs/regions/southwest/pdf/rel_2007033_sum.pdf.

6

Coming Full Circle

Research, Discovery, and Creative Inquiry at Ohio State

Janet M. Weisenberger

What does the status of "21st Century Land-grant University" mean for the research enterprise at The Ohio State University? How has the current landscape of research, discovery, and creative inquiry been shaped by the mission of the university's earliest scholars, and how does the current state help Ohio State to envision and position itself for the future? This essay explores the evolution of Ohio State research and creative inquiry from its beginnings, provides a look at the forces that drive the current research enterprise, and suggests why Ohio State scholars can look to the future with optimism.

Introduction

Research, scholarly inquiry, and creative expression constitute a major force in the lifeblood of the modern public university. The creation of new knowledge and new discoveries injects vitality into teaching and learning and enlightens community engagement and economic health in the university region. The university is at its best when the three components of the so-called tripartite mission—research, teaching, and service—intersect seamlessly, such that each complements the other.

This ideal is one that The Ohio State University strives to implement in the early twenty-first century. As a large, sprawling, and growing entity,

Ohio State struggles with the siloes that can spring up in such a distributed enterprise. However, the university holds a strategic weapon that can bridge the divides and siloes in its research, teaching, and engagement enterprise: a zeal for collaboration that has been an integral part of the university's culture for many decades. "Collaboration is in Ohio State's DNA" is a phrase frequently heard on campus. This will to connect and collaborate can transform the potential liability of a widely distributed and comprehensive campus into a strategic asset in addressing some of the world's biggest challenges.

Ohio State is, by any accounting, one of the major research universities in the US. Since 1916, it has been a member of the Association of American Universities (AAU), a group of the top sixty research universities in the nation. Ohio State carries the Carnegie Classification of Institutions of Higher Education's designation as a "Doctoral University—Very High Research Activity (R1)," a designation based on research expenditures. In the National Science Foundation's "Higher Education Research and Development Survey" (n.d.), Ohio State ranks in the top twenty-five of all universities in the nation. Funded research expenditures at the university have increased steadily over the past several decades, and now approach $900 million annually.

This essay considers the role of research, scholarship, and creativity in the university at the time of its founding in 1870, and finds possible parallels in the present, as regional, state, and national events and priorities help to shape the research mission of Ohio State as a twenty-first-century land-grant institution.

The Role of Scholarship at the Birth of the University

To understand the university's earliest mission, we begin by painting a picture of research at Ohio State's beginnings. The Morrill Act of 1862, which established the mechanism for the creation of land-grant universities in each of the states, allowed for considerable variation in the structures and missions of the early land-grant universities, particularly with respect to areas of emphasis.

Although some of the earliest land-grant universities included explicit language about research in their original state legislative language, the state legislature's bill establishing a land-grant university in Ohio did not emphasize research as an activity of the proposed university. The Cannon Act of 1870 that created the Ohio Agricultural and Mechanical College contains a few references, such as "The board of trustees shall have the power to prescribe the nature, extent, and character of experiments to be made," that might be interpreted to refer to research activities. But by the time of the second Morrill Act in 1890, it was clear that land-grant universities were expected to perform research. The second Morrill Act specifically required land-grant universities to provide an annual report on "experiments."

Regardless, most of the original faculty of the fledgling institution were productive and well-known scholars. Although none of the first group of seven faculty members at the college had PhD degrees, "the spirit of investigation dominated them. They were disposed to seek the laws of nature in the various phenomena in which nature concealed them, rather than in the tomes of a library" (Mendenhall, 1922, 191). Perhaps the most prolific of the original faculty were Edward Orton, professor of geology, mining, and metallurgy and the institution's first president, and T. C. Mendenhall, professor of physics and the mechanical arts. Orton was an economic geologist whose scientific contributions included "anticlinal theory," which could be used to predict the most favorable locations for oil and gas drilling.

Mendenhall was a self-taught physicist and meteorologist who published more than sixty scientific papers on topics in gravity, electricity, seismology, and other areas of physics. He is perhaps best known for inventing the Mendenhall gravimeter, a device for measuring the local gravitational field of the earth. A pendulum-based instrument, it provided the most accurate gravitational measurements of the time, and was widely used in geological field stations in many countries. Mendenhall, like some other scientists of the time, was a bit of a Renaissance scholar. He also published in a field known as "stylometry," which used mathematics to analyze the word structure of the works of famous authors. Mendenhall's early work in this field suggested applications to the works of Shakespeare, Marlowe, and Bacon, and was later used by proponents of the theory that the works of Shakespeare were actually authored by Christopher Marlowe.

Other members of the original faculty of the Ohio Agricultural and Mechanical College were also productive scholars. Norton S. Townshend, professor of agriculture, was the director of the State Board of Agriculture and the author of the *Agriculture of Lorain County* (1867). He was a noted authority on agricultural education, and also published on that topic. A firm believer in the value of agricultural experimentation for future economic success, he argued that experimental farms such as the one located at the Ohio Agricultural and Mechanical College in Columbus were not designed to be economically self-supporting, but rather to provide proof-of-concept evidence for new agricultural techniques, methods, and crops. Robert McFarland, professor of mathematics and civil engineering, was noted for computing the form of the earth's orbit and the longitude of its perihelion for a period of more than five million years. William Lazenby, professor of botany and horticulture who joined the university in 1881, was a noted authority on forestry, who also served as the first director of the Agricultural Experiment Station upon its establishment in 1882. Albert Tuttle, professor of zoology, was an active scholar, publishing papers focused on small organisms such as protozoa and green algae in microscopy journals as well as in broader outlets.

The work of these early scholars was largely self-funded, or supported by state efforts, as in the case of Edward Orton's geological survey for Ohio. However, it became clear at the national level that if land-grant universities were expected to create new scholarship, particularly in agriculture, that could be shared with farmers in the state, additional funding would be needed.

The state legislature authorized the creation of the Ohio Agricultural Experiment Station in 1882, for the purposes of benefitting "the interests of practical and scientific agriculture," several years prior to the passage of the federal Hatch Act of 1887 that provided funds for agricultural experiment stations across the country. When the Hatch Act was passed, providing a funding stream for agricultural experiment stations, its language included the clear intention that agricultural experiment stations should be affiliated with state land-grant universities, although it did permit funding to be directed to preexisting experiment stations that were not officially part of universities. Ohio took advantage of this provision, and the Ohio Agricultural Experiment Station was reorganized under the directorship of Charles Thorne, moving to its present location in Wooster, Ohio, a few years later, in 1892. Similarly, the creation of the Engineering Experiment Station in 1913 provided impetus for the expansion of engineering research at the university.

Further Expansion of the Research Enterprise in the Early Twentieth Century

Much of Ohio State's current sponsored research portfolio is in the medical and health sciences. At its inception, the university did not offer medical training. However, medical research and training did occur in Columbus at Starling Medical College, established in 1848 as a combined medical school and teaching hospital, the first of its kind in the US. The college published its own scholarly journal, the *Ohio Medical and Surgical Journal,* from 1848 to 1864. In 1914, William Oxley Thompson, then president of Ohio State, integrated the medical college into the university to become The Ohio State University College of Medicine. Research activity in the early years included work in poisons, cancer, and gynecology.

The advent of World War I further expanded research at Ohio State, which was one of only six universities authorized by Congress to open aeronautics schools to train military personnel. The formal program opened in 1917 and evolved over the years into programs in aviation, aeronautics, and aerospace engineering. These programs expanded with the construction of Ohio State's airport, later named Don Scott Field, in the 1940s. The success of the Engineering Experiment Station in conducting industrial research led to the establishment of The Ohio State University Research Foundation (OSURF) in 1937. At Ohio State, OSURF focused more on managing industry-sponsored research than on commercialization of faculty inventions. The portfolio of OSURF expanded to encompass all externally sponsored research, including projects sponsored by private foundations in the years leading up to World War II. As federal funding of university research grew after World War II, eventually Ohio State's federally sponsored research far exceeded that sponsored by industry. OSURF continued to manage all of the university's sponsored research until 2008, when these functions were formally reintegrated with the university.

Curiosity-Driven Research in Biological, Physical, and Social Sciences

From the very beginning, faculty at Ohio State pursued not only research with direct practical application but also investigations that were more curiosity-driven, fundamental research. The first faculty did not view this as in any way out of sync with their overall mission to provide education to the "industrial classes." Indeed, there was a strong sense that the earliest students needed to have more than simple vocational training in their specialty field, and that faculty scholarly activity should speak to this need. It was often the very same faculty who pursued both types of inquiry, as noted above with Thomas Mendenhall. From the beginning, fundamental research and inquiry and applied research were interwoven.

Many of the other disciplines that we now view as devoted to fundamental research and inquiry did not begin that way, instead incorporating intertwined threads of basic science and practical application. Moreover, development of new research foci often occurred in response to national or state need, reflecting Ohio State's land-grant mission. This early intermingling foreshadowed the current zeitgeist of translational research, in which fundamental investigation is connected directly to outcomes and applications in the real world.

Factors That Shaped Ohio State's Contemporary Research Environment

Ohio State's research enterprise, like that of other research universities in the US, was shaped by national events, such as World War I, World War II, the Cold War, and the Moon Race. Each of these events demanded a rapid and concentrated response from university researchers, and the trajectories of research programs were altered as a result. In addition, the shift from private to federal support of research after World War II also helped to mold Ohio State's research priorities.

For Ohio State, as for many other public universities, two events were of particular importance. One significant development was the establishment of the National Science Foundation (NSF) in 1950, arising from Vannevar Bush's 1945 policy memo, *Science—the Endless Frontier: A Report to the President on a Program for Postwar Scientific Research.* The other event that helped to shape Ohio State research from the end of World War II onward was the emergence of the National Institutes of Health (NIH) from the Public Health Service, which provided significant funding for research in all areas of health and disease. Funding from these two agencies represents the bulk of federal research funding at Ohio State today.

In the research realm, Ohio State has diversified the pool of external research funding, with particular success in securing funding for industry-sponsored research projects. At present, the university has emerged as one of the nation's top-ranked institutions for total industry-sponsored research expenditures. This trend dovetails well with overall shifts in both federal funding trends and university research priorities, as discussed below.

A second influence has been a profound shift in the public's valuation of US universities. It is clear that at the time of the Morrill Act, and during the founding decades of land-grant universities like Ohio State, higher education was perceived as a so-called public good, creating an educated workforce that would drive economic prosperity, competitiveness, health, and quality of life for the citizens of the state. This contrasts with the current public emphasis on college education as training for a specific career, with subsequent comparison of the costs of attendance with the earnings and employment possibilities attached to any particular course of study. Concomitantly, public emphasis on the practical applicability of university-based research has grown.

Grand Challenges, Wicked Problems, and Convergence

Nationally, the changes in federal funding emphases and public perceptions have brought about a new call for university research to lead directly to solutions to local, national, and global problems. This has played out in various forms of "Grand Challenge" initiatives at universities. Such initiatives focus institutional resources on faculty hiring and research investments in disciplines that can contribute to solving so-called wicked problems, such as global food shortages, poverty, or complex diseases such as cancer. Grand Challenge initiatives emphasize hiring across multiple disciplines rather than concentrating hires in a single discipline. This emphasis arises from the widely held perception that wicked problems are highly complex, with solutions that cannot be found within the bounds of a single discipline.

Federal agencies are increasingly moving to support multidisciplinary approaches to address large societal problems. For example, the National Science Foundation has created a program called the Convergence Accelerator, or C-Accel, which aims to facilitate the integration of approaches and knowledge from multiple disciplines in novel frameworks to address societal needs of national importance. Corollary to the efforts in hiring to address Grand Challenges and federal agency investments in convergence-style research is a set of initiatives to magnify the responsiveness and impact of research, including HIBAR (Highly Integrative Basic and Responsive Research) and PIR (Public Impact-focused Research) (The National Academies 2017).

In the realm of research, we seem to have come full circle, back to the founding principles of the original land-grant universities: the creation and dissemination of knowledge for the benefit of the citizens. The pressure on federal agencies to drive their funding toward issues of practical benefit for the nation, the increasing public pressure on universities to be "relevant" to their constituencies, the growing interest—particularly among younger scholars—in collaborations that span the boundaries of disciplines, and the need to create meaningful change all come together to drive this return to basic principles.

Ohio State's most recent Grand Challenge–style program, still in progress, is the Discovery Themes. Begun in 2014, this program was a mix of bottom-up and top-down direction. Three broad Grand Challenge themes were identified by the board of trustees and university leaders, encompassing food safety and security, health and wellness, and energy and environment. Each was targeted for significant faculty hiring. Within those themes, faculty groups submitted ideas for specific focus areas, which were competitively reviewed. Two foci were developed under the food safety and security area, Foods for Health and the Initiative for Food and AgriCultural Transformation (InFACT). In the health and wellness area, focus topics in Chronic Brain Injury and Infectious Diseases emerged, and under energy and environment, foci in Materials and Manufacturing for Sustainability and Sustainable and Resilient Economy were established. In addition, two other foci were created: Translational Data Analytics and Global Arts and Humanities. Each of these latter areas was viewed as cross-cutting, connecting all the other foci.

Fast-forward to the present, and each of the themes is faced with determining how it will evolve to realize the full potential of the new expertise that has entered the university. Three of the focus areas have morphed to become institutes that foster multidisciplinary collaboration among new and existing faculty across colleges. Others are pondering their next move. The overall goal is to find ways to create lasting impact from the university's investment, using the research generated under each theme to create interventions, cures, and discoveries that will address the global problems each was designed to tackle. While other universities are making Grand Challenge–style investments as well, the magnitude of Ohio State's commitment to this initiative gives it national visibility, with the hope that the impact will be particularly significant.

The Discovery Themes are completely consistent with a return to the university's original mission—to improve the lives of citizens. Although at its founding Ohio State's constituency was defined as the citizens of the state of Ohio, the intervening years of research that addresses national priorities (as in World Wars I and II, the space race, etc.) and the increasing realization that we are an interconnected global society have expanded and combined to redefine the university's constituency. Today we speak of Ohio State's mission to improve the lives of the people of Ohio, the nation, and the world.

Further signs of Ohio State's recommitment to its original land-grant values are seen in the university's response to urgent priorities of the city, region, and state. For the past several years, the state has invested several million dollars each year in university research that can shed light on the causes of harmful algal blooms in Lake Erie and other bodies of water across the state, as well as on possible mitigation strategies. These grants are managed by Ohio State's Stone Laboratory.

Other major challenges face the people of Ohio. At the present time, opioid addiction is a blight on the state, consuming the lives of thousands of people. The consequences of addiction include loss of valuable workforce, criminal activity, and death. The consensus is that it will require the efforts of a dedicated and multidisciplinary team that includes not only the university but also community and government agencies, all working together to address the problem. Ohio State leads a consortium of six universities, together with government and community partners, in an intervention project in nineteen Ohio counties. This consortium is funded by the National Institutes of Health's HEALing Communities Initiative as one of four such collaborations across the nation.

Other concerns facing the state (and the nation and world) include ones related to workforce in the light of the already-occurring revolution in automation, as well as how the state and the country will maintain a strong economy in the face of an aging demographic. Both of these issues are on the minds of the university's researchers. Investments in research expertise in automation, artificial intelligence, and human-machine teaming are underway. Ohio State has also developed research expertise to serve the largest economic sectors of Ohio. The largest industry sectors statewide include automotive, manufacturing, agriculture, and aerospace. The university is strong in all of these sectors, and has created research centers that offer expertise to industry and student talent for Ohio's workforce. Materials development, particularly in polymers, is another strong economic sector; Ohio State today has more than 200 materials researchers on campus. In addition, in the Columbus region, the private sector includes financial services, logistics, insurance, and health care.

The university has engaged extensively with industry for almost 100 years, so much so that in 2019 Ohio State ranked third in the nation in industry-sponsored research expenditures. Ohio State has moved beyond a desire to limit engagement with industry to one-time research project funding, however. Increasingly, the university is exploring the development of deeper partnerships with chosen industries. Deep partnerships between industry and university ensure that both entities will derive benefits from joint projects and initiatives. Concomitantly, innovation and commercialization activities derive from university research and are valued contributions to knowledge and society.

Another aspect of this full-circle return to applications-oriented, problem-focused discovery is the realization that university researchers cannot solve these problems alone. As is the case with university partnerships with industry, research that aims to have community impact is now being designed and performed with collaboration and involvement from the end users in the community. Within the university, collaboration is everywhere, and the opportunities to connect are pervasive in a university with fifteen colleges located in close proximity. Although engagement in the community has been a hallmark through the years of some of Ohio State's colleges, in areas such as agriculture, education, and medicine, community engagement has been a more recent development for other units of the university. At present, engagement is seen across the university as a crucial component in research, maximizing its impact. The involvement of the community in both the design and the execution of research is fundamental to initiatives such as the NSF Convergence program and the HIBAR and PIR efforts.

The State of Curiosity-Driven Research, the Arts, and the Humanities

This chapter has focused largely on research in its traditional sense, with paradigms of theory and experimentation, driven by hypotheses and producing data that are amenable to statistical analysis and modeling. Numerous discoveries have resulted from this work, expanding our understanding of fundamental phenomena of our world, providing insights into the workings of the human mind, and unraveling the genetic signatures of thousands of species.

In a time when the university's, and the government's, research investment priorities are increasingly shaped by the factors described in the previous sections, what is the fate of fundamental, curiosity-driven research? The answer to this question is not straightforward, because research costs money, and dollars are more and more being directed to these so-called wicked problems. Nonetheless, researchers understand that without solid fundamental research that drives our understanding forward, the solutions-oriented work that directly addresses large societal problems will not succeed. Most researchers, regardless of the discipline in which they work, believe it imperative that we continue to invest in fundamental science and social science. In a society in which immediate outcomes are increasingly demanded, it can be difficult to justify fundamental science and social science, where the potential applicability may be many years into the future. Nonetheless, the research enterprise depends on the continuing pipeline of new knowledge, from which applications, translations, and innovations arise.

Even more endangered are funds to support scholarship and creative inquiry in the arts and humanities. Justin Morrill placed considerable emphasis on the importance of the liberal arts in higher education, as evidenced by an 1887 address. In the original concept of the land-grant college, teaching and scholarship in the liberal arts were deemed necessary in order to introduce the industrial classes to common cultural referents, making these referents available to all social and economic levels. Even at the beginning, there was dissent; many of Morrill's contemporaries did not share this view. However, questions about the relevance of these disciplines have grown over the past few decades. Fogel (2012) notes that professors in such fields as modern languages, history, art, philosophy, dance, and creative writing have felt "increasingly marginalized and embattled" (247).

The creation and production of art, dance, music, and theater offer insights into the creative process that define our very humanity. In offering a world of cultural experiences, the arts and humanities bring together and unite humanity in ways not possible via other means. It could be argued that the arts and humanities are more crucial for society today than ever in the past, when global tensions and societal divisions threaten the very fabric of life. Ohio State's Global Arts and Humanities Discovery Theme addresses these concerns, promoting a "different set of methodological possibilities and practices that attend to human entanglements with technology and ecological systems, cultural belonging and place making and the legacies of domination and displacement" (Hesford n.d.).

Universities must find the equilibrium that allows them to continue to support scholarship and education in the arts and humanities, and must present the arguments that underscore their value in an environment that views education as increasingly utilitarian and vocational. The creativity that is evident in arts and humanities scholarship and creative inquiry can be a powerful force in innovation, bringing a new perspective to problems more typically viewed through a science lens. Increasing collaboration has produced, and will continue to produce, solutions that would not have been envisioned if addressed from a single discipline. In the same vein, the intermingling of arts and humanities with science and technology has led to new artistic endeavors not envisioned otherwise. The value of these endeavors must be articulated in a compelling way to a dubious public.

Rosenberg (2003) has argued that the responsiveness of US public universities to their local and regional economies is their "most distinctive feature" (113). His argument stems from the observation that in the absence of a federally funded and managed university system, each university was much more dependent on its state legislature and local industries and economic forces than was the case for universities in other countries. The land-grant concept and the emphasis on meeting the needs of the state's economy have placed land-grant universities, including Ohio State, in a position to move discoveries into innovations that can lead to products and services that enhance a region's economy.

A remaining question is how to define Ohio State's global footprint in a changing national context. After World War II, it became increasingly clear that the US had an important role to play in world events, and universities expanded their perspective to encompass a global mission. Over the course of the past few decades, researchers realized that many of the problems they studied were global in scope, and it was not possible to pursue solutions without considering global interconnections. Researchers across all disciplines have become global in their thinking, and Ohio State has a large network of international connections in both teaching and research endeavors.

But in the past few years, a rising trend of "deglobalization" has begun to emerge on the national political scene, with concomitant consequences for federal research funding. This trend has already impacted the recruitment and retention of students and faculty from particular countries, and may help to fuel a loss of US competitiveness on the global stage. Ohio State, like most US universities, has sought to attract the brightest and most innovative talent for its faculty and student ranks, regardless of where those individuals come from, but this is becoming more difficult in the present political climate. How this trend will evolve is unclear, but it underscores the fact that universities, including Ohio State, are not insulated from the winds of politics. If federal support for international initiatives declines, faculty will shift their efforts to other interests, to the detriment of comprehensive solutions for wicked problems.

The Future of Research at Ohio State

The preceding sections have outlined factors and trends that have shaped Ohio State's present course in research and discovery. As discussed, the university's past has inevitably formed its present, and by the same token, its present will surely shape its future. So which features of the current research landscape will shape Ohio State as it reaches toward the future of research?

First, Ohio State's well-ingrained impetus toward collaboration, particularly across disciplinary boundaries, will position the university to meet future complex challenges. The co-location of fifteen colleges and the ease of transcending those boundaries will be necessary to maximize research impact in addressing challenges in areas such as health and wellness, environment, and the social fabric in the future. Breadth and depth are assets, but only if they are underwoven with the spirit of collaboration.

Second, the university's long-standing history of partnerships with external entities, particularly industry, should continue and expand into the future. As federal support for research continues to slip, the need for industry to step in to partner with universities to address national imperatives will grow, to meet mutual goals. The intersection of government, industry, and university working together will increasingly be needed to address our biggest challenges.

Finally, the growing emphasis on excellence in both the student body and the faculty research enterprise will afford Ohio State a leadership position in many research areas. Ohio State is already well known in a variety of research specialties, and the university's ability to invest to create deep faculty clusters in chosen areas will cement that leadership position. Further, an expanding interest in innovation and entrepreneurship will provide a boost of creativity to the research enterprise, accelerating impact.

However, the current landscape requires universities to operate in an adaptive and flexible manner in order to respond to rapidly changing research issues. To be a true leader in the future of research, Ohio State will need to create frameworks for faculty success that are not limited to traditional disciplinary siloes, with performance metrics that transcend the traditional "publish or perish" in specified outlets. Universities do not let go of tradition lightly, but the pace of change will necessitate a willingness to move beyond tradition.

In *The New ABCs of Research* (2016), Shneiderman outlines several trends and practices that should magnify the impact of research, and should thus serve as a set of ground rules for future research activities. First, he argues that combining basic and applied research in pursuit of a problem will increase impact compared to pursuing each separately. Shneiderman notes that pursuing applied research often leads to basic research breakthroughs that have broad impact. Second, Shneiderman advocates combining science, engineering, and design approaches in addressing a problem. Each of these approaches has a different set of techniques, methods, and ethics, and blending them will produce more creative efforts to find solutions. Third is the imperative to form diverse teams of researchers to attack problems. Teams that include diverse disciplines, gender diversity, a balance of junior and senior researchers, and varied internal and external partners are likely to have greater success in achieving solutions. Finally, attention to the metrics chosen to measure success and the need to adopt agile processes are noted as essential to a highly functioning research effort. All of these recommendations are things that Ohio State is well positioned to incorporate into research strategy.

Staley (2019) insists that in the future, all universities need not be the same in structure, goals, or approaches. This argument is consistent with that regarding the land-grant university mission, as articulated by Gee (2012). Gee argues that just as the state and regional environments in which universities find themselves are not homogeneous, the mission of the university should be tailored first and foremost to the needs of those state and regional environments. It is not necessary, he contends, for all public universities to be identical, and particularly not for land-grant universities. These two complementary notions open up a wide array of possibilities for imagining the future Ohio State. Just as Orton, Mendenhall, Townshend, and the other original faculty could not have envisioned the Ohio State of today, it is likely that we cannot truly imagine the Ohio State of 50 or 100 years hence. Nonetheless, the seeds that are sown in the present will surely help to create the Ohio State research enterprise of the future.

As the university celebrates its sesquicentennial year and the many accomplishments of Ohio State research, discovery, and creative inquiry over the past 150 years, it also celebrates the impact of this research enterprise on society. From this vantage point, Ohio State can look back with gratitude to the pioneers who created and shaped the present, and look forward with optimism to continuing contributions to solutions for the biggest problems facing Ohio, the nation, and the world.

References

Brown, Sandra. 2018. "APLU: Public Impact-Focused Research." Presentation at the APLU annual meeting, November 11, 2018. http://www.aplu.org/members/councils/research/cor-meetings/cor-2018/Public%20Impact%20Focused%20Research_111118.pdf.

Cannon Act. 1870. H.B. No. 29, 59th General Assembly, Regular Session. https://library.osu.edu/documents/university-archives/Cannon_Act_1870_bill.pdf.

Coon, John. 2015. "Top 5 Industries in Ohio: Which Parts of the Economy Are the Strongest?" *Newsmax,* April 13, 2015. https://www.newsmax.com/FastFeatures/industries-in-ohio-economy/2015/04/13/id/638126.

Fogel, Daniel Mark. 2012. "Challenges to Equilibrium: The Role of the Arts and Humanities in the Public Research University." In *Precipice or Crossroads: Where America's Great Public Universities Stand and Where They Are Going Midway through Their Second Century,* edited by Daniel Mark Fogel and Elizabeth Malson-Huddle, 241–57. New York: SUNY Press.

Gee, E. Gordon. 2012. "The Modern Public University: Its Land-Grant Heritage, Its Land-Grant Horizon." In *Precipice or Crossroads: Where America's Great Public Universities Stand and Where They Are Going Midway through Their Second Century,* edited by Daniel Mark Fogel and Elizabeth Malson-Huddle, 51–62. New York: SUNY Press.

Health Sciences Library, The Ohio State University. n.d. "Starling Medical College." https://hsl.osu.edu/mhc/8-starling-medical-college.

Hesford, W. (n.d.). https://globalartsandhumanities.osu.edu/about/discover-global-arts-humanities.https://globalartsandhumanities.osu.edu/about.

Lazenby, W. 1913. "The Forests and Forestry of Germany." *Popular Science Monthly* 83, 590–98. https://en.wikisource.org/wiki/Popular_Science_Monthly/Volume_83/December_1913/The_Forests_and_Forestry_of_Germany.

Mendenhall, T. C. 1887. "The Characteristic Curves of Composition." *Science* 9: 237–46.

———. 1901. "A Mechanical Solution of a Literary Problem." *Popular Science* 60 (December). https://en.wikisource.org/wiki/Popular_Science_Monthly/Volume_60/December_1901/A_Mechanical_Solution_of_a_Literary_Problem.

Mendenhall, T. 1922. "The First Faculty of The Ohio State University." In *History of The Ohio State University v.3: Addresses and Proceedings of the Semicentennial Celebration, October 13–16, 1920,* edited by Thomas C. Mendenhall. Columbus, OH: The Ohio State University Press.

The National Academies. 2017. "HIBAR Workshop—Developing HIBAR Partnerships: Lessons from Experience. https://vimeo.com/224698537.

National Science Foundation. n.d. "Higher Education Research and Development Survey Fiscal Year 2017." https://ncsesdata.nsf.gov/herd/2017/html/herd2017_dst_05.html.

———. 2018. "NSF Convergence Accelerator (C-Accel)." https://www.nsf.gov/od/oia/convergence-accelerator/index.jsp.

Orton, E. 1884. The Massilon Coal Field. *Ohio Mining Journal* 3, no. 1 (November): 32–38. https://kb.osu.edu/handle/1811/32288.

———. 1885. Salt and Bromine Production in Ohio: Salt Wells of the Pomeroy District. *Ohio Mining Journal* 3, no. 2: 7–14.

———. 1887. *Preliminary Report upon Petroleum and Inflammable Gas.* Columbus, OH: A. H. Smythe. https://archive.org/details/PreliminaryReportUponPetroleumAndInflammableGas1887/page/n8.

Paulson, George W. 2010. *In Pursuit of Excellence: The Ohio State University Medical Center—from 1834 to 2010.* Fremont, OH: Leshner Printers.

Rosenberg, Nathan. 2003. "America's Entrepreneurial Universities." In *The Emergence of Entrepreneurship Policy: Governance, Start-Ups, and Growth in the U. S. Knowledge Economy,* edited by David M. Hart, 113–40. Cambridge: Cambridge University Press.

Shneiderman, Ben. 2016. *The New ABCs of Research: Achieving Breakthrough Collaborations.* Oxford: Oxford University Press.

Staley, David J. 2019. *Alternative Universities: Speculative Design for Innovation in Higher Education.* Baltimore: Johns Hopkins University Press.

Townshend, N. S. 1867. *The Agriculture of Lorain County.* Columbus, OH: Nevins & Myers.

Tree, D. Alan. 2014. "Research and Other Scholarship." In *The Modern Land-Grant University,* edited by Robert J. Sternberg, 35–58. West Lafayette, IN: Purdue University Press.

Tuttle, A. H. 1872. "One of Our Common Monads." *The American Naturalist* 6: 286–89.

———. 1926. "The Reproductive Cycle of the Characeae." *Science* 60, no. 1557: 412–13.

US Department of Agriculture, National Institute of Food and Agriculture. n.d. "The Hatch Act of 1887." https://nifa.usda.gov/program/hatch-act-1887.

7

Engagement

The Land-Grant Compact through Time and Change

STEPHEN C. MYERS

Engagement, through time and change, is at the core of what makes The Ohio State University prominent and unique. Engagement involves a special compact between the public and the university, a belief that societal challenges are best solved through meaningful partnerships that bring together a diversity of talents and ideas. As societal challenges have changed over time, The Ohio State University has repeatedly established relevance through just such partnerships with the people and institutions of Ohio, the nation, and the world. That these partnerships have always been able to adapt to change in ways relevant to society is the essence of what keeps The Ohio State University prominent and unique.

As we celebrate 150 years since the founding of The Ohio State University, it is worth noting that 2012 marked the sesquicentennial of the Morrill Act establishing land-grant universities across the United States. A vision promoted despite the turmoil of the Civil War, the new land-grant universities would develop the expertise that the public could count on to assist them in solving pressing societal challenges. At the outset, this expertise mirrored emerging nineteenth-century ideas of the importance

The author acknowledges the contributions of Karen Bruns, Julie Carpenter-Hubin, Darrell Gray, Bobby Moser, Randy Moses, Melinda Nelson, Roger Rennekamp, Dick Stoddard, and Barbara Vieira.

of science and technology to manufacturing and agriculture with the aim of better preparing the public for these enterprises through education.

Embodied in this aspirational mission of the 1862 Morrill Act to serve societal needs, engagement was the crucible from which leaders forged the form and function of the new "land-grant university." As socioeconomic shifts occurred in society, the land-grant university was to evolve accordingly. This made land-grant universities fundamentally different from the exclusive model of higher education that existed before the Morrill Act. The imperative to change in response to societal issues provided land-grant universities with a competitive advantage because, as University of Georgia chancellor W. B. Hill stated in 1905, "It will connect its activities more closely with the business and life of the people" (Mawby 155).This unique approach to change over time fostered the relevance of these new universities and placed them front and center as engines of innovation.

While the land-grant mission to serve society was the paradigm across the country, states were free to develop their land-grant institutions in a manner best addressing their unique local needs. One can easily imagine the variety of debates that occurred across our country as various interest groups voiced opinions about what their land-grant university should be or do. This "national vision customized to local needs" approach, along with the constant change in public needs and perceptions over time, is well illustrated in Ohio.

The tension about the form and function of The Ohio State University began with its establishment in 1870 and continues to the present. Initially called the Ohio Agricultural and Mechanical College, the nascent institution inspired vigorous conversation about resources, location, and curriculum. Existing Ohio universities competed for allocation of funding made available through the Morrill Act. Various industrial interests sought favorable siting for the new university. There was also a sharp divide about what the university would teach: Should it offer just the agricultural and mechanical arts, consistent with its name, or should its curriculum be broader?

Ultimately, the legislature placed the new university in the state capital of Columbus, supporting the governor's view that the central location would keep the university more independent from vested interests across the state. A board of trustees initially composed of members representing each congressional district decided to offer a more wide-ranging curriculum. As a result, in 1878 the institution's name was changed to The Ohio State University. The visionary leaders of the nineteenth century positioned The Ohio State University well, enabling it to develop into

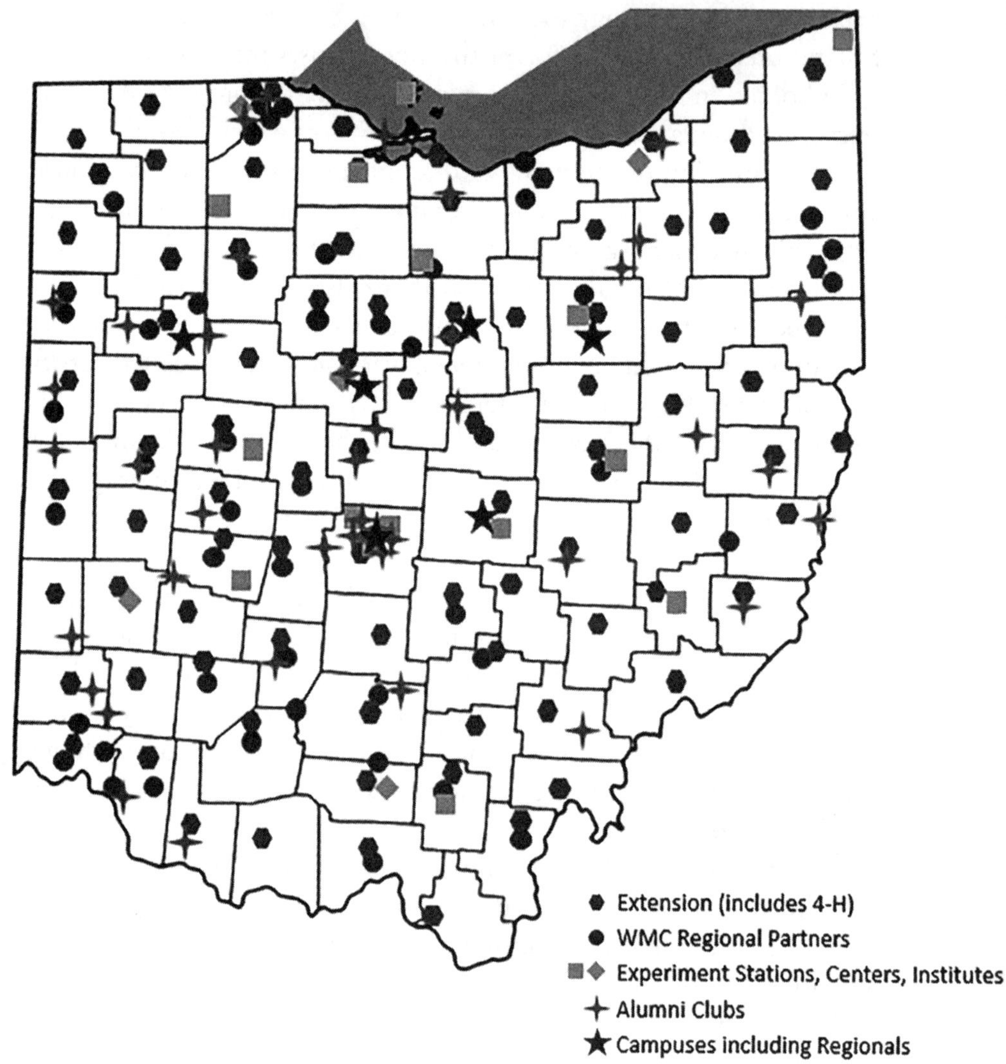

FIGURE 7.1. Ohio State presence across Ohio communities

a comprehensive university well suited to address a broad range of challenges that would come to shape the following century.

However, the various tensions among location, activities, and resources would continue to drive the need for significant engagement between the university and the public both then and now. The inclusion of research and outreach to complement the original land-grant focus on teaching was eventually supported by funds authorized by both state and federal legislation. In the early 1880s, the state legislature allocated monies to establish agricultural experiment stations, initially developed to better serve the agricultural industry across the state (figure 7.1).

In 1887, the Hatch Act provided land-grant universities with federal funds to support agricultural experiment stations and to share information with the agricultural industry. Similarly, the Ohio legislature ultimately passed legislation to support the development of an engineering experiment station, which was intended to share practical applications of research with the engineering industry. The federal government strengthened the emphasis on research with the Adams Act of 1906 and then expanded the outreach mission of land-grant universities through the 1914 Smith-Lever Act that established Cooperative Extension Services.

As the importance of research expanded, the university began to offer graduate degrees. In 1906, the Ohio legislature passed the Eagleson Bill, which established that research and doctoral education among the public universities would be the sole purview of The Ohio State University. Ohio State established a graduate school in 1912 to support the rapid enrollment for master's and doctoral programs. The impact of the Eagleson Bill lasted until the middle of the twentieth century, when other Ohio-based universities developed and expanded graduate programs in response to population growth in the state.

It is worth noting that state and federal legislation involving land-grant universities created a unique partnership that continues to shape the public and private sector dialogue in Ohio. The Cooperative Extension model places Ohio State University–affiliated professionals with expertise in youth development (4-H), agricultural production, and community development directly into Ohio's eighty-eight counties. The historical role of these professionals was twofold. Not only were they supposed to share newly discovered knowledge with the public, but they were also on the "front line" in terms of assessing emergent public needs and then reporting those findings to colleagues on the campus in Columbus. Such partnerships fostered a unique level of engagement, accountability, trust, and relevance among various business and industry stakeholders as well as partners at the local, county, state, and federal levels.

Similar narratives regarding engagement and the development of collaborative partnerships have emerged across other academic areas within Ohio State. Community health and wellness, led by the Wexner Medical Center and the associated health science colleges, is another area that highlights Ohio State's ability to address the needs of the public. Medicine's history as part of a land-grant university tradition is notable. In 1904, there were 160 institutions in the US that granted medical degrees. By 1935, only sixty-six medical colleges remained, and fifty-seven of those had merged with universities.

This transformation resulted from the 1910 Flexner Report, a document that called for more uniform and rigorous training in an academic setting, closer alignment with scientific research, and state regulation of medical schools (see Ellison's essay in chapter 9 for more details). In 1918, the Starling Medical College merged with Ohio State to establish a new College of Medicine (along with a new College of Dentistry). Over time, The Ohio State University has evolved to have one of the largest, most diverse, and preeminent academic medical centers in the country. Building on the land-grant model of partnering to better serve the community, the Wexner Medical Center launched a new alliance in 2018 with Mercy Health, part of Bon Secours Mercy Health. This partnership leverages Ohio State's highly specialized academic research, teaching, and clinical capabilities with Mercy Health's geographical footprint across the region, proven clinical service, and robust health care business acumen. Ultimately, the partnership will leverage strengths to create healthier communities.

Rapid growth and global conflicts during the twentieth century have had a significant impact on Ohio State as it evolved to serve the needs of the country. In 1917, Ohio State was one of six universities selected by the War Department to establish a School of Military Aeronautics. In 1939, Ohio State took part in the Civilian Pilot Training Program with the Civil Aeronautics Administration to promote private aviation. In WWII, graduates of this program could enter the service as commissioned pilots. (Ohio State is one of the few universities with an airport that continues to develop aviation professionals through its training program as well as provide specialized corporate partnerships.) During WWI, Ohio State developed a two-year medical degree to support the significant demand of the war. Following the war, a massive influx of students taking advantage of the GI Bill resulted in a 67 percent increase in enrollment from 1940 to 1946. The Columbus campus was transformed to serve this growth with new housing, expansion of the library, and relocation of agricultural facilities west of the Olentangy River. The university, led by the Office of Military and Veterans Services, continues to partner with Ohio communities in serving the needs of veterans and their families.

A study conducted in the early 1950s by Ohio State showed that the state population had grown dramatically during the postwar period, but residents were faced with the prospect of moving away from their communities to attend college, which limited many. In response to this need, the Ohio State Board of Trustees established regional campuses in partnership with local communities. Today, students can attend The Ohio

State University at campuses in Mansfield, Lima, Marion, Newark, or Wooster to earn a degree or ultimately transfer to the Columbus campus to finish their degree. From an original class of twenty-four undergraduate students at a single campus in 1873, Ohio State now has a typical student population of 60,000 at six campuses across Ohio participating in educational programs at the undergraduate, graduate, and professional levels. Today, Ohio State has one of the largest alumni bases in the world, and the relationship with this group is stewarded by the Alumni Association.

The latter part of twentieth century witnessed the beginning of a disconnect between the public and a range of institutions, including public universities, which continues to reverberate across university campuses. An "age of accountability" has developed with a call for universities to take on characteristics more common in private enterprises, including but not limited to an emphasis on national rankings. Universities have reacted in ways that have tended to move public universities further away from their original public serving and inclusive nature. A notable change in public funding has been addressed in many cases by increases in student tuition as well as an emphasis on new modes of revenue generation. Combined with economic recession, declines in disposable income and major shifts in workforce trends have led to student debt being at an all-time high, student completion rates remaining an issue, and major questions about the relevance of certain degrees. In effect, a perception has emerged that public universities have become what they were created *not to be.* Public opinion surveys in 2018 have shown a continued decline in confidence in higher education including a range of perceptions from a loss of relevance to a biased campus environment.

During these times, Ohio State has been a leader in shaping the conversation about the contemporary role of land-grant universities at the local and national level. In the 1990s, the institution participated in the national conversation about the need to redefine the priorities of public universities, including the importance of engaged scholarship. In 1995, senior leadership established an Ad Hoc Committee on University Outreach that advanced the importance of the term *engagement,* defined as meaningful and mutually beneficial collaboration with partners in the implementation of the university's mission across research, teaching, and service. In 1996, Ohio State had a senior leadership role on the Kellogg Commission on the Future of State and Land-grant Universities. The commission report, published in 1999, urged the expansion of the land-grant university beyond outreach and service to full engagement with communities. Universities were encouraged to consider engagement as central to their mission based on defined characteristics of the engaged institution. Guiding characteristics were established that included:

- Responsiveness
- Respect for Partners
- Academic Neutrality
- Accessibility
- Integration
- Coordination
- Resource Partnerships

In 1996, Ohio State partnered with Pennsylvania State University and the University of Wisconsin to establish the National Outreach Scholarship, which eventually became the Engagement Scholarship Consortium, a 501(c)(3) nonprofit composed of forty state public and private universities that work to advance the importance of strong community-university partnerships anchored in the rigors of scholarship.

The early part of the twenty-first century has been an exciting time for Ohio State as an engaged university. In 2001, the university formalized a university-level Office of Outreach and Engagement. Led by that office, Ohio State received the Community Engagement Classification in 2008 from the Carnegie Foundation; that classification was renewed in 2015.

Also in 2001, with support from the W. K. Kellogg Foundation, the Association of Public and Land-grant Universities established the C. Peter McGrath Award for Community Engagement. In 2013, Ohio State established the University Engagement Recognition Awards program and won the McGrath Award with its Young Scholars Program.

In 2015, a College Engagement Council (CEC) was established involving representatives from all colleges and regional campuses. That group has driven the development of a new university-wide vision for engagement based on the theory that the complexities of societal challenges are best solved through meaningful partnerships representing a diversity of ideas and talents. These meaningful partnerships, which enhance impact by promoting innovation and relevance, are built on fundamental principles:

- **Awareness of partner needs** associated with values, assets, and challenges
- **Shared resources and responsibilities** leveraging strengths for mutual benefit and collective impact

- **Accountability through evidence** in practice and evaluation
- **Commitment to stewardship** ensuring trust, compromise, efficiency, and sustainability of partnerships
- **Recognition of successes** affirming the value of partnerships

The CEC has led the establishment of a new University Community Engagement Conference that brings together faculty, staff, students, and their community partners to network and share best practices. With the creation of *Engaged Scholars,* an online, searchable catalogue housed at the university library, the university-community activities presented at the conference are being accessed and shared widely. The university's Institute for Democratic Engagement and Accountability has been established to create and disseminate knowledge that supports democratic governance. The institute advances the belief that when community dialogue and deliberation allow citizens to share perspectives and values with each other, they will be better able to appreciate reasonable differences and reach areas of common ground. The institute has partnered with the Kettering Foundation to utilize National Issues Forums to promote public deliberation and civic professionalism.

University-community partnerships that have generated new funding sources have had a dramatic impact on Ohio State and its ability to fulfill its land-grant mission. In 2012, the Discovery Themes became one of the largest initiatives in the university's history designed specifically to address compelling challenges of the twenty-first century. For example, using external and internal scans, the area of data analytics was identified as a rapidly emerging area, one with the power and potential to broadly transform society. From Ohio State's investment in this area, a new Translational Data Analytics Institute was formed with significant public-private support. Concurrently, one of the nation's first undergraduate majors in data analytics was created, informed by external feedback and trends to enhance relevance and student success.

As part of its land-grant mandate, the university is deploying novel strategies to address the issues of access and affordability for students. Funds from public-private partnerships are being used to transform the university's commitment to student success, with a focus on enhancing the learning environment. Major funding is being redirected to support students in addressing the issue of affordability and retention. Ohio State is providing leadership at the national level. As part of the University Innovation Alliance, Ohio State and other public universities are sharing best practices such as predictive analytics to enhance the success of students who identify as low income, first generation, or students of color. The American Talent Initiative, a consortium of universities launched in 2016, seeks to attract, enroll, and graduate 50,000 additional high-achieving, low- and moderate-income students by 2025.

Throughout the twentieth and now into the twenty-first century, The Ohio State University has maintained a notable sense of the inevitability of change and the imperative to engage society. Through engagement with society and the meaningful partnerships that emerge, Ohio State has changed in form and function while maintaining a strong sense of mission. As we celebrate the sesquicentennial, the university is integral to socioeconomic realities shaping Ohio, the nation, and the world. As in the past, Ohio State is employing the "land-grant approach" in forming partnerships between the university and the public. If the past is a predictor of the future, the unique perspective to adjust to the needs of society will position The Ohio State University at the forefront of relevance and preeminence as a public-serving institution. With an extensive presence across the Ohio communities steeped in history and tradition, The Ohio State University and the public have the building blocks to form further meaningful partnerships in ways that will renew the "land-grant compact" and have a transformational impact in the twenty-first century. Time and change will surely show.

References

Mawby, Russell G. 1996. "The Challenge for Outreach for Land-Grant Universities as They Move Into the 21st Century." *Journal of Public Service & Outreach* 1, no. 1: 46–56.

Manifestation of the Mission

8

Engaging Ohio's Youth and Fulfilling the Land-Grant Mission through 4-H Youth Development

KIRK BLOIR AND SCOTT D. SCHEER

Both 4-H Youth Development (4-H) and The Ohio State University (OSU) share foundations that are firmly rooted in the power of engaging with learners in pursuit of a practical education. At once a mandate and enduring mission, the Morrill Act established that the people's institutions should "teach such branches of learning . . . to promote practical education . . . in the several pursuits and professions of life." This core philosophy gives significant priority to deepening understanding and developing new knowledge.

4-H advances youth development through its four *H*'s: Head (cognition), Heart (social-emotional), Hands (service, citizenship), and Health (physical and mental). While once a lofty ideal, the mandate of engaged scholarship, realized through the four *H*'s, is now an everyday occurrence and also a driving force of modern land-grant universities.

4-H is one of four core programs of The Ohio State University Extension. The Cooperative Extension Service (CES) was created as a national effort with the passage of the Smith-Lever Act in 1914. Over the course of the past century, 4-H has reached youth in every county, town, and city in Ohio to promote positive development by delivering on the promise of OSU's land-grant mission thanks in large part to the foundational work and articulate tenacity of an Ohio and OSU pioneer, Albert B. Graham.

The Birth of Boys' and Girls' Agricultural Experiment Clubs

The first prototype of what would come to be known as 4-H took root in Clark County, Ohio, in 1902. Graham was a schoolmaster from rural Ohio who, like the authors of and those who would work to implement the Morrill Act, envisioned a practical education that would embrace the learner in an educational process aimed at helping to enrich and enlarge their prospects and prosperity. At age seventeen, Graham began teaching in a one-room schoolhouse. The years he spent toiling in spartan township school buildings crystalized his beliefs that young people would learn and retain more when they were more fully engaged—with heads, hands, and heart—in the learning process.

When Graham became superintendent of Springfield Township, Clark County, Ohio, he took steps to enrich the learning environment and experience. Graham drew upon the existing resources of the communities he served—parent volunteers who worked alongside businessmen from the township and the school buildings that were vacant after school hours and in the summer—to provide students with opportunities for deeper learning by exploring topics that were of interest to them. Chief among these experiential learning opportunities was Graham's Boys' and Girls' Agricultural Experiment Club.

Early in 1902, Superintendent Graham had talked with his teachers, parents, and local business leaders about his idea of bringing boys and girls together during after-school hours to do experiments in agriculture. He then invited students from all his township schools to the county building on a Saturday while their parents were doing their weekly shopping in town. About thirty students attended the first meeting. Graham gave them litmus paper he obtained from a local drug store and showed them how to test their home garden soil for acidity. He also worked with those who were interested to make plans for growing experimental plots of corn and flowers. Later club activities included learning to tie knots and splice ropes, collecting insects, and identifying trees. Interest in the club grew, and Graham welcomed the help of parents and teachers working alongside him to guide the youths' many varied explorations and experimentation.

Connecting with Ohio State

Graham, who had read about the work being done by researchers at the Ohio Agricultural Experiment Stations in their popular bulletins (which were funded by the Hatch Act), wrote to Thomas Hunt, dean of the College of Agriculture at OSU, to request assistance with his club efforts. Dean Hunt connected him with the OSU Agricultural Student Union, which was affiliated with OSU's Agricultural Experiment Station. Graham requested and received several varieties of seeds from the experiment station to give the youth in his clubs. The student union provided planting instructions and systematic observation report forms that Graham modified for his students' use. Club members planted and made systematic observations of their plots—temperature, precipitation, signs of pests, and yields.

One of the more important aspects about Graham's boys' and girls' club is the fact that they were both coeducational and integrated at a time when US society was still largely divided along gender and racial lines. From the beginning, Graham's clubs were integrated and open to both genders. Pictures of his early groups of youth show both boys and girls, both black and white, side by side and partners in the pursuit of horticultural enlightenment.

Word of mouth, largely spread by members of the OSU Agricultural Student Union in their own counties, eventually resulted in Dean Hunt receiving many requests for information about how to replicate the agricultural experiment club in Springfield Township in Clark County. Dean Hunt responded to the influx of inquiries by publishing "Rural School Agriculture," a bulletin that described Graham's boys' and girls' club so that other interested teachers and superintendents could start their own. The bulletin was revised, expanded, and reissued in March 1904 by the new dean of the OSU College of Agriculture, Homer Price. Graham had written a large section of the updated bulletin. It included a sample club constitution and an offer by the college to provide observation report forms and seeds for one club per township so long as the club had at least ten members, with none younger than age eight. In return, the college requested each club to report the name of the club; names of its president, vice president, secretary, and all other members; and the date it was organized.

In the fall of 1904, Dean Price reported to the US Department of Agriculture (USDA) that Ohio had "16 regularly organized clubs with a membership of 664, distributed in 10 counties" and that the college had provided seeds for 2,838 experiments with vegetables, corn, and flowers (McCormick and McCormick 1984, 62). Perhaps because of the growing popularity and success of Graham's ideas, speeches, and writings on boys' and girls' agricultural experiment clubs, Dean Price and OSU President

Oxley Thompson began to have conversations with Graham about joining OSU.

OSU's First Superintendent of Extension

In April 1905, the OSU Board of Trustees appointed Graham as Ohio State's first superintendent of agricultural extension. He began that job on July 1, 1905. On Sunday, July 2, 1905, Graham wrote OSU's first extension plan of work, which included the goal, "To acquaint boys and girls with their environment and to interest them in making their own investigations" (Christian 1959, 3). Records also reveal that Graham intended for The Ohio State University Extension to maintain a focus on youth, "to take care of as many boys and girls in agriculture clubs as practicable (Christian 1959, 3)."

Graham led efforts to institutionalize the creation of educational materials boys and girls could use, with guidance and support from trusted adults, to deepen their knowledge and skills through hands-on learning, resulting in their own mastery of the content. His core belief in hands-on learning through the application of systematic production trials combined knowledge and technology transfer to change people's practices—not only the youth, but also their parents, who tended to be more resistant to change. These foundational elements continue to provide an organizational framework for today's 4-H community clubs.

Nine years before the Smith-Lever Act would create the national extension system within the USDA, OSU recognized the importance of investing in outreach and engagement efforts and that reaching youth with knowledge derived from the application of systematic observation and hands-on discovery would improve people's practices and increase their livelihood.

OSU Influence on 4-H Youth Development

Once Congress passed Smith-Lever, administrators at USDA looked to the nation's land-grant institutions for proven outreach leaders. They saw an ideal candidate in Graham. Drawing on his years of extension leadership at OSU, he helped shape the fledgling national Cooperative Extension Service. His boys' and girls' clubs model quickly took root throughout the nation as Smith-Lever funding flowed to embed CES workers in each county and parish across the nation. Graham's formula of success—hands-on learning, systematic observation and record keeping, combined with community volunteers and support, backed by the discoveries and advances developed at the nation's land-grant universities, incentivized by competitions and awards—was promulgated far and wide. The Ohio-grown and OSU-endorsed community 4-H club became a proven delivery mechanism to help the nation continue to improve agricultural and domestic science practices that resulted in increased production to help ensure a safe, dependable, abundant food supply.

Graham's vision, combined with the land-grant DNA of OSU and ongoing public commitment to continue to fund positive youth development work in every county across the state, have allowed the 4-H program to remain consistently true to core philosophical beliefs about engaging youth in hands-on learning while remaining relevant through continual adaptation and evolution to meet the current needs of "today's" youth. With firm grounding in agriculture, which serves as a continual connection with the power of growth, perseverance, and renewal, 4-H as an integral part of OSU, helping to make the land-grant mission a living reality.

4-H Youth Development Partnerships

Partnerships are a cornerstone of 4-H. Research has shown that one youth program alone is not the best way to achieve positive youth development outcomes. 4-H has numerous partnerships with youth-serving organizations. A few noteworthy ones in the limited space of this essay include the Ohio National Guard with the Ohio Military Kids program (OMK) to support the youth of military families throughout the deployment cycle; Five Rivers MetroParks in Dayton, Ohio, with the Adventure Central program that uses an environmental foundation in a welcoming, safe, fun, active setting that utilizes volunteers and community resources; and County Agricultural Societies in all eighty-eight counties and the Ohio State Fair to promote youth activities through educational demonstrations, public speaking, and competitions. These are just a few examples of the strong partnerships with 4-H.

Ohio's 4-H Youth Development in 2020

The 4-H program currently serves youth through many delivery settings—clubs, after-school programs, camps (overnight and day camps), and school enrichment. Community clubs are the cornerstone of 4-H programs as they provide consistent exposure and structure to foster positive youth development. Particular attention is given to the inclusion of essential elements in all delivery settings to bring about positive youth development: (1) a positive relationship with a caring adult (youth learn and develop in adult leader–directed environments that are caring, supportive, and fun; (2) an inclusive environment (using learning techniques for the youth to work as team and with others while valuing and respecting the diversity of all participants); (3) a safe emotional and physical environment (meeting the needs of the youth where they are emotionally, physically, socially, and cognitively); (4) opportunity for mastery (allowing for creativity following the experiential learning cycle through the activities; (5) engagement in learning (using fun, positive experiences across many subject areas); (6) opportunity to see oneself as an active participant in the future (encouraging choices, decision-making, and leadership roles and exploring future career interests); (7) opportunity for self-determination (promoting activities that contribute to intrinsic motivations); and (8) opportunity to value and practice service to others (engaging in volunteer and civic activities in youths' local communities).

The target audience for the 4-H program today are youth ages five to nineteen years old. The 4-H Cloverbud program is designed to be developmentally age appropriate for children ages five to eight years. Even though the youth are clearly the focus of the 4-H program, the volunteers and professionals who are involved in the planning, delivering, and evaluating of the program are vital contributors for the outreach arm of the land-grant mission.

A sesquicentennial snapshot of OSU's 4-H program can be measured by the number of participants, volunteers, and support professionals. Enrollment data from 2018 indicate that 557,927 Ohio youth (an even 50–50 split of girls and boys) participated in clubs, group, and special interest programs, including food and nutrition programs. 4-H club membership totaled 69,826 youth, while 15,735 youth were involved in 4-H camping programs. A total of 15,988 adult volunteer leaders were active in 4-H and 6,074 youth also volunteered their time. Content-oriented projects are selected by 4-H youth each year. Of the 654,227 4-H projects completed in 2018, 54 percent focused on healthy lifestyles, 30 percent on science, technology, engineering, and mathematics (STEM), and 16 percent on citizenship. Each of these categories contains numerous projects related to each general content area. More than 170 4-H professionals provided leadership at the local and state levels and include extension educators, program assistants/coordinators/mangers, and state specialists.

The impact of The Ohio State University's 4-H program is best expressed by 4-H youth voices. Once such youth voice is 4-H member Ava Loneman, who was selected by national 4-H council as winner of the "Youth In Action Pillar Award" for STEM. She was recognized nationally for establishing herself as a leading youth advocate and organizer for STEM education, reaching more than 1,600 youth with hands-on programming in three years by founding the Bio-Med Science Academy 4H Afterschool Makers Club. She stated in the *4-H Today Blog,* "When I was young, I remember hearing from a classmate, 'STEM isn't for girls.' But even from an early age, I knew that STEM was my passion. My goal is to help other young people—and especially other girls—realize that STEM is fun, and that success is within your reach" (4-H 2017, para. 3).

A key stakeholder is Dr. Cathann Kress, OSU's vice president for agricultural administration and dean of the College of Food, Agricultural, and Environmental Sciences (CFAES). She stated in a CFAES News Release website, "I've said that the lyrics of 'Carmen Ohio,' the alma mater of OSU, truly live within our community. . . . 'Time and change will surely show, how firm thy friendship' applies to our 4-H alumni and supporters. . . . I consider 4-H to be the first CFAES class youth can take" (Frey 2018, para 4).

4-H Youth Development in the Next 150 Years

If the past is the best predictor of the future, then the future is bright for the next 150 years of OSU's 4-H program. Mapping out how 4-H has evolved since its roots in Clark County is truly amazing, going from corn crop and canning clubs to eclipse balloon–launching projects sanctioned by NASA. To continue the manifestation of the land-grant mission through 4-H, it will be critical to adapt and evolve with Ohio's youth and their communities over time. 4-H's humble roots started with the need for programs after school at a time when most of Ohioans lived in rural, farm communities. These first clubs were experimental clubs connected to the needs in the early 1900s, which usually centered on agriculture. One focus on the clubs was to develop and grow better and more corn and improve methods of food preservation. The youth were able to demonstrate ways to do this and develop better farm and food practices that were ultimately adopted by the adult community. This illustration of 4-H's start that grew out of meeting a community need is what has driven the evolution of 4-H over time.

Today, there is much focus on science, technology, engineering, and math. There is a demand for workers to earn degrees and fill the many open STEM positions in Ohio and beyond. An example of how 4-H has impacted the current and future state of STEM is evident in Ohio 4-H alumnus and chief engineer of a space-based manufacturing company, Michael Snyder. He started out in 4-H Cloverbuds and advanced to doing robotics and engineering projects for over ten years, ultimately earning his bachelor's and master's degrees from OSU in aeronautical and astronautical engineering. He spoke to Jennifer Sirangelo—President and CEO of the National 4-H Council—about the future, saying that "I feel like we may go full circle from living off the land and going completely technological in society and then going back to figure out how to regain the land. I feel like there's opportunity in the future to pave the way for what STEM looks like 200 years from now" (Sirangelo 2019, para. last).

The strength of OSU's 4-H program is that it meets the needs of the youth and their communities at the local level while supporting the national mission of 4-H's guiding principles: positive youth development, partnerships, learning, and youth potential. As a result, there are specific programs that are unique at the local level and others statewide. These 4-H programs have distinct objectives and outcomes. Examples of these include pet therapy programs, bioenergy education, rocket science, and urban gardening. It would be naïve to deliver identical programs or one program the same way in post-urban Youngstown, Ohio, as in rural Appalachian Jackson, Ohio. This approach has led to strong support through funding and volunteer efforts that have taken on many forms that vary from county to county. Some counties have commissioners that generously fund 4-H, while other counties have tax levies that are voted on by their citizens giving their stamp of approval (4-H may be the only youth-development program in Ohio and the US that is voted on by its citizens for tax-levy support in some counties).

The future of OSU's 4-H program rests in its ability to keep current and future-focused through statewide guidance by serving youth at the local level through county-directed 4-H programs. While 4-H has done this for over a century, youth development was recently expressed in terms of positive individual cognitive, social, psychological, and physical outcomes (Lerner et al. 2018). Amazingly, these are similarities between the past and today that can serve as a guiding foundation forward or back to the future.

References

4-H. 2017. "Ohio's Ava Lonneman Selected as 4-H Youth In Action Winner for STEM." *4-H Today* (blog). *National 4-H Council.* February 22, 2017. https://4-h.org/media/ohios-ava-lonneman-selected-as-4-h-youth-in-action-winner-for-stem/.

Christian, Carlton F. 1959. *History of Cooperative Extension Work in Agriculture and Home Economics in Ohio.* Columbus, OH: The Ohio State University Extension.

Lerner, Richard M., Brian M. Burkhard, Elise D. Murray, and Kathy M. Robinson. 2018. "Positive Youth Development." In *The Sage Encyclopedia of Lifespan Human Development, Vol. 4,* edited by Marc H. Bornstein, 1691–94. Thousand Oaks, CA: Sage.

Frey, Beth. 2018. "You Did it again, Ohio! $20,000 Raised for 4-H." May 17, 2018. https://cfaes.osu.edu/news/articles/you-did-it-again-ohio-20000-raised-for-4-h.

McCormick, Virginia E., and Robert W. McCormick. 1984. *A.B. Graham: Country Schoolmaster and Extension Pioneer.* Worthington, OH: Cottonwood Publications.

Sirangelo, Jennifer. 2019. "4-H Expert Series: Michael Snyder, 4-H Alumnus and Co-Founder of Made in Space, on the Making of a STEM Leader Yesterday, Today, and Tomorrow." *4-H Today* (blog). *National 4-H Council.* Accessed September 17, 2019. https://4-h.org/about/blog/4-h-expert-series-the-making-of-a-stem-leader-yesterday-today-and-tomorrow/.

9

The "Flexner Effect"

Medical Educational Reform and the Land-Grant Universities

E. Christopher Ellison

The creation of the land-grant universities by the Morrill Act of 1862 is one of the legendary stories in higher public education in the US. The land-grant universities enhanced access to affordable, local, and high-quality public education. Similarly, the Flexner Report on North American medical schools, published in 1910, had a profound effect on medical education. Although nearly a half a century apart, these visionary and innovative actions came together in the twentieth century to allow university leaders to create one of the greatest systems of public medical education, research, and health care in the world. Further, expansion of land-grant's agrarian roots to include medicine would in the future allow them to more effectively meet their missions and societal covenant, particularly in urban communities.

Based on the Flexner Report, the medical schools ideally would need to merge with the universities. This was the case for the Starling–Ohio Medical College that was founded in 1907 and The Ohio State University in Columbus, Ohio, into which it merged in 1914. This effort was led by The Ohio State University's fifth president, William Oxley Thompson, and clearly was prompted by Abraham Flexner's visit to the medical college in December 1909. In the report, he rated it in Division 2 of his three divisions because it required a high school diploma rather than a university education for entrance, as required to be in the top tier, Division 1. "It had reasonable laboratory facilities," and Flexner thought that "vigorous measures might however produce here a good institution." (Flexner [1910] 1972, 287). He further stated, "The state of Ohio has a duty in reference to medical education and public health, the performance of which is made comparatively simple by the appropriate location at Columbus of the most important of its three state universities" (Flexner [1910] 1972, 288).

Additional medical college and university mergers occurred throughout the US in the early twentieth century. It is likely that the fierce commitment to the land-grant missions by the university presidents and chancellors and the fortuitous co-location of medical schools and the land-grants accelerated these affiliations and hence the transformation of medical education. Likewise, as medical knowledge exploded in the mid-twentieth century and the population grew in the twenty-first century, there was a demand for education and clinical training of more physicians. Hence, given the locations of the land-grants and their innovative leadership, they were readily available to serve as vessels to expand medical education. The resulting development of new medical schools by the existing land-grants made possible the accelerated realization of a model of distributed public medical education in the US.

This essay will review the evolution of medical education from the nineteenth through the twentieth centuries and put a spotlight on the role that the land-grants played in catalyzing the reforms emanating from the Flexner Report as well as meeting the public need to expand medical education. Secondly, using the example of medical education at The Ohio State University, this essay will show how medicine was and continues to be a major contributor to the success of this institution in meeting its land-grant missions and service to the rural and increasingly urban community. Other land-grants have also incorporated medicine as a fundamental pillar, and still others may learn from this experience and seek this strategy in the future.

Evolution of the Role of Land-Grant Universities in Medical Education

As originally established in 1862, land-grant universities were focused on agriculture, mechanical arts, and military science. The educational programs were to include liberal arts and other sciences. However, medicine was not specifically included. This is not surprising as at the time of the passage of the Morrill Acts of 1862 and 1890, medicine was very early on in its development as a discipline and with few exceptions was not taught at universities but rather in private professional schools that were not affiliated in any way with the universities. There were some exceptions, such as John Hopkins University, and in addition several early land-grants had medical schools (table 9.1).

However, in general, medicine was not included in the founding disciplines of the land-grants. Medical education in the nineteenth and early twentieth centuries in the US is described as being proprietary, orthodox, and sectarian. However, several coordinated efforts in the early twentieth century brought it under scrutiny. The publication of the Flexner Report in 1910 led to regulatory standards for medical education, including the recommendation that the proprietary medical schools be merged with universities that had a full-time faculty and that clinical faculty do bedside teaching in affiliated hospitals. Over time this led to establishing schools of medicine and academic health centers at some of the largest and most successful public universities, including the land-grants. Although a few land-grants had medical schools prior this report, the key recommendation that existing and new schools be part of a university was likely viewed by forward-thinking university leaders as a major opportunity for the land-grant universities to initiate, evolve, and expand medical school programs.

The Flexner Report and the Evolution and Regulation of Medical Education

In 1904 the American Medical Association (AMA) created the Council on Medical Education (CME). At this time, US physicians varied substantially in their understanding of human physiology, pathology, and disease. Frankly, the practice of medicine in the US was not uniformly scientifically or evidence based. With the exception of a few clinics, physicians in the US had a poor public reputation. Hence, the main objective of this group was to restructure US medical education. At its first annual meeting, the CME adopted two standards. They first specified the minimum prior education required for admission to a medical school. The second defined a medical education as consisting of two years' training in human anatomy and physiology followed by two years of clinical work in a teaching hospital.

In 1908, the CME requested that the Carnegie Foundation for the Advancement of Teaching survey North American medical education. The president of the Carnegie Foundation, Henry Pritchett, a staunch

TABLE 9.1. Land-grant universities with medical schools (based on dates of university affiliation, 25)

LAND-GRANT UNIVERSITY	CAMPUS	FOUNDED	AFFILIATES WITH UNIVERSITY
Maryland		1807	1812
Vermont		1822	1822
Missouri	Columbia	1845	1875
UC San Francisco		1864	1873
Minnesota		1888	1889
Nebraska		1881	1892
Illinois		1882	1897
Cornell		1898	1898
West Virginia		1902	1902
Wisconsin		1907	1907
Arkansas		1879	1911
Tennessee		1850	1911
Ohio State		1846	1914
Louisiana State (LSU)	New Orleans	1931	1931
Puerto Rico		1950	1950
UC Los Angeles		1951	1951
Florida		1956	1956
Kentucky		1960	1960
Connecticut		1961	1961
Massachusetts		1962	1962
Penn St		1963	1963
Michigan St		1964	1964
Hawaii		1965	1965
UC Davis		1966	1966
UC Irvine		1896	1967
Arizona	Tucson	1967	1967
UC San Diego		1968	1968
LSU	Shreveport	1969	1969
Nevada	Reno	1969	1969
Missouri	Kansas City	1971	1971
Texas A&M		1977	1977
UC Riverside		2008	2008

(TABLE 9.1. *continued*)

LAND-GRANT UNIVERSITY	CAMPUS	FOUNDED	AFFILIATES WITH UNIVERSITY
Virginia Tech Carilion		2008	2008
Arizona	Phoenix	2012	2012
Rutgers	NJ Med School	1954	2013
Rutgers	Robert Wood Johnson	1961	2013
Nevada	Las Vegas	2014	2014
Washington State		2015	2015

* Cornell is a private school. ** UC = University of California. Campus shown if more than one location. Reproduced with permission. Ellison, E. C. 2019. "Time and Change: The Importance of Innovation and Leadership to the Future of Surgery." *Annals of Surgery* 270, no. 3 (September): 394.

advocate of medical school reform, chose Abraham Flexner to conduct the survey. Flexner was not a physician, scientist, or medical educator, although he held a bachelor of arts degree. He was born in Louisville, Kentucky, on November 13, 1866, and was the first in his family to complete high school and go on to college. In 1886, at age nineteen, Flexner completed a bachelor of arts at Johns Hopkins University. In 1905, he pursued graduate studies in psychology at Harvard University and at the University of Berlin. As he had studied and traveled in Europe, he was likely well aware that one could not practice medicine in continental Europe without having undergone an extensive specialized university education. One can speculate that this is one reason why Pritchett chose him to lead the effort. Flexner would ultimately recommend that North American medical education conform to prevailing practice in continental Europe.

At the time of the report in 1910, there were 155 medical schools in North America (the US and Canada). The estimated US population at the time was about ninety-two million people. Per capita this is nearly two medical schools per million people (1.7 per million population). Flexner visited most, if not all, of these schools. He found that each of these schools differed greatly in their curricula, methods of assessment, and requirements for admission and graduation. Many of the medical schools were small "proprietary" and for-profit trade schools owned by one or more physicians. In general, they were not affiliated with colleges or universities. A degree was typically awarded after only two years of study. Laboratory work and anatomic dissection were not necessarily required. Many of the instructors were local doctors who taught part-time

For many of these physicians, their own training was marginal. In addition, there was little or no regulation of the medical profession by state governments.

Nevertheless, several schools received praise for excellent performance, including Western Reserve (now Case Western Reserve), Michigan, Wake Forest, McGill, Toronto, and especially Johns Hopkins, which Flexner described as the "model for medical education" (Raffel and Raffel 1994, 11). In addition, there were nine 1862 land-grants that had affiliated with or developed medical schools prior to the Flexner Report. Of note, all remained open after the report was issued. These include the following universities, shown by the year the medical school was affiliated: Maryland, 1812; Vermont, 1822; Missouri, 1872; Nebraska, 1892; Minnesota, 1889; Illinois, 1897; Cornell, 1898; West Virginia, 1902; and Wisconsin, 1907.

After Flexner studied the situation, he issued the following recommendations.

1. Reduce the number of medical schools (from 155 to thirty-one) and reduce the number of medical school graduates to 2,000 per year, from 4,400.
2. The proprietary medical schools should either close or be incorporated into existing universities. Medical schools should be part of a larger university with a full-time faculty hired with high credentials.
3. Give medical schools control of clinical instruction in hospitals.
4. Medical schools should appoint full-time clinical professors.
5. Increase the prerequisites to enter medical training.
6. Train physicians to practice in a scientific manner and engage medical faculty in research.
7. Strengthen state regulation of medical licensure.

It was Flexner's opinion that admission to a medical school should require, at a minimum, a high school diploma and at least two years of college or university study, primarily devoted to basic science. When Flexner researched his report, only sixteen out of 155 medical schools in the US and Canada required applicants to have completed two or more years of university education. By 1920, 92 percent of North American medical schools required this of applicants. Flexner also argued that the length of medical education should be four years, and its content should be what the CME agreed to in 1905.

Impact of the Flexner Report

Flexner sought to reduce the number of medical schools in the US from 155 to thirty-one and to cut the annual number of medical graduates from 4,400 to 2,000. A majority of US institutions granting MD or DO degrees as of the date of the report closed within two to three decades. In 1904, there were 160 MD-granting institutions with more than 28,000 students. By 1920, there were only eighty-five MD-granting institutions, educating only 13,800 students. By 1935, there were only sixty-six medical schools operating in the US.

Thus, between 1910 and 1935, more than half of all North American medical schools merged or closed. An important factor driving these mergers and closures was that state medical boards gradually adopted and enforced the report's recommendations. Of the sixty-six surviving MD-granting institutions in 1935, fifty-seven were part of a university. Of these, nine schools were part of the original 1862 land-grants. During a second of three waves of expansion of medical education between 1951 and 1980, there were an additional sixteen medical schools that affiliated with the land-grants, and in the period from 2001 through 2019, there have been an additional seven land-grant medical schools.

The Current State of Medical Education in the US

There are currently 149 medical schools in the US for a population of about 328 million people. This is approximately 0.4 medical schools per million populations, or four times less on a per capita basis than in 1910, when the Flexner Report was published. Today, the land-grants play a major role in public medical education. Of the original 1862 land-grant universities, twenty-eight have a total of thirty-eight medical schools today. In 2018–2019, there were 20,742 students enrolled in medical schools at land-grant universities, representing 22.7 percent of the total US medical school enrollment. In addition, many of these universities have developed academic health centers that provide health care, graduate medical education, and other services to the communities and states in which they are located.

Several of the land-grant colleges, including The Ohio State University, have developed other health sciences, including colleges of nursing, pharmacy, optometry, public health, dentistry, and veterinary medicine, further strengthening the delivery of the land-grant missions. Hence today, the land-grants compose 25 percent of the universities in the US with medical schools and account for nearly 23 percent of the enrollment. There is no doubt that incorporating medicine as a core discipline has helped the land-grants meet their societal covenant in the rural and particularly in urban settings. In addition, depending on the organizational structure and operational efficiency, a medical center also provides a revenue stream to the university.

Over a Century of Medicine and Community Service at The Ohio State University

On January 10, 1913, the board of trustees of the Starling–Ohio Medical College submitted a proposal to the board of trustees of The Ohio State University offering to the latter its rights, titles, and property of its College of Medicine, Dentistry, and Pharmacy. Arguably, the former was ahead of its time as it was the first medical school in US to erect and have exclusive control of its own hospital (The St. Francis Hospital, Columbus, Ohio), which was completed in 1855. The offer was accepted and an act of the General Assembly enabled the trustees of The Ohio State University to organize and maintain this college.

Beginning with this merger, there has been a continuous expansion of medical education, research, and service on the Columbus campus. The first graduating class of the College of Medicine in 1915 consisted of forty-five students, including one woman. Today, approximately 200 students graduate each year. About 50 percent of the graduates are women and 25 percent are underrepresented minorities in medicine.

The medical center has become a leading academic health center as a direct result of the university leadership prioritizing its land-grant mission. The growth in physical plant on the campus is divided into phases for ease of presentation. The first hospital on campus was the Cleveland Pulte Medical College, acquired in 1914. In Phase 1, construction began on the Starling Loving Hospital in 1917 and was completed in 1923, with an addition in 1924. By 1926 it had 296 inpatient beds, operating rooms, a maternity ward, and laboratories. In Phase 2, a new hospital opened in early 1951, adding additional beds and operating suites as well as expanded maternity wards. After a north wing addition was completed in 1960, it was officially named University Hospital in 1961 and later, in 1984, Doan Hall. A new medical school building and research labs (Graves Hall and Meiling Hall) were constructed in the 1960s.

Phase 3 consisted of the university hospital expansion named Rhodes Hall in 1976, which was completed in 1979. The James Cancer Hospital and Solove Research Institute opened in 1990 as the only freestanding cancer hospital in central Ohio, and the Harding Psychiatric Hospital opened in 1991. New additional research buildings were also added: Tzagournis Medical Research Facility in 1999 and the Davis Heart and Lung Institute in 2000. Phase 4 saw the opening of a Ross Heart Hospital in 2004 and its later expansion, and the state-of-the-art Biomedical Research Tower was completed in 2006. Phase 5, in 2012 through 2018, was heralded by the completion of a new 300-bed James Cancer Hospital and Solove Research Institute in 2014 and a Brain and Spine Hospital.

The Ohio State University College of Medicine employs a full-time faculty of 1,946 (122 full-time basic science faculty, 1,763 full-time clinical faculty, and 61 full-time other faculty) to teach 800 medical students, numerous graduate students, and over 800 residents and fellows annually. The faculty received over $106 million in research funding from the National Institutes of Health (NIH) in 2017 and has averaged over $94 million in annual NIH research funding since 2009. Currently the faculty oversees more than 2,000 active research studies and clinical trials.

Today, The Ohio State University Wexner Medical Center has 1,506 beds and provides tertiary care to central Ohio. It is one of the largest employers in the region, with over 29,000 employees. It offers the only solid organ transplant center and burn center in the region, a Level I trauma center, and a state-of-the art critical care service and leads community efforts to reduce infant mortality. It is home to the only freestanding and National Cancer Institute (NCI)-designated cancer center in central Ohio. In fiscal year 2018, it recorded 64,529 admissions, 130,916 emergency room visits, and 44,888 surgeries. In fiscal year 2017, it provided a community benefit of over $215 million, including charity care as well as over $70 million for medical education and $40 million for research.

Conclusion

Leadership commitment to missions outlined in the Morrill Act of 1862 has allowed the land-grant universities to play an important role in the transformation and expansion of medical education that followed the implementation of the recommendations in the 1910 Flexner Report. Such commitment by the leaders of The Ohio State University allowed them to have the vision and fortitude to merge the Starling–Ohio Medical College in 1914 and evolve from those organizations' roots as one of the largest and most eminent public medical centers in the US. Incorporating medicine ultimately helped this land-grant to better fulfill its missions of education, research, and service to its rural and urban communities.

References

Association of American Medical Colleges. 2017. "2017 U.S. Medical School Faculty." https://www.aamc.org/data/facultyroster/reports/486050/usmsf17.html.

Barzansky, Barbara, and Norman Gevitz. 1992. *Beyond Flexner: Medical Education in the Twentieth Century*. New York: Greenwood Press.

Bland, K. I. 2011. "Preserving Surgical Academia in the Centenary of the Flexnerian Academic Health Center." *Annals of Surgery* 254, no. 3: 393–409.

Blue Ridge Institute for Medical Research. 2018. "Ranking Tables of NIH Funding to US Medical Schools in 2017." http://www.brimr.org/NIH_Awards/2017/NIH_Awards_2017.htm.

Council on Medical Education, American Medical Association. n.d. "About the Council on Medical Education." https://www.ama-assn.org/councils/council-medical-education/about-council-medical-education.

Duffy, Thomas P. 2011. "The Flexner Report—100 Years Later." *Yale Journal of Biology and Medicine* 84, no. 3 (September): 269–76.

Edwards, Linden F. 1952. "Centenary Anniversary of the Oldest Medical College Hospital in the United States—St. Francis Hospital, Columbus, Ohio." *Bulletin of the History of Medicine* 26, no. 3 (May–June): 269–76. https://www.jstor.org/stable/pdf/44446400.pdf.

Flexner, A. (1910) 1972. *Medical Education in the United States and Canada: A Report to the Carnegie Foundation for the Advancement of Teaching.* New York: The Carnegie Foundation for the Advancement of Teaching. http://archive.carnegiefoundation.org/pdfs/elibrary/Carnegie_Flexner_Report.pdf.

Luoma, Harrison. 2007. "The Ohio State University Medical Center Biomedical Research Tower [Columbus, OH]." *Healthcare Design,* August 31, 2007. https://www.healthcaredesignmagazine.com/architecture/ohio-state-university-medical-center-biomedical-research-tower-columbus-oh/.

The Ohio State University Wexner Medical Center. n.d. "Our Facilities." Retrieved from https://wexnermedical.osu.edu/about-us/our-facilities.

———. 2019. "Key Facts and Figures." https://wexnermedical.osu.edu/mediaroom/facts.

Raffel, Marshall W., and Norma K. Raffel. 1994. *The US Health System: Origins and Functions*. 4th ed. Albany, NY: Delmar Publishers.

Rodgers, Kristin. 2011. “Starling-Loving University Hospital.” *Historical Reflections,* October 31, 2011. https://library.osu.edu/blogs/mhcb/2011/10/31/starling-loving-university-hospital/.

———. 2012a. “Arthur G. James Cancer Hospital and Richard J. Solove Research Institute” *Historical Reflections,* April 3, 2012. https://library.osu.edu/blogs/mhcb/?s=James+Cancer+Hospital.

———. 2012b. “Tzagournis Medical Research Facility.” *Historical Reflections,* June 4, 2012. https://library.osu.edu/blogs/mhcb/?s=Tzagournis+Medical+Research+Facility.

———. 2014a. “Charles Austin Doan.” *Historical Reflections,* April 13, 2014. https://library.osu.edu/blogs/mhcb/?s=Doan+Hall.

———. 2014b. “Harding Hospital.” *Historical Reflections,* September 17, 2014. https://library.osu.edu/blogs/mhcb/?s=Harding+Hospital.

———. 2014c. “John Howell Janeway Upham.” *Historical Reflections,* February 16, 2014. https://library.osu.edu/blogs/mhcb/?s=Davis+Heart+Lung+Institute.

Wikipedia. 2019a. “1910 United States Census.” https://en.wikipedia.org/wiki/1910_United_States_Census.

———. 2019b. “Abraham Flexner.” https://en.wikipedia.org/wiki/Abraham_Flexner.

———. 2019c. “List of Medical Schools in the United States.” https://en.wikipedia.org/wiki/List_of_medical_schools_in_the_United_States.

World Population Review. 2019. “United States Population 2019.” http://worldpopulationreview.com/countries/united-states-population/.

10

Social Impact and Inclusive Excellence

Thomas K. Gregoire

The social work profession began in poor urban and often immigrant communities, largely concurrent with the emergence of the public land-grant university in the mid-to-late 1800s. As land-grant initiatives were promoting access to higher education and the dissemination of scholarship for society's benefit, social workers were taking up residence in high-need neighborhoods to work as members of the community addressing local needs in what became known as settlement houses. This approach—of living among those we serve—parallels the extension movement's efforts to bring knowledge and expertise from the university into the community. Godman Guild, the first Columbus settlement house, was founded in 1898. Additional settlement houses followed throughout Columbus—many of which remain today—and are important partners for the College of Social Work in our teaching, research, and engagement missions.

Social Impact

While the land-grant tradition is guided by an aspiration to disseminate the expertise of the university for the benefit of the community, we recognize that our greatest impact could be as convener and collaborator, not just expert. This approach of doing *with* and not *for* acknowledges the inherent strengths of residents in communities, the desire and capacity of diverse groups to lead efforts that affect them, and the potential of a university-community collaboration for generating effective and sustained interventions reflecting the unique needs of that community.

Many scholars in our university employ community-based participatory research strategies, which emphasize joining with the community as equal partners throughout the research process to engage communities in their own destiny. The College of Social Work along with our university colleagues have considerable impact as community partners. A brief and limited overview of our social impact reveals our capacity to bring scholarship to important questions in immediately relevant ways.

LiFE*sports*—Learning in Fitness and Education through Sports—is a partnership of social work, athletics, and extension. The LiFE*sports* program is a national model for community-engaged research, teaching, and learning. This is A+ in evidence-based, positive youth development through sports. Over 600 at-risk youth attend a four-week summer camp hosted at Ohio State athletics facilities, followed by monthly community-based "booster sessions." In addition to the many benefits for the youth participants, The Ohio State University (OSU) students from across disciplines do internships with the camp, and many complete an undergraduate minor in positive youth development that evolved from the program.

A collaboration with the College of Food, Agricultural, and Environmental Sciences employed a geospatial mapping strategy to identify food deserts, areas with limited access to healthy and affordable food. That work was followed with the development of community gardens, created with members of each community that reflect the unique needs of that neighborhood.

Age-Friendly Columbus and Franklin Country is a global initiative of the World Health Organization and the first program to be housed at a land-grant university. The initiative supports the redesign of the built, social, and service environment for an aging population and reconceptualizes older adults as partners and assets rather than as problems to be solved. Led by the College of Social Work, faculty, staff, and students from fourteen different academic units engage older adults in the community with a motto of "Nothing for us without us." Early impacts include informing the city planning budget for sidewalk repair and design; a Better Business Bureau designation of "Age-Friendly Business"—meeting specific senior-centered criteria; and public transportation routes redesigned with input from seniors.

The Champion Intergenerational Enrichment and Education Center provides joint programming for young children and older adults to build relationships across generations and a sense of purpose among older adults. The innovative center is located in a low-income neighborhood on the city's Near East Side, and is defying traditional models of day care that separate children and adults. Scholars from many disciplines—including social work, medicine, and nursing—study the benefits of intergenerational programming, while students learn to work in a low-income, intergenerational, and interdisciplinary context. Perhaps most importantly, the center enables older adults to remain in their homes and caregivers of children and adults to remain in the workforce.

For communities struggling with an emergent problem, we are of most benefit when our research is nimble and quickly adapted to the needs of its communities—defying the stereotypes of higher education as slow to change. When the Columbus City Council needed to quickly understand the needs of the growing New Americans population (immigrants and refugees), they funded social work faculty to conduct interviews across the city and convene community meetings with forty-five providers who serve this population to provide recommendations for supporting these new neighbors. This research is now informing city policy and has led our college to develop a collaborative agenda for community-university partnership. Similarly, social work is at the forefront in the fight against the opioid epidemic in Ohio. With colleagues from across disciplines, social work scholars are collaborating with hard-hit rural communities to test and disseminate interventions that help families recover and remain intact.

Navigating the current service system is a challenge for vulnerable persons. Services are often not located where and when they might be most readily accessed, individuals have multiple needs, and transportation is a challenge. We are undertaking a number of experiments with community partners to make services more accessible:

- The Columbus Public Library hosts social work interns, placing social workers where persons who are homeless often congregate.
- Pets play a significant role in many of our lives, and that includes persons who are homeless. Our faculty participate in an established and highly effective program in veterinary medicine to bring care directly to pets and their humans in camps where many persons who are homeless live. Students from the nursing, veterinary medicine, and social work programs are making home visits to older adults to test the benefit of a comprehensive approach to home-based assessment and care.

- At the request of the Columbus Fire Department, social work interns are deploying with Emergency Medical Services bringing resources immediately to bear in a crisis.
- Franklin County currently leads Ohio in evictions. In response, social work interns and Legal Aid staff are present in the hallway outside eviction court. Data show that an intervention—even at this late point—can be a significant benefit to residents.

These few examples reflect our land-grant commitment to partner with communities in the application of research, teaching, and engagement for relevant, timely, and transformational social impact.

Our Social Context in a Turbulent Time

As we consider our obligations as a twenty-first-century land-grant, we do so in turbulent and divisive times. Our capacity to engage in civil and evidence-informed discourse feels diminished. Ideology seems valued over scientific knowledge—particularly in areas such as social, economic, and immigration policy. Race and religion continue to be sources of significant conflict. Social media is used to inflame and radicalize. In this divisive context, the land-grant aspires to be the university of all the people.

The land-grant university emerged and the social work profession exists because the status quo does not work for many. Income inequality and a declining manufacturing base threaten the well-being of entire communities. We can predict—with reasonable accuracy—an individual's educational and health outcomes, life-span, and likelihood of incarceration on the basis of their race and ethnicity and the neighborhood where they reside. A fierce twenty-first-century land-grant could reflect upon its potential, and responsibility, to promote society's capacity to engage in civil and informed discourse, advance a just society, and overcome ideological differences that thwart progress, oppress people, and divide our nation.

As a public institution, the land-grant is responsible to a state legislature and executive branch and dependent on both for considerable support. We benefit from the advocacy and philanthropy of influential individuals, foundations, and corporations. Ohio State enjoys the support of hundreds of thousands of alumni and others across the region who have no direct affiliation but closely identify with Ohio State. Each group has widely varying influence and competing expectations of the university. While replete with expertise that makes the land-grant uniquely positioned to respond to the needs of our communities, it is so broadly accountable that it struggles with becoming risk averse.

A case in point. Preliminary findings of a federally funded study conducted by two tenured faculty members—one from the OSU College of Social Work and the other from a non-Ohio public university—appeared to identify the failings of one state's economic policies for low-income families after the 2008 Great Recession. Faced with empirical findings that challenged the efficacy of that state's policy, the faculty members were assailed by state officials and legislators from the state and federal levels. A state legislator threatened to block further federal funding for the project and the state administration retained other scholars to attack the research publicly, while concurrently the state declined to release data that might confirm or refute the preliminary findings. This is the type of inquiry a courageous land-grant must support for the betterment of all people.[1] While not all conflicts are played out at such a high level, the challenges of teaching, research, and engagement in our polarized environment will test the commitment of the land-grant to all persons and our presumed desire to promote a just society.

Inclusive Excellence

Beyond reflecting a shared societal value, a growing body of evidence supports the positive impact of a diverse environment upon improved organizational performance (Valantine and Collins 2015). Our commitment to inclusion occurs in the same ideologically fraught context. Today's student body may be the most diverse group of students ever enrolled at Ohio State, and our students, faculty, and staff encompass a broad range of identities. Each experiences the environment differently. Many with diverse identities do not enjoy the same sense of safety and support that is assumed among members of the mainstream culture, some of whom struggle to understand the challenges of being different. We recognize in particular the negative impact of today's divisive discourse and violent events upon students of color, members of the LGBTQ communi-

1. As of this writing, subsequent data collection and analysis support initial conclusions. The findings have the potential to change the lives of thousands of children and families for the better, if science can precede ideology.

ties, women, and students and faculty from the international community, among others. Yet, the modern land-grant does not have the luxury to see today's social upheaval and inequality as occurring "out there." Many students come to our campus with an expectation that their experience be understood and supported by the university and that we commit time to the difficult conversations that arise in our classrooms. The quality of their educational experience and their ability to thrive in our university often mandate it.

Although inclusion need not be viewed as zero-sum, change informed by a commitment to inclusion of one group can be perceived as a threat by others. Ohio State's commitment to remove bias and barriers for women in our academic workplace may threaten some white men who have benefitted from past practices, or are simply unaware of the impact of privilege. Hiring and recruitment that focuses on creating a more diverse faculty and student body can be derided as sacrificing quality. While few white men likely work or study under the label of an "affirmative action" selection, many women and people of color do.

With a view of these challenges as learning opportunities, we make considerable efforts across the university to promote thoughtful and evidence-informed conversations on implicit bias, privilege, and the impact of our social environment upon everyone in our community. And to be clear, inclusion means all people. In social work, our conversations on supporting all students include those from traditionally conservative backgrounds who may feel painted with a broad brush, excluded from dialogue on inclusion, and marginalized. We are most inclusive when everyone is heard, and most effective when everyone listens.

In our zero-sum national dialogue, conversations on national movements such as #MeToo, same-sex marriage, Black Lives Matter, immigration, and privilege can be acknowledgments of lived experiences and supportive for members of diverse groups, and conversely can be subversive and threatening for others. In social work, our efforts to support diverse groups through community conversations, displays, and accommodations have been greeted with approval and controversy. Black Lives Matters posters have been vandalized, signage for gender-neutral restrooms were repeatedly destroyed, the dean's participation in the annual Columbus Pride Parade always seems to prompt a strident email from the community. The twenty-first-century land-grant requires courage to teach and study, and the creativity to promote the challenging conversations of our time.

Access

Inclusion starts with access. We are proud to work in a university that matches its commitment to access and affordability with substantial investment. We are moved by our ability to promulgate generational change when we graduate the first member of a family to earn a college degree. Presently, 38 percent of all undergraduates in the College of Social Work are first-generation students, who with Ohio State's support are accomplishing a formerly unattainable outcome in their family.

As profound as generational family change might be, we recognize that our potential impact extends beyond the student and their family. Students selecting a helping or healing profession—such as social work—did so with a commitment to serve. Many of our first-generation students come with the goal of returning home to bring change. Access at Ohio State can mean transforming students, their families, and entire communities.

We are preparing students to work in the most challenging of environments. In social work, we are advancing the construct of "educating the whole student" as our A+ in access and inclusion for students. Educating the whole student means graduating students with competencies and life skills that extend beyond those acquired in a traditional academic setting. It includes instilling in them skills for managing the demands of higher education, and later, challenging careers. It teaches financial wellness, so that decisions made during college are not impacting the student twenty years later. We promote positive mental health by providing—through our college and in collaboration with our university—timely access to wellness, prevention, and early intervention activities. Discipline-specific career mentoring is particularly important for students from families without a history of employment in the professional sector. This includes the Social Work Career Closet, a large repository of professional attire provided free to students who lack the resources to purchase clothing needed for interviews and first jobs. An excellent experience for our low-income and first-generation students is an excellent experience for everyone.

The Land-Grant of the Future

Among the many questions to contemplate for the land-grant of the future, two in particular stand out for this chapter. First, how can we come together as a society? As described throughout this chapter, it is not hard to conclude that the way our society is working to solve deeply challenging problems is not benefitting, or including, wide sections of our population. The challenging problems of our social and physical environments are not well suited for the simple solutions proffered from today's conflicting ideological perspectives. Precisely because these problems are complex, the twenty-first-century land-grant may be uniquely situated to lead through science, through partnership with communities, and by training the next generation with a commitment to a just society and the skills to promote a civil discourse.

Second, what is the future of community? Many individuals live meaningful lives in virtual communities. For many, the digital environment is the dominant source of knowledge, support, and identity. Yet, much of our societal discord is sown in that community and there is great polarization on the value of technology and virtual space. As with other communities, a divide exists between those who have the ability to access and master virtual communities and those who do not. The land-grant of the future will teach, research, and engage in the emerging virtual community. Today multiple College of Social Work scholars study virtual communities, the digital environment, and the role of technology in promoting change. The land-grant university has evolved from its original agricultural and mechanical mission to include an identity as an urban land-grant, and could now explore its potential as a virtual land-grant. The future is largely unknown, yet no future exists that would not be enhanced by the work of the modern land-grant.

References

Valantine, Hannah A., and Francis S. Collins. 2015. "National Institutes of Health Addresses the Science of Diversity." *Proceedings of the National Academy of Sciences* 112, no. 40 (October): 12240–42.

11

Food and Nutritional Security

Still the Grand Challenge for Land-Grant Universities

Casey Hoy and Brian Snyder

An internationally accepted definition of food security is when all people at all times have ready access to a culturally appropriate diet that will promote a healthy and active life. Despite progress in the last century or two, our species has never achieved food security by this definition, and progress has slowed. Food security is not a simple problem of production with primarily technological solutions. Rather, it is a challenge filled with complex trade-offs and laden with conflicting values, particularly when the goal is to achieve this sustainably and with resilience in the face of climate change. Contributions from all academic disciplines in land-grant universities, and extensive partnerships that are rooted within communities, will be needed to continue progress toward food and nutrition security for all.

Introduction

According to the United Nations (UN) definition, the "right to food is the right of every individual, alone or in community with others, to have physical and economic access at all times to sufficient, adequate and culturally acceptable food that is produced and consumed sustainably, preserving access to food for future generations" (De Schutter 2014). This definition also applies to nutritional security, which requires both quality and quantity of food that is "sufficient" and "adequate" to support a healthy and active life. Global food security for all people has never been achieved. Currently, a large percentage of people in the world have neither food nor nutritional security. By the most recently published Food and Agriculture Organization (FAO) statistics, approximately one in eight people in the world are obese, one indication of a lack of nutritional security, and at the same time one in nine people are chronically undernourished.

According to comparable US Department of Agriculture Economic Research Service (ERS) figures, the situation in the US is not much better than in the world as a whole—in Ohio approximately one in seven households experience low food security, lacking nutritional security, and about one in sixteen households experience very low food security, meaning chronic hunger. Our nation, despite having a land-grant university system that has an expressed charge of assisting the population achieve food security, is one of the few in the world and the only developed country that does not formally recognize a right to food (FAO 2015).

The conditions that ensure the right to food for all people at any given time and place include availability, access, and adequacy of both nutritional quality and an appropriate fit with cultural needs. For these conditions to be met over time, both sustainability and resilience must be qualities of the food system as well. So what is missing? Availability appears to be sufficient at a global scale, at least in caloric terms, because FAO estimates of 2,940 kcal/person/day in global production are more than sufficient for caloric requirements of all *Homo sapiens.* Nutritional quality of this production, however, would need to be considered as well, and these estimates are more difficult to find. Access and adequacy, and the sustainability and resilience of food systems, appear to be the more challenging properties to achieve at this point.

People are food insecure because they either don't have the money or appropriate access to purchase food, or they don't have the land and other resources (seeds, tools, etc.) to produce it themselves. Therefore, food and nutritional security is impossible to disentangle from poverty and other indicators of social disparity. Globalization might be expected to alleviate these issues by keeping prices low through global competition that minimizes production costs, although depending entirely on governmental regulation to subsidize some of those costs such as fossil fuel derivatives and to avoid external costs like environmental harm, public health challenges, and a dramatically skewed distribution of wealth. Global systems have grown tremendously over recent decades because they create equity for shareholders, equity in this case meaning wealth. But they also leave a great deal of inequity among both consumers and producers.

The global economy does not have any direct responsibility for ensuring livelihoods, providing food security, or meeting any other specific needs for any population or place, except as required through government regulation or encouraged by collective consumer action. Cultural change influenced by political and economic forces, as well as broader awareness of and attention to human health and ecological factors, will be needed to ensure the well-being of the large percentage of the population whose needs are not being met by the current system.

Agriculture and Food Systems

A food system extends from the natural resources on which production depends forward through the entire complex human food supply chain. Beyond consumers, the system functions include the eventual health outcomes of diet for individuals and populations, and ideally with a return of resources back to production—compost, for example. Scholars taking a systems approach to understanding food system dynamics consider the broad terms *availability, access,* and *utilization* to represent critical segments along the continuum from production through distribution to consumption and its results. Agriculture in the narrow sense, with a focus on production, exists at the availability end of the continuum. But in a broader sense, we consider such related activities as the supply chains that begin with agricultural production, and food, fiber, feed, and other agriculturally derived products, as well as strategies to recycle food waste back through the system, to be part of agriculture. All of these activities and more are considered to be encompassed by agricultural ecosystems, or agroecosystems.

Healthy Agroecosystems

Agroecosystems include farms and neighboring lands, both farmers and nonfarming neighbors and ultimately, all members of a community that are linked by the human food chain. The agroecosystem functions through relationships between people, many other organisms, and the land, the ultimate source of food. Although there is no clearly preferred geographic boundary that encompasses both the biophysical and social interactions in an agroecosystem, relevant scales include the proximate watershed or production region, or metropolitan region including the urban-to-rural continuum. Sometimes these systems are best defined by waterways, and sometimes by highways. Healthy agroecosystems function in ways that meet human needs. Past descriptions and definitions of healthy agroecosystems have relied on either a description of the properties that arise because of how they function (like sustained productivity), or on constraints that limit the function (like the prevalence of degraded natural systems). New models of healthy agroecosystems are clearly needed to address the dual challenges of achieving both food security and environmental resilience.

A Wicked Problem Requiring a Systemic Approach

Wicked problems are characterized by complexity, many undefined causes, trade-offs that vary because of different values, and no singular solution because the best solution depends on one's resources and values. Food security is a good example of a wicked problem, because it arises from infinite combinations of land, culture, agriculture, trade-offs, inconsistencies, and values that vary at all social levels from individuals to nations. For example, food insecurity exists throughout the urban to rural continuum in the US, but for various reasons that are tied to poverty, racial disparity, social support, and more. As a result, there is no single or simple solution, like producing more food or expanding charitable food-distribution networks. But there are many ways that a land-grant university can contribute to the varied and complex solutions that address the needs of any given segment of the population.

Successful solutions must balance consideration of externalized costs within a system, which usually accrue over the longer term, with the shorter-term benefits offered by food-production gains, expanded processing options, and the relative success of retail markets. There must also be consideration for the well-being of all members of the community, from the production to consumption ends of the supply chain, including transient members of a community, like many farmworkers. These types of analyses require simultaneous consideration of perspectives from many different academic disciplines, and from outside academia altogether. It is like a complex set of simultaneous equations that must be solved together in an interconnected way, but for which no exact solution exists.

Transdisciplinary Research and the Land-Grant Future

A modern land-grant university encompasses many disciplines. The sciences range from natural and physical to social and behavioral, with mathematics as a language that unites all of these disciplines. Although it is comforting for some to think that everything can be boiled down to equations, in fact many phenomena are not best represented quantitatively, and the incidence of these increase in the social and behavioral sciences. Moreover, disciplines such as philosophy, theology, and ethics challenge even our standard ways of knowing what the problems are and how to solve them. More qualitative explanations of the world become increasingly important in the social and behavioral sciences and are the basis for scholarship in the arts and humanities, which stress imagination and both a conceptual and an emotional understanding of the world. Tackling a challenge like food security is profound enough that there are roles for every discipline represented in land-grant universities.

It is little wonder, given the variation in approach to knowledge and description of the world around us, from presumed objective mathematics and data at one extreme to acknowledged emotion and imagination at the other, and with limitless combinations across the continuum in between, that universities struggle with finding common ground across the full range of academic disciplines that they encompass. Yet these are all academic disciplines, and the knowledge they represent is incomplete. The idea of the engaged university has gained a following in higher education, but our challenge as land-grant universities is to find ways to accept, honor, and integrate the knowledge and wisdom that exist outside of academic disciplines, both in historic and contemporary contexts, with the knowledge that stems from scholarship of many forms, from science and technology to the arts and humanities (figure 11.1). That is the meaning of transdisciplinary inquiry—a profound challenge, but not insurmountable.

A friend, author, and Amish farming neighbor who uses a horse-drawn plow likes to point out that he uses precision agriculture equipment—it's between his ears and he knows where every rock in the field is because he's hit them all multiple times while plowing, and they get your attention! Even when the goal of our technology is to automate the response to such variation in the environment, the variation remains and the personal experience with place and context extends well beyond the patterns that we work with in scientific investigation. In a similar vein, much of the knowledge that stimulated impressive advances in the past, from

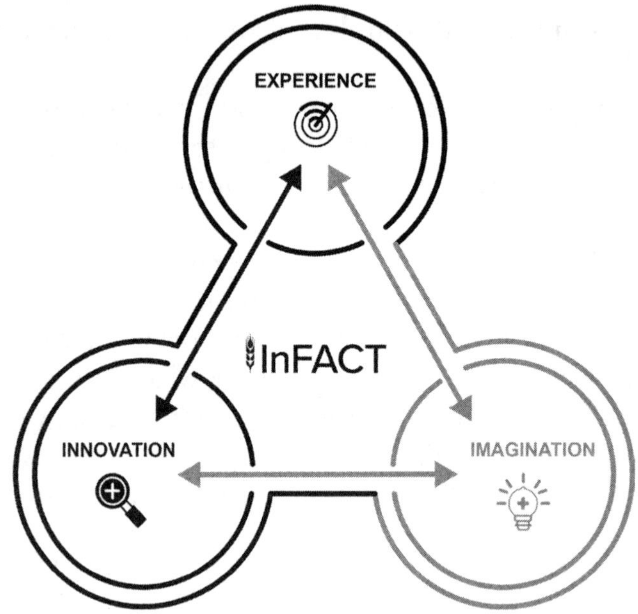

FIGURE 11.1. InFACT as a transdisciplinary endeavor, embracing each of the continua bounded by the innovation inherent in science and technology, the imagination inherent in the arts and humanities, and the experiential knowledge that exists beyond academic disciplines

construction of Roman aqueducts that are still in use today to the food-production systems that fed entire civilizations for many centuries, are not fully captured in current theory or practice. Addressing the wicked problem of food security will require balancing indigenous knowledge with scientific discovery. Robin Wall Kimmerer, who is a professor of environmental and forest biology at the State University of New York College of Environmental Science and Forestry and also an enrolled member of the Citizen Potawatomi Nation, speaks eloquently on the importance of such balance today. For instance, she explains in an interview in the *Sun*:

> Western science explicitly separates observer and observed. It's rule number one: keep yourself out of the experiment. But to the indigenous way of thinking, the observer is always in relationship with the observed, and thus it's important that she know herself: As I watch that bee and flower, as I study how water moves, as I observe the growth of the grass in this meadow, I understand that the kind of being I am colors how I see and feel and know. Furthermore, my presence might even be influencing how the world is working around me.
>
> It's important to recognize the relationship that exists between the observer and the observed. In Western science we believe our technologies

InFACT

INITIATIVE FOR FOOD+AGRI**CULTURAL** TRANSFORMATION

CORE VALUES

- **Innovation, Leadership and Ecological Awareness** in our academic endeavors and engagement with communities.
- **Equity and Social Justice** for all.
- **Diversity, Transparency and Continuous Improvement** in farming & food systems.
- **Indigenous Knowledge balanced with Scientific Discovery** to honor diverse sources of knowing as well as generations of students, teachers, communities, families and farmers working together.

FIGURE 11.2. The core values of InFACT, including respect for different ways of knowing the world

> and how we frame our hypotheses will eliminate our bias. A traditional perspective instead celebrates the relationship. A young person is going to see things differently than an old person. A daughter and a mother and a grandmother will see in different ways. All of these perspectives should be brought to bear. Rather than isolate them, we can incorporate them into the learning process. (Tonino 2016)

The Ohio State University's Initiative for Food and AgriCultural Transformation, InFACT, began as a faculty-driven systemic and transdisciplinary approach to the food security challenge, supported by impressive financial resources. The university's investment included a commitment to thirty new faculty in many departments and colleges. Each of these hires was envisioned as a position that would bridge current areas of strength, acting as points of connection for faculty teams across colleges who could bring the breadth of the university to bear on food security.

The areas in which these hires cluster, although representing the areas of greatest opportunity at Ohio State, are indicative of the breadth of scholarly activity needed to address the wicked problem of food security. But for each of the broad areas of investigation and work that will be discussed below in outlining the breadth of academic contributions needed to impact food security, keep in mind that there is a complementary depth of experience associated with each that exists in people but well outside the boundaries that are somewhat artificially drawn by academic disciplines. Our core values (figure 11.2) include a commitment to the balance described above between academic and indigenous knowledge and experience.

In brief, the clusters include the following categories.

Climate-resilient agricultural production. Agriculture, natural resources, and ecosystem services on which our food supply depends are critical for ensuring food security. The problem is *not* primarily crop yields or even the amount of land in production; rather, it is the number of people healthfully fed per acre that is a more accurate and rarely used metric for the efficiency of agricultural production with respect to food security. A sustainable food supply depends on existing and renewable natural resources, and the ingenuity of people in managing natural resources. The effects of climate change, which are already being observed in the form of more frequent and severe storms and droughts, will challenge not only the sustainability of current production systems but their resilience, both the stability of the system in the face of small shocks and its ability to adapt and maintain key functions when the environment changes to the point that the current system no longer functions. A resilient agriculture and food system would feature diversity at all scales, in terms of what is produced, who is producing, and where.

Health and nutrition. The nutrient density and diversity of food is at least as important as the number of calories available. Hunger and malnutrition result from a diet insufficient in quantity or quality, or both. Furthermore, food and its effects on physical health cannot be separated from a wide range of behavioral and lifestyle contributing factors as well as mental health outcomes, which must be considered given increasing rates of suicide and conflict in otherwise stressed populations, including on university campuses. Health care really does fundamentally depend on food, as recognized by Hippocrates.

Policy and planning. Public policy governing food systems should achieve equitable food access while enabling long-term viability for farmers, but no such comprehensive policy platform exists at either the state or national level. Economic inequality is usually the root cause of food insecurity. As a result, the cost of food, particularly when one includes what it takes to obtain it, varies considerably as a percentage of income. These issues have a history in policy and public investments that have left entire communities vulnerable to food insecurity and related public

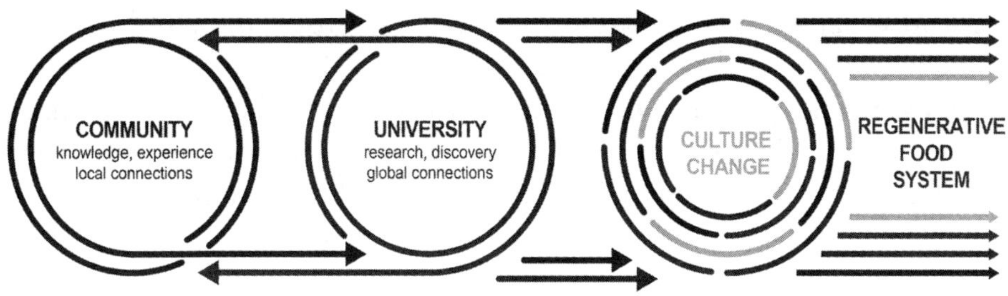

FIGURE 11.3. InFACT's theory of change, with solutions springing from outside the university and propelled by transdisciplinary collaboration toward the culture change needed for a food system that resolves food security challenges

health concerns. Better food policy is needed at local, state, national, and international levels.

Business ecosystems and entrepreneurship. Business ecosystems include the business environment and relationships along food value chains. They feature many steps between the farm and fork, and extend to many other sectors that are not typically associated with food or agriculture. For example, commodity crops like corn are fed to animals and processed into food ingredients but also biochemical feedstocks and transportation fuel. Transforming our system of food and agriculture to achieve food security will create enormous challenges, but also plenty of opportunity for innovation and entrepreneurship in businesses and economic strategies along food value chains, from local to global scales.

Culture, art, and design. Cultural norms and values are at once both the cause and the effect of our current food system. The fact that Ohio has rates of household food insecurity above the national average, while very few people know about it, is a cultural issue. Food insecurity and outright hunger are beginning to engender a simultaneous response from faith, art, social justice, and other communities, including those defined by racial and ethnic heritage. We have an opportunity to raise awareness of food security from a wide range of perspectives, with the arts and humanities as a key means for exploring and understanding where transformation is needed and what outcomes could be possible. Culture and food are intertwined in ways that provide many fruitful openings for academic exploration and artistic expression.

As noted, each of the areas of scholarship described above can be matched and enriched with deep knowledge and experience connected with particular times, places, and peoples. So our challenge, if we are to address the wicked problem of food security, is to combine efforts across networks that include the breadth of academic disciplines, and beyond, to the experience and solutions that can be offered by those who are most affected by and in whose hands the real response to food security challenges depends (figure 11.3). This is why land-grant universities exist, with many colleges and a mission to perform on behalf of society.

References

Coleman-Jensen, Alicia, Matthew P. Rabbitt, Christian A. Gregory, and Anita Singh. 2018. *Household Food Security in the United States in 2017*. Economic Research Report No. ERR-256. https://www.ers.usda.gov/publications/pub-details/?pubid=90022.

De Schutter, Olivier. 2014. "The Transformative Potential of the Right to Food." Report of the Special Rapporteur on the right to food, Olivier De Schutter (A/HRC/25/57). https://www.ohchr.org/EN/HRBodies/HRC/RegularSessions/Session25/Pages/ListReports.aspx.

Ericksen, Polly J. 2008. "Conceptualizing Food Systems for Global Environmental Change Research." *Global Environmental Change* 18, no. 1 (February): 234–45. https://doi.org/10.1016/j.gloenvcha.2007.09.002.

FAO. 2015. "The Right to Food around the Globe." http://www.fao.org/right-to-food-around-the-globe/en/

FAO, IFAD, UNICEF, WFP, and WHO. 2019. *The State of Food Security and Nutrition in the World: Safeguarding against Economic Slowdowns and Downturns.* Rome: FAO. http://www.fao.org/state-of-food-security-nutrition/en/.

Hoy, Casey W. 2015. "Agroecosystem Health, Agroecosystem Resilience, and Food Security." *Journal of Environmental Studies and Sciences* 5, no. 4 (December): 623–35. https://doi.org/10.1007/s13412-015-0322-0.

Tonino, Leath. 2016. "Two Ways of Knowing: Robin Wall Kimmerer on Scientific and Native American Views of the Natural World." *The Sun,* April 2016. https://www.thesunmagazine.org/issues/484/two-ways-of-knowing.

Vadrevu, Krishna Prasad, John Cardina, Fred Hitzhusen, Isaac Bayoh, Richard Moore, Jason Parker, Ben Stinner, Deb Stinner, and Casey Hoy. 2008. "Case Study of an Integrated Framework for Quantifying Agroecosystem Health." *Ecosystems* 11, no. 2 (March): 283–306. https://doi.org/10.1007/s10021-007-9122-z.

12

Reinventing the Regional Campus

Norman W. Jones

One must keep in mind the daunting collection of challenges currently facing higher education as a whole in order to understand the vital role played by the regional campuses of The Ohio State University. Costs have risen steadily due to multiple factors. These include the need for ever-more-sophisticated computing infrastructure and services as well as instructional technology software and support personnel; the increasing cost of health care; and the demand for more extensive student support services to address critical issues such as sexual assault, mental health, and food insecurity. Colleges and universities are also being called on to refashion the traditional undergraduate curriculum to prepare students more fully for increasingly technological workplaces. In addition, students now expect higher-quality residential and recreational facilities than ever before. While such costs continue to rise, the revenue side of the business model for higher education is under intense pressure: Public funding of public universities has dropped substantially even while those of us who serve such universities are working harder than ever to keep tuition and fees low to decrease student debt.

Meanwhile, we also face external demands from businesses to produce more college graduates to meet workforce needs at the same time as demographic changes in many areas of the US are shrinking the traditional pipeline for college students. The most promising way to meet this challenge is to expand the pipeline by increasing the diversity of college students in terms of income, age, race, and ethnicity. We must increase the number of "first-generation" college students as well—students whose parents never earned a college degree. In short, if we are to meet the needs of tomorrow's economy, then we must graduate more students from groups that have historically been underrepresented on college campuses.

An added benefit of this solution, according to well-researched studies such as Scott E. Page's *The Diversity Bonus* (2017), is that we can boost problem-solving skills and outcomes by increasing the diversity of our problem-solvers. Moreover, innovations in higher education such as those embraced over the past decade by Georgia State University demonstrate that colleges and universities can reduce and even eliminate achievement gaps between higher- and lower-income students. All we need to do is improve our teaching methods and streamline students' interactions with the bureaucracy of higher education. These strategies can increase academic excellence by clearing away unnecessary bureaucratic obstacles to help students focus on and engage more actively in their learning.

Such innovations require resources that are in short supply, given the budgetary strains previously noted. It's a time that calls for creative solutions, and Ohio State's regional campuses are helping to lead the way. In the process, we are reinventing what being a "regional" campus can mean—particularly what it means to be regional campuses of a great twenty-first-century land-grant university.

It was clear what *regional* meant in the late 1950s and early 1960s when Ohio State's regional campuses were established in Lima, Marion, Mansfield, and Newark. The population of Ohio had increased by more than 10 percent since the end of World War II, and smaller cities and towns did not offer enough postsecondary educational opportunities to meet the growing demand. A report on this situation by an Ohio State professor, Kenneth Arisman, convinced the university's board of trustees to establish regional campuses. They were designed especially for students who needed to remain employed while pursuing a college degree: Most courses were offered after regular work hours. One of the first four-year degrees offered entirely at an Ohio State regional campus was in education. The growing "baby boom" generation needed more primary and secondary teachers.

Today, our mission has important continuities with these original aims. Ohio State's regional campuses provide Big-Ten-quality educational opportunities in a small-campus setting open to any Ohioan who has completed high school. Our tuition and fees are substantially lower than those paid by students on the Columbus campus. Students can now finish more than ten majors entirely on a regional campus, and education is still a popular choice. At the same time, many students "campus change" to Columbus after spending a year or two on a regional campus: They can thereby complete any of more than 200 majors offered at Ohio State, which is one of the most comprehensive universities in the nation. We call this a "campus change" to Columbus rather than a "transfer" because we are not separate institutions but rather one university in several locations, teaching the same courses with the same academic standards. The diploma is the same whether students complete their degree on a regional campus or the Columbus campus: No specific campus is named on our diplomas because we are all The Ohio State University.

More than 6,000 students enroll each year on Ohio State's regional campuses, and at the end of the academic year, roughly 1,500 of those typically campus change to the Columbus campus. This number of campus-changers, considered alongside the hundreds of students who complete their degrees entirely on the regional campuses each year, means that a significant number of Ohio State graduates completed some or all of their Buckeye experience on a regional campus.

We work hard to ensure that these students receive the same top-quality academic experience at the regionals as students receive on the Columbus campus. The regional campuses focus especially on providing personalized attention to each student. The average class size on the regional campuses is approximately nineteen students. Taken together, we employ more than 150 tenure-track and clinical faculty, a substantial number of whom have earned the University Alumni Distinguished Teaching Award and many of whom are nationally and internationally known experts in their fields. We also employ more than 200 additional teaching faculty and 300 staff. Tenure-track faculty on the regional campuses hold terminal degrees in their field and are reviewed and tenured by their respective departments on the Columbus campus; they are full members of those departments, which maintain academic oversight of all courses and programs on the regional campuses. Regional campus faculty keep their courses aligned with Columbus standards.

In short, Ohio State's regional campus structure remains true to the land-grant vision whereby the regional campuses provide an Ohio State education at an affordable price to any Ohioan willing and able to do the required work. Over the past two decades, however, a fundamental aspect of Ohio State's regional campus mission has expanded because admission directly to the Columbus campus has become increasingly selective. A growing number of students each year choose to begin their Buckeye college experience on a regional campus because we provide not only small class sizes and personal attention but also an "open access" admissions policy: Anyone with a high school diploma or its equivalent can enroll at Ohio State through one of its regional campuses. As a result, the regional campuses experience a wide variety of academic preparation levels, from high-performing students to those for whom Ohio State's regionals offer an opportunity to prove that their previous academic performance does not represent their full potential.

This range of student preparation levels, combined with the high-quality Ohio State academic instruction we offer, contribute to our status as pacesetters among open-access public colleges and universities. Ohio State's regional campuses hold top spots relative to other open-access campuses both statewide and nationally in terms of our retention rates, which measure the percentage of students who complete their first year of college and continue into their second year—one of the key indicators of student success in higher education.

The regionals have witnessed an additional change that is related to but also larger than changes resulting from the increased selectivity of Columbus-campus admissions. Namely, the regional campuses have experienced an increase in the number of students coming from outside our home and adjacent counties, which is undoubtedly the result of not only the limited capacity for new students on the Columbus campus but also the increased capacity for student housing on the regionals.

This necessarily raises a question: If *regional* means *localized*—existing within a limited area or geographic region—then how far can the reach of a regional campus extend before we are no longer able to consider it merely "regional"? At Ohio State, *regional* no longer means what it once did because our regional campuses are not only serving our respective regions but are also serving the entire state of Ohio.

This change is exciting and beneficial to students. Regional campus students now have the benefit of meeting classmates who come from a greater variety of areas in Ohio, which directly contributes to the richness of their college experience. Indeed, the diversity of regional campus students—geographic, economic, racial, and ethnic—has increased in richly productive ways. In addition, this change has resulted in more activities on campus as we have added a growing number of residential students in addition to our more traditional commuter population. There are new opportunities to create a stronger sense of community and belonging by expanding activities that build campus life opportunities for both commuter and residential students. Technology also makes it increasingly easy to connect regional campus students to their peers on the Columbus campus, with events "streaming" live from Columbus to one or more regionals now a regular occurrence.

These changes at Ohio State's regional campuses take on national significance when viewed in light of the broader challenges facing higher education as a whole—especially the increasing need for a more highly educated workforce in both the state of Ohio and nationally, and the growing recognition among higher education leaders that our colleges and universities can only meet that need by graduating much larger numbers of students who historically have been underrepresented on college campuses, such as students of color, financially underresourced students (typically defined as students who receive federal Pell grants), and students who are among the first generation in their family to attend college.

Contrary to some sensational headlines, research shows that earning a college degree is tremendously valuable. Statistics from the Bureau of Labor demonstrate that unemployment rates are dramatically lower for those with college degrees than for those without them, and most new jobs go to college graduates. Yet as a study by the Jack Kent Cooke Foundation explains, "high-achieving lower-income students" are "less likely to complete a bachelor's degree than their higher-income peers (54 percent versus 78 percent)" ("Achievement Trap" 2007). Many college and university leaders attest to the severity of this problem most eloquently through their actions: They have banded together to try to solve the problem by forming organizations such as the University Innovation Alliance (UIA), the American Talent Initiative, and Complete College America. Many of the nation's most recognized colleges and universities are members of at least one of these organizations; Ohio State has been strongly involved in all three. We are committed to making a substantial difference.

The UIA exemplifies this work: It is a consortium of eleven large public universities dedicated to increasing educational attainment rates for financially underresourced students. The UIA vision holds that "by piloting new interventions, sharing insights about their relative costs and effectiveness, and scaling those interventions that are successful, we will significantly increase the number of low-income Americans graduating with quality college degrees and that, over time, our collaborative work will catalyze systemic changes in the entire higher education sector." So far, the eleven UIA members collectively have achieved a 29 percent increase in the number of degrees earned by financially underresourced students. Ohio State's regional campuses are at the heart of this vision for the catalytic relevance of our twenty-first-century land-grant mission.

As a land-grant university that has achieved an exceptional level of academic excellence, Ohio State plays a special role in this work because we combine the academic rigor of flagship research universities that have highly selective admissions (on the Columbus campus) with the open-access admissions policy and affordability of public institutions that aim to serve as gateways to opportunity for everyone (on the regional campuses). As such, we have much to offer to the national conversation about the future of higher education in the US—let alone the future of land-grant institutions. Indeed, as the Columbus campus has become increasingly selective in its admission process, Ohio State's regional campuses now play the lead role in fulfilling the university's land-grant mission as an open-access gateway to educational opportunities. For many prospective students living in communities hard-hit with economic reversals, we are also the more affordable education option.

We are proud that our regional campuses typically achieve student retention rates at least 10 percent higher than the national average for open-access college and university campuses, and that we rank among the top state and national open-access campuses for our graduation rates. Yet we are also proud that we refuse to rest on our laurels: We continue to innovate to help even more of our students achieve their dreams.

President Michael V. Drake spurred this effort by expanding the President's Affordability Grants, extending their reach so that more than 1,000 regional campus students receive these scholarships each year. He made sure that regional campus students were also included in the Digital Flagship Initiative that provided a free iPad to every new student on the regional campuses. He committed financial support for a three-year pilot to increase innovative student success initiatives on the regionals. He ensured that regional faculty are incentivized for completing teacher training workshops the same way Columbus faculty are. He also committed millions annually to help pay all of the tuition for regional campus students who demonstrate the greatest level of financial need and who prove themselves by successfully completing their first semester at Ohio State: The Buckeye Opportunity Program creates what amounts to a tuition-free college experience for such students. Taken together, President Drake's commitments are unprecedented and mark an exciting change in the university's stance toward its regional campuses.

At the same time, Ohio State's regional campuses recognize that our student success innovations depend significantly on our being equally ambitious and innovative when it comes to engaging regional businesses and other community stakeholders to create meaningful partnerships in support of workforce and economic development. Such engagement currently includes real estate development, workforce development in manufacturing and health care, and student and faculty involvement in addressing community challenges. We have created a new degree program whose graduates will be trained for roles in manufacturing leadership, for example. We have also undertaken a multimillion-dollar community agriculture initiative that uses an entrepreneurial business model to create jobs. We are partnering with real estate developers and municipalities to expand economic activity in our local regions. Finally, the regional campuses continue to work with public school systems to support primary and secondary education, for instance by training K–12 teachers how to teach math more effectively.

In short, our regional campuses serve a crucial function in helping The Ohio State University achieve its status as a leader in higher education. As a whole, Ohio State is a uniquely comprehensive flagship land-grant university distributed across multiple geographic locations that serve a mix of urban, suburban, and smaller rural communities. The regional campuses provide this internationally respected education in an open-access, affordable, personalized, and supportive setting. We motivate students to become part of a transformational university whose reach is spectacularly vast. Put differently, we motivate students by offering a goal genuinely worth achieving, a challenge in which they can take pride. Equally important, we offer this educational opportunity to all students, including those who may not previously have seen higher education as a real possibility for themselves.

In light of the many challenges currently facing higher education, providing these educational opportunities, which forms the heart of Ohio State's regional campus mission, grows only more deeply urgent and meaningful every day.

References

Page, Scott E. 2017. *The Diversity Bonus: How Great Teams Pay Off in the Knowledge Economy.* Princeton, NJ: Princeton University Press.

Wyner, Joshua S., John M. Bridgeland, and John J. DiIulio, Jr. 2007. "Achievement Trap: How America is Failing Millions of High-Achieving Students from Lower-Income Families." Jack Kent Cooke Foundation. https://www.jkcf.org/research/achievement-trap-how-america-is-failing-millions-of-high-achieving-students-from-lower-income-families/.

13

The Science of Families

Work-Family Balance and the Twenty-First-Century Land-Grant Mission

Claire Kamp Dush and Stephen M. Gavazzi

Throughout this book, and across the higher education literature, the dominant narrative is that land-grant universities were designed to help the working class realize the American Dream through an affordable and practical college education. Yet as historian Nathan Sorber suggested in his 2018 book on land-grant universities, initially there was some noteworthy controversy about how much of this access to postsecondary education should have been afforded to women. In the words of Sorber:

> Pioneering land-grant women challenged both sides of a gendered debate on the purpose of the Morrill Act, which conceptualized land-grant colleges as intertwined with career preparation. Within the cultural context of a separate-spheres ideology that confined women to the private world of family and home . . . women were questioned as to why they would prepare for careers that were closed to them. . . . [L]and-grant coeducation would become the rule by the turn of the century, as young women overcame exclusionary discourses and practices, created unique spaces on campuses, and challenged the gendered foundation of the land-grant idea. (16–17)

At present, more than 50 percent of all undergraduate and graduate degrees conferred by Ohio State are awarded to females. One would assume then that our university has been living up to the land-grant ideal that all our graduates can achieve their highest work-related potential. Yet, it is our belief that only one degree program—Human Development and Family Science (HDFS)—has been systematically preparing students for the realities of work and family life in the twenty-first century.

We begin this essay with a brief examination of the history of family science, which is bound inextricably to the history of home economics within the land-grant university. Next, we discuss the unique ways that the field of family science reflects the tripartite land-grant mission, including how family science instructors teach students to understand the critical balance between work and family issues, how family scientists provide cutting-edge research on families that is translational in its orientation, and how family therapists and other family-serving professionals are applying such knowledge in efforts to improve the lives of children, adolescents, and families. We end this short essay by examining the evolution of family science at The Ohio State University. Included in this final section are some vibrant examples of how HDFS faculty, staff, and students are contributing to a twenty-first-century land-grant mission that places work and family issues at the very center of our teaching, research, and community engagement activities.

The History of Family Science and Home Economics

The science of studying families is almost as old as the land-grant universities themselves. According to family scientist Bill Doherty and colleagues:

> Contemporary family science in America was born in the progressive era, from 1880 to 1920, during the same period that sociology and home economics became disciplines. . . . [T]he progressive era was marked by a strong concern for social reform in the face of the problems created by industrialization and urbanization . . . [and] the family was viewed as an endangered institution that required social theory (created by social scientists) and social therapy (conducted by social workers, from whom sociologists had split off). (Doherty et al. 2009, 7)

Historians such as Nathan Sorber (cited above) and Megan Elias (2008) have framed the rise of home economics as having both gender-specific and scientific underpinnings. On the topic of gender, home economics as an academic program was initiated in large part to provide women with the opportunity to apply their college experiences in the work world as teachers and Cooperative Extension Services personnel. The science within home economics programs, then, was applied particularly to those issues that pertained to household matters: cooking and nutritional health, sewing and textiles, home management and decoration, family financial matters, and child rearing.

Family science thus emerged from the initial examination of factors related to the child's development within the home. It is now its own discipline, complete with a distinct professional organization—the National Council on Family Relations (NCFR; https://www.ncfr.org), which bills itself as "the premier professional association for understanding families through interdisciplinary research, theory, and practice." As we shall see in the next section of this essay, this simultaneous focus on theory, research, and practice seamlessly matches the tripartite mission of the land-grant university.

Family Science and the Tripartite Land-Grant Mission

Three federal acts provided land-grant universities with a three-part mission. The Morrill Act of 1862 was designed to provide the "industrial classes" (what today we would term working-class families) with access to an affordable education. This means that land-grant universities have a primary teaching mission. The Hatch Act of 1877 provided federal funding to establish experiment stations that formed the basis for the research mission of the land-grant institution. Special emphasis was placed on solving the pressing problems that impacted those citizens of the states served by these universities. Finally, the Smith-Lever Act of 1914 brought Cooperative Extension Services into existence, creating the mechanism by which knowledge generated by the university could be disseminated directly to families, farms, businesses, and communities. This became the community-engagement component of the land-grant mission.

Family science programs offer coursework designed to provide students with a greater understanding of children and adolescents and the families in which they grow and develop. There is a strong commitment to excellence in the teaching mission, as evidenced by activities surrounding the Family Science Association (FSA; https://www.familyscienceassociation.org), an organization dedicated to discovering and disseminating best practices in teaching and learning family science topics. The FSA does this through two primary mechanisms: the stewardship of *Family Science Review,* a journal focused on the teaching and scholarship of family science, and the hosting of the annual Teaching Family Science Conference.

Family scientists who contribute to the research mission of land-grant universities do so through the production of both basic and applied research pertaining to families. The previously mentioned NCFR organization hosts three refereed journals that touch on all aspects of the scholarship continuum. The *Journal of Marriage and the Family* is the flagship journal dedicated to the publication of basic research generated by the family field, *Family Relations* is the journal dedicated to the publication of applied family research, and the *Journal of Family Theory and Review* publishes articles that integrate various disciplinary approaches to the study of the family.

That said, the empirical products of family science continue to trend toward a more applied focus, what more recently has been termed *translational research.* In large part, this is due to the more applied nature of family science, which is to say that the application of family science teaching and research fits well within the community engagement component of the land-grant mission. Family science departments have had a long history of housing couple and family therapy training programs, for example, and there are many individuals (like the second author of this paper) who are trained as both family scientists and family therapists.

Family Science and the Work-Family Interface

From the outset, a land-grant education was designed to be practical. Graduates of land-grant universities were supposed to make an immediate contribution back to the communities from which they hailed, including as participants in the workforce. We make the assertion here that no woman or man will be able to achieve their full potential at work until they understand how to make family life more work friendly and, in turn, to make work more family friendly. As a result, we believe that the family science field must facilitate the achievement of this deepened balance between work and family issues by enacting changes at various points between the individual level and the societal level.

Family science has taught us that our family relationships influence our work performance; individuals who are more stressed in their personal life are less productive at work. Further, family science has taught us that our work lives impact our family relationships such that individuals who are more stressed at work have poorer interactions with their partners and children. Yet very little is done at Ohio State and other land-grant universities to prepare students to be *both* productive workers and healthy family members. Due to the rise in women earning college degrees and the fall in the wages of men without bachelor's degrees since the 1970s, in 2019, for the first time, the number of women with college degrees in the workforce outnumbered men. College-educated women with children are working both because they enjoy their work and because their income is necessary to support their families. In 2017, women outearned men in 26 percent of US families. Teaching OSU students, and for that matter, the general public, strategies for creating a division of household labor, childcare and parenting, and household management that works for both partners is critical to the health and well-being of both these individuals and their families.

The Evolving Science of Families at Ohio State

Family science at Ohio State has its roots in the establishment of the Department of Domestic Economy in May of 1896 by the board of trustees at the recommendation of Ohio State president James Canfield. An author in the *Farmers' Review* commented at the time that "the course in domestic science is a course in language and science with the application of the latter to the practical affairs of women" (Hunt 1896, 388). In 1897–1898, the first courses were offered, and President Canfield's own daughter was a member of the first class. Dorothy Canfield Fisher said on the occasion of the program's fiftieth anniversary that her father was "much criticized—laughed at heartily, many times, for his radical and absurd idea. And I am personally more and more thankful for it, because in the first class . . . I saw the dignity and value of skillful and intelligent homemaking" (Ashcraft 1970, 2). The first bachelor's degree was granted in 1900 to Laura Anna Weisman and the first master's degree in 1905. Extension work in domestic science began in 1909 in Amesville in Athens County. In 1913, the name of the department was changed to Home Economics. A home economics building was completed in 1917, with an appropriation from the Ohio legislature, and was named Campbell Hall in 1921 after the deceased wife of Governor James E. Campbell. Campbell Hall was renovated in the 1960s, and is still the home of family science at Ohio State. In 1922, the first childcare courses began, and the laboratory nursery school was established in 1925. In 1926 funds became available for research in home economics through the Purnell Act and home economics grew. The School of Home Economics was established in 1929. The first PhD was awarded in 1949. As early as 1945, family and child development was a division in the school. Family and child development became a department of its own in 1975 and changed its name to Family Relations and Human Development. The name was changed to Human Development and Family Science in the early 1990s. In 2013, HDFS became a part of the Department of Human Sciences. As of spring 2019, HDFS had over 400 undergraduate majors, 100 undergraduate minors, and more than twenty-five graduate students working toward doctoral degrees.

Teaching about Families and the Land-Grant Mission

Faculty and instructors in the HDFS program at Ohio State are some of the best educators at OSU, with students rating their classes highly and making comments including "Everyone at OSU should have to take this class!" Majors are also highly satisfied at the time of their graduation; in 2017–2018, 95 percent of HDFS majors said they were satisfied or somewhat satisfied with their experience as a student at Ohio State. Ohio State teachers are also driving family science education across the country. The first author of this chapter founded and moderates a Facebook group for family science educators around the country that includes over 300 members. Family Development, a general education class, regularly enrolls over 300 students in fall and spring semesters. The class teaches students about the science and research behind marital quality and divorce, and importantly, how to balance work and family life. Students learn the importance of having both spouses/partners share housework and household management tasks such as making doctor and dentist appointments for children so that both partners have the time and energy to perform at work, and the emotional energy to nurture their couple relationship. Students also learn in this class how gender and parental status can negatively affect women's career trajectories and positively affect men's career trajectories. Students also learn concrete strategies for calling out bias and microaggresssions at work so that they can make the world a better, more equitable place for all. For example, if an alumni hears a woman's status as a mother suggested as a reason that she is not productive at work, students learn to gently point out that parental status was not used as a reason that a man was not productive, so the group should stay away from using parental status for women. Finally, students in this class reflect on expectations for marriage today by comparing modern marriage vows to those from the 1980s or 1990s. Students learn that marital scholars have suggested that we have higher standards for marriage today, and students write down their own vision of a perfect partner and reflect on whether their expectations of the perfect partner are actually realistic. Thus, this class is just one example of how HDFS helps students to create work lives that support their families, and family lives that support their work.

Research about Families and the Land-Grant Mission

To get better answers to the question of how present-day couples are balancing work and family, and how it compares to previous eras, researchers in the HDFS program are collecting innovative, contemporary data on work and family life in the US. With funding from the Eunice Kennedy Shriver National Institute on Child Health and Human Development, Ohio State family scientists led by this chapter's first author are leading the National Couples' Health and Time Study. For the first time in the US, Ohio State family scientists will collect a sample of partners who are in different-gender and same-gender couples from across the US. Individuals will report on their health, their relationships, and how they spend their time, and researchers will connect their time to their satisfaction with their relationships and their work to both physical and mental health outcomes. This study is also collecting dried blood spots from participants to test for stress biomarkers to learn how stress gets under the skin of individuals who are sexual and gender minorities, as well as individuals who are racial and ethnic minorities. This important study will shed much-needed light on how couple relationships can buffer or exacerbate health disparities related to race and ethnicity and sexual and gender minority status.

Further, the Work and Family Life Study will leverage population-level data collected in 1980, 2000, and new population data to be collected in 2020 to examine how work and family life in the context of marriage has changed over the past forty years. Although there are theories that today's couples have too high of expectations for their intimate relationships, there are no data available to test these theories. With funding from the National Institute on Aging pending as of this writing, Ohio State family scholars led by this chapter's first author will be the first to look at family functioning over the past forty years, and its implications for health. This study will also include a sample of same-gender married couples, which will be the largest sample of its kind.

Engaging Families and the Land-Grant Mission

Family scientists at Ohio State regularly work with communities to improve the lives of Ohioans. With funding from the US Department of Agriculture (USDA) and the Aetna Foundation, Professor Deanna Wilkinson designed and implemented Urban Gems, an after-school academic enrichment and a summer program for youth ages ten to seventeen in two urban neighborhoods with high poverty in Columbus. Students run a mini-farm using an aeroponic system as well as an outdoor garden. Students learn (1) the science of gardening as well as research skills through tracking crop yields, (2) entrepreneurship through running a small business selling their yield, (3) the importance of healthy eating and living, (4) teamwork and leadership skills, and (5) problem-solving abilities in the context of a growth/fixed mindset curriculum. Finally, community service is weaved throughout. About 180 youth have been served annually by Urban Gems since 2016.

The PROSPER Ohio program led by Professor Michael Betz is aiming to address Ohio's opioid crisis. PROSPER stands for PROmoting School-community-university Partnerships to Enhance Resilience. With PROSPER Ohio, Betz is implementing family and school programs in twelve communities. The programs build youth competencies and prevent problem behaviors including opioid and other drug use and delinquent behaviors by focusing on supporting positive youth development and family functioning. One important aspect of the program is that it does not focus only on "at risk" families, but is designed to help all youth and families. PROSPER Ohio has funding from the USDA's National Institute of Food and Agriculture, the Ohio Department of Higher Education, and the Substance Abuse and Mental Health Services Administration.

The Couple and Family Therapy program has served countless central Ohio couples and families directly, and couples and families all over the nation through the alumni of the program. Couple and family therapists take a holistic approach to helping individuals and families, addressing the behaviors of all family members to improve the well-being of individual family members and the family as a whole. Graduate student therapists at the OSU Couple and Family Therapy Clinic see individuals, couples, and families on a sliding scale from campus and across Central Ohio. Professor Keeley Pratt and her graduate students also work with patients and families in the Ohio State's Comprehensive Weight Management Program to help both patients and families support patient weight-management goals.

The Future of Family Science at Ohio State

The HDFS program at Ohio State is uniquely situated to improve the lives of Ohio State students, Ohio families, and indeed, families around the US. With an interdisciplinary focus on the intersection of families, work, and health, and a social justice thread, HDFS is preparing the next generation of husbands, wives, fathers, mothers, and employees to balance their work and family lives and their health and well-being, to achieve their full potential. By enacting the three-part land-grant mission, OSU's HDFS faculty and students will continue to be some of the most engaged citizens in the world, improving it for the good of all. If Dorothy Canfield Fisher were alive today, she would likely be surprised that the work of "skillful and intelligent homemaking" is now shared by both men and women in most US couples because both men and women engage in paid work, but she would be disappointed that higher education in general has neglected their focus of educating the whole person for all aspects of their professional and personal lives. That said, she would likely be gratified that her own degree program was continuing to holistically enact her father's "radical and absurd idea" to help prepare individuals to be engaged family, community, and global citizens.

References

Ashcraft, Kathryn Gorrell. 1970. *The Ohio State University School of Home Economics: A History 1896-1970.* https://kb.osu.edu/bitstream/handle/1811/75726/ARV_OSU_Centennial_Histories_HomeEconomics.pdf;sequence=1.

Doherty, William J., Pauline G. Boss, Ralph LaRossa, Walter R. Schumm, and Suzanne K. Steinmetz. 2009. "Family Theories and Methods: A Contextual Approach." In *Sourcebook of Family Theories and Methods: A Contextual Approach,* edited by Pauline G. Boss, William J. Doherty, Ralph LaRossa, Walter R. Schumm, and Suzanne K. Steinmetz, 3–30. New York: Plenum.

Elias, Megan. 2008. *Stir It Up: Home Economics in American Culture.* Philadelphia: University of Pennsylvania Press.

Hunt, J. H. 1896. *Farmers Review.* "Domestic Science at the Ohio University." May 27, 1896. https://books.google.com/books?id=jULLuNLIkb4C&pg=PA338#v=onepage&q&f=false.

Sorber, Nathan M. 2018. *Land-Grant Colleges and Popular Revolt.* Ithaca, NY: Cornell University Press.

14

Agriculture as the Cornerstone College in the Twenty-First-Century Land-Grant Mission

Cathann A. Kress and Graham R. Cochran

Imagine if you will a world in which—by simply eating the right combination of delicious foods—we could prevent cancer. Or one in which a lowly dandelion could be harvested to create high-quality sustainable rubber. Imagine a world where the single deadliest animal to humans—the mosquito—has been neutralized and we don't spray insecticides to eliminate them from transmitting dengue, malaria, and Zika, but can shorten their life-span by short-circuiting their systems, leaving honeybees and other pollinators untouched. Or imagine a world where soil structure and microbes help us manage specialized agriculture resulting in less need of irrigation, fertilizers, and herbicides.

We don't have to imagine these things because, at land-grant universities across the nation, colleges of agricultural sciences are working on them right now. For almost any problem you can think of related to food, agriculture, health, and the environment, the land-grant colleges of agriculture have talented students, staff, and faculty working on solutions and exploring new technologies—just like we've done for the past 150 years.

This is what we do in colleges of agriculture. We carry on the critical work of the human species, begun around 12,000 years ago, with the simple but essential activity of harnessing the sun's energy—the basis of all energy on the planet—and converting it for human use. Or, to put it more simply: We sustain life.

FIGURE 14.1. Thompson Library with triangle—Knowledge at the base, Agriculture, Arts, Science, Letters

When humans began to use agriculture as a means for nourishing not just individuals, but whole communities, human life changed dramatically. Farming made it possible for us to live together in larger and larger groups, for towns to form, for our populations to grow, *for us to learn from each other.* Those connections—the collective learning shared about new tools, new uses for clay and metal, new techniques—increased the rate of innovation. Without having to constantly search for food, humans began to explore new modes of travel on land and on sea, the written word, the arts and literature, the evolution of religion, and the sharing and preservation of information. Agriculture is the cornerstone of all learning and knowledge (figure 14.1).

So, it is no surprise that colleges of agriculture served as the focus of land-grant universities as they developed across our nation. In 1870, when the Ohio Agricultural and Mechanical College was founded, the population of the US was much like it was in Ohio, which had less than three million citizens and most of them, about 80 percent, called rural areas home, with farming largely their main occupation. The other 20 percent lived in urban areas, including the future metropolitan cities of Cincinnati (population in 1870, 216,000), Cleveland (93,000), and Columbus (31,000). Ohio farmers grew corn, wheat, oats, and barley among their crops. They raised cattle, sheep, and pigs. Some of the farmers grew tobacco, some grew hemp. Soybeans had just started to find their feet.

Cooperative Extension was added as an arm of land-grant universities in the early 1900s to bridge a gap between research at land-grant universities and the people who needed it the most—rural citizens engaged in agriculture. Extension developed deep relationships with the communities they served, sharing their findings on a new crop or planting practice, and working side by side with farmers to refine and apply those results in the field.

In the first century of the land-grants, colleges of agriculture focused heavily on one significant goal across most disciplines: yield. This singular focus on yield, driven by a need to feed a growing population, led to dramatic increases in farm production during the twentieth century. For example, we were quickly growing more food from the same or fewer acres and producing more milk from fewer cows.

The unprecedented success of colleges of agriculture throughout the land-grant system—home to research and new technologies developed to increase the production of food, fiber, and fuel—helped our country grow, innovate, and become an economic powerhouse.

Today, Ohio's population is more than four times greater than it was in 1870, or nearly twelve million. The state's largest city is Columbus, with a population of some 890,000, and the three *C* cities (Cleveland, Columbus, and Cincinnati) each have more than two million people in their wider metropolitan areas. And the ratio of who lives where has flipped 180 degrees: About 80 percent of Ohioans live in urban areas, 20 percent in rural areas.

Ohio farmers produce many of the same types of crops and livestock as they did 150 years ago. But thanks to improvements driven in large part by land-grant research and development, the specific crop varieties are healthier, their yields are higher, production practices have improved, and livestock lines are healthier and more productive, too. There are booms, to name a few, in urban farms, organic farms, Farm-to-School farms, greenhouses, vineyards, plant nurseries, and Ohio's already huge food-processing industry. The number of farms in the state producing those crops and feeding so many of us stands at only about 78,000, according to the US Department of Agriculture's most recent Census of Agriculture, or about one farm for every 150 Ohioans. While fewer people are directly involved in farming, Ohio's agricultural and food-production industry remains a vital part of the Ohio economy, contributing one in eight jobs and $1 out of $13 of Ohio's gross state product.

While the original focus for land-grants was improving rural life and increasing crop yields, we no longer face one main goal. Changes in our society, the interconnection between urban and rural communities, and the challenges we face are complex. And while agriculture in the traditional sense—the agriculture of 150 years ago—is still a central part of our college's purpose, we as a collective group of agricultural colleges must apply our education, translational research, and engagement with communities to address many of the grand challenges now facing our world.

With a burgeoning population, the need for sustainability in our agricultural practices remains strong. The first grand challenge touches on our most fundamental human need—food security, which includes the production, distribution, accessibility, and safety of our food. Unfortunately, amid our great agricultural story here in the US and all our efforts to efficiently produce high-quality, affordable food, food insecurity persists. Over forty-two million people live in food insecure households in the US. Nearly six and a half million are children for whom nutritional deficiency has developmental consequences that will impact them for the rest of their lives. Ohio ranks third in the nation for food insecurity, impacting both urban and rural communities alike.

Another facet of the first grand challenge, environmental and ecosystem sustainability, includes the importance of water quality. Whether harmful algal blooms in Lake Erie, hypoxic (low-oxygen) areas in the Gulf of Mexico, or the health of local rivers and streams, there are no simple solutions. Sociologists call issues like this one "wicked problems," where the solutions often generate more problems. A wicked problem has innumerable causes, is tough to describe, and doesn't have one right answer. Sounds like a perfect challenge for a scientist!

We live at a time when there is a greater probability of a pandemic than ever before, mostly because of the concentration of populations, both human and animal. At the same time, our science has managed to eradicate only two diseases, one human and one animal—smallpox and rinderpest, respectively. Meanwhile, it's estimated that about 150 pathogens exist with the potential to cause epidemics in humans. Additionally, it is increasingly understood that agriculture plays a significant role in disease prevention not only through the promotion of good nutrition but through a greater understanding of the role foods can play in treating diseases like cancer. Only 5 percent to 10 percent of all cancers can be attributed to genetics; the rest have their roots in the environment and lifestyle. Colleges of agriculture, through partnerships with other departments at our universities, are poised to focus on this second grand challenge: One Health—the integration of human health, animal health, and environmental health.

As a result of changing demographics, another challenge facing agriculture in the next decade is improving the consumer's perception of modern agriculture. With fewer of us engaged in agriculture, the gap between consumers and farmers has grown, with misperceptions and misunderstandings about where food comes from, whether it's safe to eat, and how well we care for the land and water entrusted to our care.

No longer can we expect that our suburban and urban neighbors have a connection to a farm and appreciate what it takes to provide them with food, fiber, and fuel. Sometimes, even our rural neighbors don't have a connection to a farm other than that they drive by them. Consumer perceptions commonly reported by the media include animal welfare issues, environmental degradation, and safety of genetically engineered crops.

Most negative perceptions are based on a distrust of technologies that improve agricultural efficiency. In order to overcome the long-term challenges facing agriculture, it is imperative that consumers become more confident in modern agricultural practices. Consumers often believe modern agriculture has a more negative environmental impact than traditional agricultural practices of the early to mid-1900s. In reality, virtually all agricultural practices have decreased their environmental footprint, often driven by discoveries from the land-grants. While many understand this about our work, our remarkable success at sustaining life in increasingly efficient ways has meant fewer of us are needed to do it, fewer of us understand what it takes to do it, and fewer of us appreciate what must be done to preserve our ability to continue to do it well.

Shifts in our demographics and industry mean that for the first time in our nation's history, a strong production agriculture does not necessarily guarantee a strong economy for rural America. And so, we have rural communities struggling to find a foothold in today's economy. These communities have perhaps been most heavily impacted by agriculture's efficiency, as the need for work and workers has shifted.

Slightly more than a fifth of the nation's people live in rural America. Rural places make up 97 percent of our nation's space—places where we grow our food and where we go to play. Rural, however, no longer means farm—although most policy makers and urban dwellers believe it does. If we look at rural counties that count agriculture as their major source of income, the US has gone from 2,000 of those counties in 1950 to just 556 when the 1990s began. That's out of slightly more than 3,100 counties and county equivalents total nationally.

At the same time, nearly 60,000 high-skilled agriculture job openings are expected annually, yet our agricultural colleges produce only about 35,000 graduates each year. Many of the jobs are not traditional production agriculture jobs but are driving the innovations and technology required to feed the world's growing and increasingly diverse population. This new agriculture represents an opportunity that could be leveraged in favor of rural America.

The final grand challenge directly impacts the success with which we will be able to address our current wicked problems and future challenges. With unprecedented research opportunities ahead of us, to find solutions to the grand challenges facing our world, there is a great need to continue to attract and prepare students for the future, many of whom have little to no background in agricultural or environmental issues. These new jobs in food, agricultural, and environmental sciences include work with drones for remote crop sensing, greenhouse control systems that use machine learning to dispense fertilizer when needed in precise amounts, horticulturists and food scientists working together to create more nutritious foods that combat cancer, and much more.

Given the scope and complexities of these challenges, we have a compelling mandate to broaden and refine our extension, engagement, and outreach efforts. We need to include more university resources, technology transfer, and industry partnerships so that a broader audience can appreciate and value what we do. We must balance related and significant goals of viable agricultural production, food security and safety, human and animal health, and environmental and ecosystem sustainability. Addressing the challenges represented in each area is critically important for our colleges, our universities, our communities, our country, and our world—meaning the relationship between the university and surrounding communities remains just as relevant today as it was 150 years ago.

We need to continue our on-ground presence of university extension professionals, a tremendous asset to fostering collaboration across the university and with communities that is paramount for long-term engagement. This connection to communities, already in place and fully leveraged, will result in a more engaged institution, addressing vital community needs.

Colleges of agriculture, in whatever variety they exist, remain a cornerstone of the land-grant university. We need to focus our energy on "yield" once again: investing our time to yield a stronger connection to those we serve; investing in engagement with our communities to yield translational research; and investing in our infrastructure to create spaces that will yield solutions, cures for disease, and groundbreaking research. We need people willing to invest themselves and their lives in the noble enterprise of agriculture (and other emerging facets of agriculture) with the recognition that it forms the foundation of society and community. Simply put, we need scientists and leaders.

No matter what you care about—international trade, hunger, health, the environment, business, or finance—everything has its roots in agriculture. As we look to the future, it very well could be a food scientist who prevents cancer or a plant breeder who solves hunger. A soil scientist could create affordable solutions for clean water, or an economist might bring policy makers and citizens together to solve environmental problems in their community. And leaders who understand this, who value the work of our colleges of agriculture and the importance of agriculture in the fabric of our society, will be the leaders who change the world, the leaders who yield the greatest result: sustaining life.

15

At the Intersection

The Birth of Ohio's 1862 and 1890 Land-Grant Universities

Laquore Meadows

The history and significance of the land-grant institutions in the state of Ohio have a storied past—a past infused with a rich legacy positioned outside of current-day tradition while also symbolized by multiple acts of legislative influence. Said influences not only helped to build the origin narratives of Ohio's land-grant universities, but have also had a lasting impact on the fruition and vitality of these two distinct, yet vital institutions now in pursuit of a common land-grant mission.

The founding of The Ohio State University resides at the intersection of legislative action, advocacy, and geographic opportunity. Upon the passage of the Morrill Act of 1862, two of Ohio's more senior institutions of higher education, Miami University and Ohio University, sought to acquire the 1862 land-grant designation. Both institutions deemed it to be more advantageous to scale existing agricultural and mechanical programs than to create a new college solely on its own. Farmers across the state, however, were not in alignment with this proposal and instead preferred that an institution be established to solely focus on their interests. This sentiment, coupled with the advocacy of then-governor Rutherford B. Hayes, prompted the state legislature to decide that in lieu of establishing the state's land-grant in southeastern or western Ohio, it would be more advantageous to establish an institution of higher education near the state capital. Given this, The Ohio State University, originally named the Ohio Agricultural and Mechanical College, was born and ultimately situated in Columbus, Ohio, on the property once known as Neil Farm.

Ohio Agricultural and Mechanical College opened its doors under very humble conditions. The college's one and only building was not fully complete when the institution's first twenty-four students made their way to campus. The roof of the building had yet to be completed and the floors remained unfinished. Despite the ongoing construction, the college and the students excelled—however, not without concern for funding to support continued operations.

Given the land-grant dollars allocated to the college, the state of Ohio did not deem it to be the state legislature's responsibility to provide appropriations to ensure the sustainability of the institution. Given this, similar to the physical infrastructure of the college's first building on opening day, the funding that supported the first decade of the Ohio Agricultural and Mechanical College's existence was meager at best. However, with time and continued advocacy, the sentiment shifted and the state of Ohio affirmed its commitment to help ensure that the institution was positioned to flourish.

Similarly, nearly sixty miles away and seventeen years after the founding of the Ohio Agricultural and Mechanical College, the Combined Normal and Industrial Department established its roots as a part of the nation's first historically black private institution, Wilberforce University, named after abolitionist William Wilberforce. Originally founded in 1856 by the Methodist Episcopal Church, and later acquired by the African Methodist Episcopal Church in 1863, Wilberforce University was located near Xenia, Ohio, with close proximity to the Tawawa Woods, originally named as such by the Shawnee Indians.

In its early days, Wilberforce University offered classes in the areas of theology, law, and teaching; however, as a result of the need for a dramatic influx of trained African American teachers and industrial workers, nearly thirty years after the founding of Wilberforce University, the Combined Normal and Industrial Department was created and subsequently funded by the state of Ohio. True to the desire of the state, the department established its roots by providing teacher training and technical education.

Three years after the creation of the department and nearly three decades after the establishment of the first Morrill Act, the Agriculture College Act of 1890, or the Second Morrill Act, was passed to help mitigate the growing expenses of the 1862 land-grants. Most notably, however, the 1890 act allowed for the creation of seventeen "Negro colleges," later explicitly defined as historically black colleges and universities (HBCUs) in the Higher Education Act of 1965. The Agricultural College Act of 1890 specified:

> No money shall be paid out under this act to any state or territory for the support and maintenance of a college where a distinction between race or color is made in the admission of students, but the establishment and maintenance of such colleges separately for white and colored students shall be held to be a compliance with the provisions of this act if the funds received in such state or territory be equitably divided.

Given this unique opportunity, the state-funded Combined Normal and Industrial Arts Department sought to acquire the 1890 land-grant designation. Unlike many predominantly white colleges in the south, Ohio's 1862 land-grant institution practiced a non-race-based admission policy. In fact, Fred Patterson, Ohio Agricultural and Mechanical College's first black student, was admitted in 1889, one year prior to the passing of the 1890 land-grant act. Given this, the college qualified to receive the funds associated this legislation. At the urging of then–former US president and OSU board of trustee member Rutherford B. Hayes and others, the Ohio legislature ultimately decided to award the Ohio Agricultural and Mechanical College with the $25,000 associated with this act, leaving the Combined Normal and Industrial Arts Department to continue on its current trajectory. Despite not receiving the land-grant designation or the funding that accompanied it, the department continued to flourish and became Central State College in 1951 and later Central State University in 1965.

Fast forward nearly 125 years, due to the devout advocacy of Congresswoman Joyce Beatty, Congresswoman Marcia Fudge, Senator Sherrod Brown, and many others, on February 7, 2014, the 113th Congress of the US voted to approve the 2014 Farm Bill, wherein Section 7129 read as follows:

> (Sec. 7129) Designates Central State University (Ohio) as an 1890 land-grant institution.

As a result of this bill introduced by Representative Frank Lucas (R-OK-3), the Combined Normal and Industrial Arts Department at Wilberforce, now Central State University, became an 1890 land-grant institution.

Ohio, the US's Newest 1862/1890 Land-Grant State

February 2014 will always serve as an important period in history for the state of Ohio and more—namely, the Cooperative Extension community. At the signing of the 2014 Farm Bill (HR 2642), Central State University, Ohio's only public historically black institution, received its land-grant designation, thus joining The Ohio State University in the pursuit of the accomplishment of a tripartite mission: teaching, research, and service.

Since receiving the 1890 land-grant designation, both Central State University and The Ohio State University have worked to establish the policies and procedures needed to help facilitate the physical and procedural infrastructure of their new dual land-grant kinship. In an effort to accomplish its objectives as it relates to the work of Cooperative Extension, an early act on behalf of Central State University was to identify, hire, and co-locate personnel in five pre-existing extension offices to serve the residents of Butler, Cuyahoga, Franklin, Hamilton, Lucas, and Montgomery Counties. Plans have also been established to build a stand-alone office for Central State University Extension in Greene County, Ohio, and to co-locate with local community-based organizations.

While achievements have been significant in charting a pathway forward, the future of Ohio's land-grant institutions continues to be immense. As a result of the advocacy of Senator Sherrod Brown (D-OH) and Senator Rob Portman (R-OH), a provision was added to the Agriculture Improvement Act, also known as the 2018 Farm Bill, to modify the funding formula used to help fund 1890 land-grant institutions. As a result of said provision, Central State University became the recipient of additional USDA funding, most notably without jeopardizing the funding allocation to other 1890 land-grant institutions.

Emerging from a building with a roof under construction and a state-funded department situated in the midst of a private institution, both The Ohio State University and Central State University have transitioned a mighty long way from their respective origins. Furthermore, unlike other 1862/1890 land-grant partnerships in Southern states, the state of Ohio's dual land-grant kinship has been established in a societal context set apart, yet unfortunately not completely void of the racial context that existed when the original legislation was established. While this is important to note, optimism prevails. As both institutions look to the future, many opportunities await to leverage each other's strengths in an effort to be of service to the citizens of Ohio. Each institution individually and collectively possesses the intellectual and social capital needed to make a sustained impact on the future of our state. It is at the intersection of both that this impact will be fully utilized.

References

"A Century of Lawmaking for a New Nation: U.S. Congressional Documents and Debates, 1774–1875." Library of Congress. Accessed April 18, 2017. http://memory.loc.gov/cgi-bin/ampage?collId=llsl&fileName=012/llsl012.db&recNum=535.

H. R. 2642. Agricultural Act of 2014. Accessed January 10, 2010. https://www.congress.gov/bill/113th-congress/house-bill/2642?q=%7B%22search%22%3A%22Nuclear+power+Canada+Federal+Energy+Regulatory+Commission+%28FERC%29%22%7D&s=1&r=4.

16

Ohio State as a Twenty-First-Century Urban University

Harvey J. Miller

Introduction

Similar to other land-grant institutions in the Midwest and Western US, The Ohio State University (OSU) has traditionally been associated with agricultural extension and outreach. There is a fine record of achievements in this domain, and much work still to be accomplished. But, in the twenty-first century there are new challenges facing the world, namely, the consequences of massive urbanization. The world is now majority urban, and will be almost completely urban by the end of the century. We must determine how to live on a crowded urban planet if civilization is to survive and thrive in the twenty-first century and beyond.

The world crucially needs new knowledge and solutions to urban issues such as managing growth, providing access to opportunities, social equity and inclusion, sustainability and resilience, and health and wellness. Many of these solutions will require university partnerships with business, governments, and community stakeholders located in urban

Some of the material in this chapter is based on the archival records of The Ohio State University. Thanks to Katie Reed (Office of Academic Affairs, or OAA) for her research support. Also thanks to Randy Smith (OAA) and Morton O'Kelly (College of Arts and Sciences) for their input and comments.

areas. The Ohio State University is well prepared to be a leader in twenty-first-century urban scholarship and outreach. It is a comprehensive, well-respected public university with a main campus located in a major city and branch campuses in diverse, moderate-sized cities. Ohio State's footprint also encompasses the globe; it can serve the needs of Ohio cities and beyond. The university recognizes these challenges and opportunities, and has been building new capabilities for urban scholarship and outreach.

This chapter discusses Ohio State as a twenty-first-century urban university. We begin with a discussion of the major issues facing an urbanized world, laying out a broad agenda for urban scholarship and outreach. We also discuss the scientific revolution occurring in urban science, enabled by new data sources and powerful technologies such as geographic information systems (GIS). We will then make a case for Ohio State as an urban university in the twenty-first century. We review the evolution of Ohio State's capabilities in urban scholarship and outreach. We conclude this chapter with a discussion of Ohio State moving forward as an urban university: why Ohio is a good setting for urban scholarship, and the role that Ohio State can play in this new era.

Twenty-First-Century Urban Challenges: A World of Cities

For most of human history, a very small minority of the population lived in what we now call towns and cities. This changed with the Industrial Revolution in the eighteenth and nineteenth centuries and the Great Acceleration of population, urbanization, socioeconomic activity, and environmental impacts in the mid-twentieth century and beyond. An epochal moment occurred in 2008: For the first time in human history, the majority of the world's population lived in cities. By the end of the twenty-first century, the vast majority of eleven billion people will live in urbanized areas: The earth will essentially be an urban planet.

Cities have a universal scaling quality: Wealth creation and innovation have positive returns to growth, while infrastructure costs enjoy economies of scale. This slight advantage of benefits over costs with growth is the magic that fuels urbanization. But these forces also create challenges that will become acute, if not existential, in the crowded urban world of the twenty-first century.

Growth and Stasis

The world's cities are growing in number and size. In 1900, London was the largest city in the world, with over six million inhabitants. The first few *megacities,* with ten million or more inhabitants, emerged in the twentieth century. In 2018, there are over thirty megacities; this is expected to grow to over forty cities by 2030. This explosive urban growth creates unprecedented challenges, particularly since much of it is occurring in middle- to low-income regions. Closer to home, Columbus, Ohio, is one of the fastest growing cities in the US: It is expected to add 500,000 to one million people by 2050. What will be the impacts on quality of life?

Although some cities are growing rapidly, other are dealing with a different problem. *Legacy cities* such as Cleveland, Youngstown, and Akron (Ohio), Buffalo (New York), Leipzig (Germany), and Manchester (UK) may never be quite what they once were. But, many legacy cities have positive features such as dense, walkable centers; underutilized housing and infrastructure; and skills, values, and networks from their industrial past and immigration history. How do we transform these cities into lively, livable, and sustainable communities?

Mobility and Accessibility

People crowding into cities for access to opportunities bring the ironic fate of congestion. The average American spends more time in traffic every year than on vacation, sapping productivity, harming wellness, and raising the cost of business. Congestion also has equity implications: The ability to pay for housing determines whether you can avoid or mitigate traffic and long commutes in a city. It is clear that the world cannot handle another billion or more cars that could be added in the twenty-first century; how do we create efficient, inclusive, and sustainable mobility systems for a crowded urban world?

Polarization and Inclusion

The positive and negative feedback loops that generate urban growth and stasis also generate increasing polarization within cities. In *The New Urban Crisis* (2017), Richard Florida describes the implications of what he calls *winner-take-all urbanism*: greater inequity, housing affordability crises, a disappearing middle class, and a patchwork metropolis with small areas of privilege and large swaths of distress and poverty. This hits close to home: Florida identifies Columbus as the second most unequal city in US. How do we leverage the benefits of urbanization while ensuring our cities are just and inclusive to all?

Sustainability and Resilience

The drive for spatial proximity at the heart of urbanization also creates the potential for greater environmental sustainability: Density and proximity lower per capita resource consumption and waste generation required for mobility and interaction. Urban sustainability is essential in a crowded urban planet that is already experiencing massive ecosystem diversity loss and the ravages of human-induced climate change. Cities must also build resilience to shocks: Coastal cities are facing rising sea levels, while interior cities such as Columbus are likely to experience severe storm events, urban flooding, and dangerous heat, impacting human lives and infrastructure.

Health and Wellness

For most of human history, cities were unhealthy due to diseases and poor environmental quality. While we have (mostly) solved this problem through modern sanitation, water systems, and environmental protection laws, we have introduced a new threat to human health: lifestyle diseases due to built environments that discourage healthy, safe, and convivial physical activity. Urban polarization is also leading to major health inequities in our cities: Social determinants of health such as the neighborhood environment, social capital, and access to education, health care, and opportunities can have larger impacts on health than clinical interventions. How do we make cities healthier, and for all?

The New Science of Cities

At the same time that urban challenges are becoming acute, we are experiencing a revolution in the science of cities. In the past, we conceptualized cities as "static aggregates": systems that move toward equilibrium and could be understood as the sum of their parts, similar to a machine. Scholars now recognize that cities are driven more by bottom-up than top-down forces: They are complex systems that are always in disequilibrium and continually emerging. They must be understood as dynamic flows, interactions, and networks. Cities cannot be engineered like machines but rather should be cultivated like gardens: This is a more intricate but ultimately more fruitful approach to shaping our cities toward more sustainable, equitable, and healthy communities.

There is a new urban science emerging that leverages expanding capabilities to capture, store, manage, process, and communicate digital geospatial and temporal data. In-situ and remote sensors, location-aware technologies such the global positioning system (GPS), mobile phones, and social media are generating rich and plentiful amounts of data about cities. We now have the computer power to simulate entire cities at the level of the individual. We are seeing the rise of *smart cities* that use data to make infrastructure more effective and responsive. The persistent data collection facilitated by these technologies allows for new types of *opportunistic science* that leverage planned and unplanned events in the real world to generate new insights and enable evidence-based policies that are sensitive to context. A new era is emerging for urban scholarship and outreach that integrates disparate disciplines and bridges the gap between university and community in meeting the challenges of the twenty-first-century urban world.

Ohio State as an Urban University

Ohio State is responding to the challenges of an urban world and the opportunities afforded by the new science of cities. In 2016, The Ohio State University Board of Trustees approved a new mission statement that reads in part:

> The Ohio State University is the model 21st-century public, land-grant, research, *urban,* community engaged institution.

The emphasis in the passage above highlights a crucial new word in this vision statement—*urban.* This simple but momentous change has profound implications for university teaching, research, and community engagement moving forward. It is also the culmination of years of concerted efforts by the state of Ohio and The Ohio State University to create new opportunities and facilities for interdisciplinary urban scholarship and outreach. These efforts build on long-standing university strengths in the social sciences, humanities, engineering, city planning, public policy, social work, education and human ecology, urban extension, and geospatial science.

Urban Universities Programs

Starting in 1979, the state of Ohio distributed funds to eight universities for urban-related studies and programs.[1] Seven of the eight universities created urban centers to distribute these funds. Ohio State chose to distribute the funds directly to faculty via the Committee on Urban Affairs (CUA). Several lost funding opportunities, a lack of visibility for urban scholarship, and minimal interdisciplinary interaction led to the view that an urban center would make OSU more effective in urban scholarship and outreach by creating a focus for interdisciplinary urban scholarship. A new center could also leverage the emergence of GIS, spatial analysis, and other data-enabled and computational methods for urban scholarship.

In 1995, a report to the Ad Hoc Committee on Applied Social and Public Policy argued that Ohio State's broad resources offer the potential to establish a nationally recognized urban research center comparable to major urban centers at other leading public universities. This was the catalyst for the creation in 1997 of the Public Policy Initiative Planning Committee (PPIPC) to evaluate the strengths of Ohio State in the public policy arena. These efforts concluded that unrealized potential for a nationally recognized urban center existed at Ohio State, but the opportunity has not been realized due to the lack of a formal structure. As Dean Randall B. Ripley, chair of the PPIPC, concluded in the committee's final report, "There is an urgent need at Ohio State for some formal structure that can further promote urban and regional research."

In 1998, the PPIPC issued a call for proposals. The CUA submitted a proposal for the formation of the Center for Urban and Regional Analysis (CURA) with a focus on urban research as a public policy initiative. In response, the Office of Academic Affairs (OAA) provided funds for an

1. The eight universities were University of Akron, University of Cincinnati, Cleveland State University, Kent State University, The Ohio State University, University of Toledo, Youngstown State University, and Wright State University.

interim organization, the Urban and Regional Analysis Initiative (URAI), led by Professors Morton O'Kelly (geography) and Hazel Morrow-Jones (city and regional planning). This resulted in the creation of CURA in 2001.

Center for Urban and Regional Analysis

The Center for Urban and Regional Analysis is an interdisciplinary research innovation hub specializing in the application of GIS and spatial analysis to urban issues. CURA's mission is to bridge urban scholarship and urban policy through spatial analysis of economic, social, environmental, and health issues in the cities and regions of Ohio and beyond. CURA maintains an active research program focusing on questions surrounding cities, transportation, and sustainability. The center successfully competes for funding from federal scientific agencies such as the National Science Foundation and the National Institutes of Health. CURA also offers support services for research, working with scholars across campus to augment their capabilities with the power of GIS and geospatial data analytics.

CURA works with community partners to identify areas of mutual concern and strategic opportunities for university-community partnerships on urban issues. This includes stakeholders such as the city of Columbus, the Mid-Ohio Regional Planning Commission (MORPC), the Central Ohio Transit Authority (COTA), the Ohio Department of Transportation (ODOT), Action for Children, and Age-Friendly Columbus.

CURA facilitates conversations among a diverse group of urban scholars on campus and thought leaders and stakeholders in Columbus, throughout the state of Ohio, and at the national and international scales. This includes public lectures, panel discussions, and workshops on topics ranging from sustainable urban transportation, cities and health, smart cities, transportation and social equity, water and cities in the era of climate change, and the future of suburbs.

Other Initiatives

Ohio State has developed other capabilities for interdisciplinary scholarship and engagement on urban-related issues. Founded in 2003, the Kirwan Institute for the Study of Race and Ethnicity is an interdisciplinary, engaged research institute focusing on social justice, equity, and inclusion. In 2013, the university created the Discovery Themes initiative to connect expertise across campus and develop new interdisciplinary research capabilities addressing major challenges facing humanity. The Discovery Themes initiative led to the creation of the Translation Data Analytics Institute (TDAI) and the Sustainability Institute (SI); both have direct relevance to the new data-enabled, interdisciplinary science of cities and the sustainability challenges facing the twenty-first-century urban world.

Coalition of Urban-Serving Universities

Ohio State is also a founding member of the Coalition of Urban Serving Universities (USU), a select organization embedded within the Association of Public and Land-grant Universities (APLU) to harness the collective power of public urban research universities. Created in 2005, USU focuses on working to advance student success through innovation and aiming to achieve community transformation through partnerships. USU is guided by the belief that public urban universities are anchors in their respective regions and can transform these communities through partnerships. USU priority areas include (1) building smart, resilient cities; (2) improving the health of a diverse population; (3) fostering student achievement; and (4) twenty-first-century workforce development. At the time of writing, USU consists over forty select US universities and medical centers (https://usucoalition.org).

As the previous discussion suggests, Ohio State has made substantial efforts to develop capabilities and networks that will help fulfill its mission as an urban university in the twenty-first century. In addition, the location of its main and branch campuses within the state of Ohio provides distinct needs and opportunities for urban scholarship and outreach.

Ohio as an Urban State

Ohio has a wide range of urban environments and trajectories. This includes fast-growing cities such as Columbus, stable cities such as Cincinnati, and legacy cities such as Cleveland and Youngstown. Ohio also has a diverse range of city sizes and geographic settings: The locations of Ohio State's branch campuses in the cities of Lima, Mansfield, Marion, Newark, and Wooster reflect much of this diversity. Ohio's history includes towns and cities developed during the river, canal, railroad, highway, and aviation eras.

Although some cities and regions in Ohio have lost population in recent decades, the future may be different. It is an unavoidable fact that the global climate is changing. Because of this, people will be forced to relocate because of too much water (the coasts) and too little water (the Southwestern US). While no region will be spared from the impacts of climate change, Ohio has features that may make it more attractive in the twenty-first century, in particular, access to freshwater—an essential commodity for the twenty-first century. Ohio cities also offer dense, historic urban cores that could (once again) be well served by alternatives to the automobile such as walking, bicycles, and public transit. These are urban features desired by younger generations. Ohio also retains skills and cultural values from its industrial past that could prove valuable in a future of small-batch manufacturing, craft, and maker communities.

Institutions such as New York University's Center for Urban Science and Progress, the Massachusetts Institute of Technology's Urban Science Institute, and University College London Centre for Advanced Spatial Analysis are part of the revolution in urban science and engagement. But these initiatives are focusing on the same problem in different contexts: how to manage growth in world cities (such as New York, Boston, London, and Singapore) and in the developing world (such as in cities in India). Less attention is being paid to the needs of other cities, such as the types of cities that are represented in Ohio.

Conclusion

Ohio State has made enormous progress in its evolution as an urban university during the closing decades of the twentieth century and the opening decades of the twenty-first century. The university is breaking down the barriers among disciplines and with the broader community that hamper progress toward meeting the urban challenges facing humanity.

Ohio State has a strong institutional culture oriented toward improving the world; this is reflected in the university motto, "Education for Citizenship." Ohio State as an urban university can continue this tradition by leveraging new technologies, data, and approaches to understanding cities, and focusing interdisciplinary scholarship and outreach on the grand challenges facing the twenty-first-century urban world. The institution is rising to these challenges. Ohio State is reimaging its mission and creating the capabilities and partnerships that can help make progress toward an innovative, socially just, and environmentally sustainable world of cities.

References

Batty, Michael. 2018. *Inventing Future Cities.* Cambridge, MA: MIT Press.

Bettencourt, Luís M. A., José Lobo, Dirk Helbing, Christian Kühnert, and Geoffrey B. West. 2007. "Growth, Innovation, Scaling, and the Pace of Life in Cities." *Proceedings of the National Academy of Sciences* 104, no. 17 (April): 7301–6.

Florida, Richard. 2017. *The New Urban Crisis: How Our Cities Are Increasing Inequality, Deepening Segregation, and Failing the Middle Class—and What We Can Do about It.* New York: Basic Books.

Halsey, Ashley III. 2018. "Has the Love Affair with Driving Gotten Stuck in Traffic?" *Washington Post,* November 7, 2018. https://www.washingtonpost.com/local/trafficandcommuting/has-the-love-affair-with-driving-gotten-stuck-in-traffic/2018/11/07/328505de-e12f-11e8-8f5f-a55347f48762_story.html.

Havens, Greg. 2019. "Land-Grant Campuses for the 21st Century: Moving beyond Rural and Semi-Rural Sites." *Planning for Higher Education* 47, no. 2 (January–March): 6–19.

Kjellstrom, Tord, and Susan Mercado. 2008. "Towards Action on Social Determinants for Health Equity in Urban Settings." *Environment and Urbanization* 20, no. 2 (October): 551–74.

Kramer, Melissa G. 2013. *Our Built and Natural Environments: A Technical Review of the Interactions among Land Use, Transportation, and Environmental Quality.* 2nd ed. Washington DC: US Environmental Protection Agency, Office of Sustainable Communities, Smart Growth Program.

Miller, Harvey J. 2017. "Geographic Information Science I: Geographic Information Observatories and Opportunistic GIScience." *Progress in Human Geography* 41, no. 4 (May): 489–500.

Sperling, Daniel, and Deborah Gordon. 2010. *Two Billion Cars: Driving Toward Sustainability.* Oxford: Oxford University Press.

Steffen, Will, Wendy Broadgate, Lisa Deutsch, Owen Gaffney, and Cornelia Ludwig. 2015. "The Trajectory of the Anthropocene: The Great Acceleration." *The Anthropocene Review* 2, no. 1 (January): 81–98.

United Nations. 2018. *The World's Cities in 2018—Data Booklet* (ST/ESA/ SER.A/417). United Nations Department of Economic and Social Affairs, Population Division.

West, Geoffrey. 2017. *Scale: The Universal Laws of Growth, Innovation, Sustainability, and the Pace of Life in Organisms, Cities, Economies, and Companies.* New York: Penguin.

17

Toward a Land-Grant Fierce Future

BE THE MODEL™ College of Veterinary Medicine in the Twenty-First Century

Rustin M. Moore

The Ohio Agricultural and Mechanical (A&M) College's School of Veterinary Science was founded in 1885, more than twenty years after President Abraham Lincoln signed the federal Land-Grant College (Morrill) Act of 1862. Despite the two decades that had elapsed, the origins of veterinary sciences at what would eventually become Ohio's first and only college of veterinary medicine were distinctly and authentically rooted in the land-grant tradition—born out of the necessity to educate individuals who would care for the many animals associated with Ohio's booming agricultural industry.

Even before establishment as a school, veterinary sciences permeated the curriculum at Ohio A&M, first through the Department of Zoology and Veterinary Science under the direction of Professor Albert H. Tuttle, a zoologist, and then through the Department of Agriculture, Botany, and Veterinary Science, under Dr. Norton S. Townshend, a medical doctor who taught courses in animal disease. Wrote Dr. Arthur F. Schalk in his 1956 *History of the College of Veterinary Medicine,* "considerable interest was exhibited in veterinary medicine" before the college's founding. Said Dr. Schalk:

> The agricultural students who came from the farms, were deeply concerned about the losses from disease in their herds and flocks . . . [and] they naturally wanted to learn as much as possible about livestock health

> and disease. Hence, it is not at all unusual to learn that large numbers of those students elected to pursue all the veterinary courses projected in the agricultural curricula; nor is it surprising to know that their numbers sometimes equaled or exceeded those who chose conventional agricultural courses. (Schalk 1957, 48)

With a petition from the board of trustees to the state legislature in 1885 and the arrival of Dr. H. J. Detmers, the first professional veterinarian on faculty, the nation's third veterinary school was founded. Renamed the College of Veterinary Medicine in 1897, today the college remains Ohio's only college of veterinary medicine, one of only twenty-five colleges of veterinary medicine at land-grant universities in the US; it prepares more than 80 percent of Ohio's veterinarians. Continuously accredited by the American Veterinary Medical Association and ranked in the top five in the nation by *U.S. News and World Report* for over a decade (currently #4), the college recently was ranked #3 among US colleges and #8 worldwide by QS World University Rankings—an external validation of our preeminence, prominence, and impact.

Since our founding, we have awarded over 9,800 doctor of veterinary medicine (DVM) degrees, more than any other US veterinary college, and nearly 1,000 graduate degrees. Our college has a reputation for "growing" leaders in academia, practice, industry, government, military, research, professional organizations, and others. Approximately thirty former veterinary or graduate students, interns, residents, faculty, and administrators have gone on to serve as deans and as thought leaders in the field, including eight who currently serve as deans of US veterinary colleges. The college's first graduate, Dr. Mark Francis, became the founding dean of the Texas A&M School of Veterinary Medicine. Two of our DVM alumni, Drs. Lonnie King and Glen Hoffsis, have served as dean at two and three colleges of veterinary medicine, respectively. Our DVM and graduate alumni work in all fifty states and in over forty countries, serving all areas of the profession.

The veterinary medical profession has evolved since the college's founding—from its beginnings of caring for horses, which provided the primary mode of transportation and plowed Ohio's fields, to serving Ohio's livestock and growing pet population, and leading research initiatives impacting animal and human health. What might Dr. Detmers have thought of today's wired classrooms, state-of-the-art therapies, and internationally recognized One Health research that translates to advances in animal and human health? He would see a continuation of the land-grant mission he was instrumental in establishing for the college. He would also see a continuous thread of teaching, research, and engagement that continues to thrive and is interwoven in everything we do in our classrooms, clinics, barns, research labs, and other areas within the college, and on farms and fields across the state's eighty-eight counties and beyond.

Within our modern land-grant university, we continue to protect animal agriculture, promote food safety, and perform agricultural and biomedical research that advances animal and human health. We preserve the human-animal bond; serve as a resource to veterinarians through referral and consultation services; provide assistance to animal owners, pet parents, and others; and provide primary, emergency, and specialty veterinary care for animals throughout our veterinary health system. Last year the system had over 45,000 patient visits and cared for over 28,000 animals on farms across Ohio. That is just a glimpse of our land-grant mission in action.

As we look to the future of veterinary medicine, with the guidance of a new, transformational strategic plan, the College of Veterinary Medicine will continue to drive progress in our communities and worldwide as we strive to BE THE MODEL™ comprehensive college of veterinary medicine in the world. Our ambition to BE THE MODEL™—to be emulated by our peers and to set the bar for preeminence—is a continual journey rather than a destination. It is also the difference between A and A+, the distinction Ohio State president Michael V. Drake has described between "doing a good job and being your best self." We simply could not accomplish this at any other institution. Our co-location with fourteen other colleges, including six other health science colleges, a nationally recognized human medical center, and numerous other exemplary colleges and programs, uniquely positions our college as a critical partner as the university strives to solve our world's most complex and pressing problems. Our college is proud to contribute to Ohio State's prominence and incredible contributions to our communities, nation, and world; that is land-grant fierce in action and impact!

Preeminent Teaching and Learning

Our college seeks to deliver extraordinary, value-driven education that prepares veterinarians to lead the field, advance science, and achieve personal fulfillment. Our graduate degree programs offer MS, MPH, and

PhD degrees in preparation for careers in biomedical, clinical, and field-based epidemiological research—and are central to the college's research agenda. Collectively, we help prepare the next generation of veterinary practitioners, specialists, scientists, and thought leaders in their respective fields.

Unique contributors to students' success include the nation's first required shelter medicine and surgery rotation for fourth-year veterinary students in partnership with Columbus Humane, a program that over the past decade has provided every student the opportunity to spay or neuter twenty-five to thirty dogs and cats under the direct supervision of our faculty. The Veterinary Scholar Summer Research Program provides mentorship and infrastructure for veterinary students to attain specific technical and conceptual skills to perform hypothesis-based research involving faculty supervised projects. Working alongside and under the supervision of our faculty scientists introduces students to research and the desire to seek advanced degrees beyond their DVM and a broader spectrum of career opportunities. The college offers a business minor in health sciences through Ohio State's Fisher College of Business. We have had and continue to have a leading professional development curriculum, and our Office of Career Management was the first to be established at a college of veterinary medicine to offer career services exclusively for veterinary students, alumni, and employers. We were one of the first to adopt and implement a health and well-being program for our DVM students, with licensed social workers embedded in the college and other mental health resources available. The Rainier Scholars Program engages professional degree/graduate students in veterinary medicine with academic, laboratory, and hands-on projects and experiential opportunities to position them for career pathways in industry.

As a land-grant college of veterinary medicine, we have moved from being state funded to state supported, and the level of support positions us at the bottom of the top 10 colleges and less than half the median regarding funding on a per student basis, and in the bottom 10 percent of all thirty US colleges of veterinary medicine. In the twenty-year span between 1999 and 2019, our state funding increased about 11 percent, or just over 0.5 percent per year. However, this clearly lags behind the 53 percent increase in consumer price index (inflation) during the same period. This results in our purchasing power from state funding being only 72 percent of what it was twenty years ago, while the costs have increased substantially. We are woefully underfunded by the state compared to peers, which has widespread negative consequences.

Fortunately, philanthropy has played a key role in advancing the college's land-grant mission areas. For example, a $39 million transformational gift from the Stanton Foundation helped establish the Building Preeminence in Veterinary General Practice Education (BPVGPE) program, which supports initiatives that result in more competent and confident, practice-ready veterinarians. Along with the Stanton Summer Externship program, which gives students hands-on experience caring for dogs and other small animals in designated veterinary practices as they help clients from a broad range of socioeconomic backgrounds provide an appropriate level of care for their pets, the BPVGPE helps students learn the art and science of how to practice along the spectrum of care.

Our college's comparative and veterinary medicine graduate program is renowned, and many of our graduates (PhD, DVM/MS, MS, and MPH) have distinguished careers in biotech/pharma, animal-health, and biomedical corporate entities, as well as in academia. Their work during their time in our college has strengthened and advanced our research and discovery and contributed to our commercialization success. Our veterinary pathology residency/PhD program is one of the premier programs in the nation preparing the next generation of board-certified anatomic and clinical pathologists with research-intensive training. Our veterinary public health specialization within the MPH program (MPH-VPH) through the College of Public Health is unique and provides students with public health credentials to serve as leaders in prevention and control of zoonotic and food-borne diseases in the US and the world. Currently, the dean of The Ohio State University Graduate School is a faculty member in our college.

Our college has been a pioneer and leader in the development of advanced clinical training by embracing and promoting the establishment of residency programs leading to specialization. In fact, this year marks the fiftieth year since the first resident in small animal surgery began his program. We have since expanded residency programs in multiple specialties throughout the college and our faculty have been leaders in these respective specialty colleges, including serving as officers and president.

Our strategic plan seeks to improve the accessibility and affordability of veterinary medical education; promote a healthy, inclusive, and supportive environment; and enhance diversity. We have limited annual tuition increases to 2 percent annually, while between 2014 and 2019, we increased philanthropic scholarship dollars awarded annually by just under 500 percent and the average scholarship dollars awarded per student by just over 500 percent to address the cost of education and debt for our students. Our college received the 2019 Award for Fundraising

Excellence in Student Scholarships from the American Association of Veterinary Medical Colleges, a testament to our commitment to help relieve our students' educational debt.

We have intentionally worked to enhance the diversity of our homogeneous veterinary profession. From students entering in 2015 to 2018 (classes of 2019 to 2022), the change in the three groups considered underrepresented in the veterinary profession by the American Association of Veterinary Medical Colleges has increased from 14 to 35 percent for underrepresented minorities; 14 to 28 percent in males; and from an unknown number to 29 percent for first-generation college students. Seventy-one percent of our class of 2022 represented at least one of these three underrepresented groups. Because of our diversity and inclusion results, we received the Health Professions Higher Education Excellence in Diversity (HEED) Award from *INSIGHT Into Diversity* magazine the past two years. Our commitment to diversifying the veterinary profession is based on scientific evidence that diversity contributes to excellence and will help the veterinary profession better serve our people and communities.

Innovative and Impactful Research

Since Dr. Detmers first studied hog cholera, our researchers have worked to solve complex problems, often across disciplines. Dr. Richard Olsen developed and commercialized the first vaccine for feline leukemia virus (FeLV), which had been the leading cause of illness and death in cats. Research into the FeLV vaccine also provided important insight into diseases that depress the immune system—such as human acquired immune deficiency syndrome, or AIDS—and ultimately led to the opening of the university's Center for Retrovirus Research (CRR, the director of which has always been one of our college faculty). The work of the CRR and research across the university were important in establishing the university's Infectious Diseases Institute, which contributes to global research in diseases impacting animals and humans. The director of this university-level institute and four of the eight program directors are faculty from our college.

The college is at the forefront of the arena known as One Health, which examines how the health of humans and animals and the well-being of the environment are inextricably linked and contribute to critical risk factors for infectious diseases. Veterinarians are broadly educated in comparative medicine and disease, and are thus are well positioned at the center of the triad to positively benefit the health and well-being of animals, people, and the environment. One way to view this is through the lens of the "Three Zs" of One Health:

- Zoonoses—infectious diseases that start in animals and are transmitted to people, which account for about 70 percent of the (re)emerging infectious diseases in people;
- Zoobiquity—because animals and people develop similar diseases like cancer, diabetes, and arthritis, it is beneficial to collaborate across human and animal health to advanced comparative medicine, including investigating naturally acquired spontaneous models of animal disease to lead to discoveries that enhance animal and human health; and
- Zooeyia—the term used to define the positive health benefits (physical, social, behavioral, emotional, mental, and psychological) on people who interact with animals.

Research increasingly shows that people with autism, dementia, post-traumatic stress disorder, and many other health conditions can benefit from interaction with a pet.

The college has led Ohio State in commercialization revenue generated from royalties on the strength of both the Olsen FeLV vaccine and tick-borne diagnostics for companion animals from the laboratory of Dr. Yasuko Rikihisa. In fact, the success of the commercial license of the FeLV vaccine was a key driver in the establishment of the university's Office of Technology and Commercialization.

Through our strategic plan, the college seeks to make Ohio State a national and global leader in animal and human health as a top research-funded college of veterinary medicine. Current outstanding research efforts include the use of host-directed therapeutics for lung infections; mitigation approaches for antimicrobial bacterial strains; environmental, bird, and swine surveillance to inform future strains for flu vaccines; various sponsored research, clinical trials, and testing services; and much more.

Caring for Ohio's Animals

Symbolic of the college's land-grant roots is our veterinary health system, which serves tens of thousands of Ohio's animals each year through the Veterinary Medical Center's Hummel & Trueman Hospital for Companion Animals, Hospital for Farm Animals, and Galbreath Equine Center on the Columbus campus; Small Animal Emergency and Orthopedic

Surgery Center at the Veterinary Medical Center Dublin location; and Large Animal Services at Marysville. With pets becoming more a part of our families, three of four households having at least one pet, and the expected US population increase, the need for veterinarians and the economic impact on communities will only continue to increase.

The veterinary health system provides a unique educational environment that prepares students, interns, and residents for general and specialty practice and careers across the breadth of the profession and spectrum of care. They learn from outstanding clinical faculty members, who have been leaders and pioneers in the development and use of plates and screws for repairing fractures in dogs and horses, and who pioneered the development and refinement of total hip replacement in dogs, among many other advancements.

A recent $33 million enhancement of the Veterinary Medical Center, predominantly funded by private philanthropy, provides additional space for care as well as a rich learning environment for students during their fourth-year clinical capstone. Supported by an investment of $6 million by the Blue Buffalo Company, the Blue Buffalo Veterinary Clinical Trials Office currently oversees twenty to thirty-five clinical trials at any one time and over sixty trials a year, with enrollment of over 700 patients per year. These trials have contributed to the development of new treatments for cancer, heart disease, and arthritis, among others, and have benefitted animal and human health.

Through our strategic plan, the college seeks to BE THE MODEL™ for excellence in academic veterinary medicine and the referral center of choice by delivering accessible, cutting-edge care in partnership with referring primary care veterinarians, while providing outstanding client experiences. Through our clinical services, we provide vital resources and assets to Ohio and beyond.

We collaborate across the Ohio State campus and with the Columbus Zoo and Aquarium, The Wilds, the Ohio Wildlife Center, and other zoos to ensure the health and well-being of wildlife and exotic animals as part of our Ecosystem Health and Conservation Medicine program. To maintain critically important animal and plant biodiversity, it is important we work together to promote a healthy and balanced ecosystem.

Engaging with Our Communities

In keeping with our land-grant responsibility, our Veterinary Medicine Outreach program seeks to improve the health of animals and people, while promoting positive human-animal interactions. Since it was founded in 2009, the program has partnered with organizations like LifeCare Alliance, Meals on Wheels, and other community organizations to care for hundreds of pets of homebound, homeless, low-income, elder, and other vulnerable people in Franklin County. Pets receive wellness care and owners benefit from pet care education and counseling. Community outreach also touches the lives of our students. Beyond the students' medical experiences, they also benefit from raising social awareness and responsibility, building cultural competencies, and instilling civic responsibility. By interacting with diverse populations, they are prepared for veterinary careers where compassion, empathy, and interpersonal skills are as essential as medical knowledge.

Our college is committed to the university's extension mission and purpose, and in our case that means generating knowledge and research discoveries, disseminating this in user-friendly and helpful methods, and assisting Ohioans to prevent animal disease, improve livestock production, safeguard animal welfare, ensure food safety, and other activities that better lives, businesses, and communities.

The college's outreach efforts also extend around the globe through the university's interdisciplinary Global One Health initiative, where one of our college faculty serves as the executive director. One example, our Ohio State/Ethiopia One Health Partnership is creating a road map for a pilot rabies prevention and control program in Gondar, Ethiopia, aimed at significantly reducing the number of cases of rabies, a preventable disease, in animals and humans, which kills 59,000 a year worldwide. The college's rabies eradication program is enhancing public awareness, improving bite wound care for optimal postexposure rabies prophylaxis, providing mass vaccinations of dogs, humanely managing the dog population, and strengthening rabies diagnostic and surveillance capacities. This pilot can lead to the development of a national plan for sustainability in other regions of Ethiopia and perhaps across Africa and beyond.

Implementation of our BE THE MODEL™ strategic plan will lead to more opportunities for students, faculty, and staff to help those who are underserved in our community and around the globe, and to engage with Ohio's veterinary community through extension services and continuing education opportunities that improve the health, welfare, and productivity of animals, food safety and security, and public health.

Toward Our Modern Land-Grant Future

As we celebrate the 150th anniversary of The Ohio State University as Ohio's initial land-grant institution, it is appropriate to reflect on this seminal piece of legislation that has greatly improved our lives yet is often underappreciated. The land-grant institutions that have served us so well in the past remain very much relevant today, although in a different context. How will our college continue to address the major challenges facing our communities, state, nation, and world? When the colleges of veterinary medicine throughout the nation fought for continued relevance in the 1920s as the importance of horses declined, Ohio State moved quickly to redefine the role of a veterinary medicine education: emphasizing the importance of the food and fiber industry and pets, and changing the principal dissection animal from horse to dog—more than two decades ahead of some other colleges.

Looking toward the future, our college will continue to innovate and move quickly and nimbly to address challenges we cannot even yet anticipate. Advancing partnerships and interdisciplinary collaborations, we will charge ahead with continued efforts to improve diversity and inclusion among students, faculty, and staff; promote the health and well-being of our students; address veterinary shortages in rural and underserved areas; and continue to lead ambitious research studies that improve the health and save the lives of animals and people. The college will continue to be a leader across all our land-grant mission areas.

Morrill Act signer Abraham Lincoln famously said, "The best way to predict the future is to create it." That's what we're doing as we aspire to BE THE MODEL™ comprehensive college of veterinary medicine in the world. As we celebrate the university's sesquicentennial, we look forward to creating, continually redefining, and modeling a preeminent modern land-grant college of veterinary medicine that addresses and finds solutions to the time's most relevant and complex issues in the twenty-first century and beyond.

References

Schalk, A. 1957. *History of the College of Veterinary Medicine, The Ohio State University, 1873–1956.* Columbus, OH: The Ohio State University Press.

18

Engineering at The Ohio State University

Driving the Economic Development of Ohio

David B. Williams

Ohio State began as the Ohio Agricultural and Mechanical (A&M) College, and agricultural and mechanical engineering are still taught today. Over the intervening 150 years, engineering has been at the forefront of the state of Ohio's economic development. Although the College of Engineering (CoE) was not formally created until 1896, three of the original A&M faculty members taught engineering, including Edward Orton, the university's first president, who was hired as a professor of geology, mining, and metallurgy. Given his metallurgical and geological backgrounds, it is appropriate that Orton is recognized by a metal plaque in Orton Hall (figure 18.1) as well in the stone strata of that building, which reflect Ohio's geology. Orton believed that his role was to have a meaningful impact on society. The words on the plaque remind us of Ohio State's land-grant role in driving the economy of Ohio and the Columbus community from its inception. Orton is recognized as "a scholar devoted to science and its applications to economic problems. A philanthropic citizen whose counsel guided the city."

Orton's fields of metallurgical and mining engineering were integral to the steel industry's rise in the US, although steel had only been manufactured in commercial quantities since the invention of the Bessemer process in 1856, just a few years before the Morrill Act. Steel soon drove the nation's economy and built the powerhouse cities of Bethlehem, Cleveland, Gary, Pittsburgh, and Youngstown. Today, *materials* engineering

FIGURE 18.1. Metal plaque in Orton Hall

remains a predominant strength at The Ohio State University and new materials continue to fuel Ohio's economy.

Engineering grew beyond A&M in lockstep with the growth of the state of Ohio. Within Ohio State's first decade, three of the seven degrees available at the university were engineering: mechanical, mining (originally), and then civil. Civil engineering was needed as our infrastructure, cities, and transportation methods grew. Over the next four decades, CoE expanded as new disciplines were created. Nikolai Tesla and Thomas Edison competed to develop the best way to move electrons around the country, bringing light and power to rural Ohio, and reflected today in the Columbus headquarters of American Electric Power (AEP).

In parallel, electrical engineering appeared at Ohio State as we found better ways to generate, distribute, and later store all those electrons. Architectural engineers, now including city and regional planners and landscape architects, ensured that what we built worked, not just for the engineers, but for the people who lived and worked in the "built environment." Chemical engineering grew as Midwestern oil was refined into different liquids to create the chemical and polymer industries, led by companies such as Standard Oil of Ohio and Goodyear (of Akron). As our industries became more complicated and the entire industrial enterprise become more complex, industrial and systems engineers developed ways to comprehend, improve, and simplify the interweaving systems we built. Nuclear power is considered one of the top ten inventions of the twentieth century. Ohio State's Nuclear Reactor Lab began operation in 1961, and our nuclear engineering graduate program was established soon after. Other new industries over the last half of the twentieth century were built on specific engineering triumphs—especially the silicon transistor and integrated circuits. Computer science and computer engineering grew accordingly.

A hundred and fifty years after A&M, as this chapter shows, Ohio State engineers are still driving Ohio's economic development. As discussed below, CoE's strategic hiring plan is aligned with Ohio's long-standing economic strengths in *materials, manufacturing, mobility,* and *medicine.* Over 25,000 architecture and engineering alumni work in the state of Ohio—nearly 40 percent of our entire alumni body of more than 60,000 people.

Two *mobility*-related industries play an important economic role in Ohio. First, we have a proud history of aviation and aerospace, including key contributions from the Wright Brothers, Jerri Mock, the Tuskegee Airmen, John Glenn, and Neil Armstrong. Indeed, Ohio's state quarter coin features the Wright flyer and a moon-walking astronaut, as evidence of Ohio's contribution to aviation and space flight. CoE boasts strong relationships with Boeing, GE Aviation, Pratt and Whitney, Honeywell, and other aerospace giants. Of all states, Ohio is the largest supplier of parts to Airbus and Boeing.

Second, the automotive industry has long contributed to our economy and is built on a foundation of Ohio innovators. John Lambert from Ohio City built the first gasoline-powered, single-cylinder automobile in 1890, which could speed at five miles per hour, and Charles Kettering invented the first automobile self-starter in 1911. Kettering held more than 300 patents, most of which were used in automobiles, and Garrett Morgan, of both African American and Native American heritages, was inspired (after observing a crash!) to develop a traffic signal in 1923. Today Honda's North American headquarters are in central Ohio. All these aerospace and automotive companies hire dozens of our graduates and invest millions of dollars in CoE research annually.

Today *manufacturing* contributes almost 20 percent of Ohio's GDP. Manufacturing research flourishes in CoE, where our faculty are part of five National Network for Manufacturing Innovation centers (https://www.manufacturing.gov/mfgov.html) and we introduce students to the fundamentals of real-world manufacturing problems in our unique Center for Design and Manufacturing Excellence (https://cdme.osu.edu). Economy-driven changes continue within CoE today, as we explore engineering's role in data analytics, integrated business systems, manufacturing technology, public policy, law, cybersecurity, cancer treatment, art and design, and other areas yet to be conceived.

The Future

The *manufacturing* and *mobility* industries will continue to rely on new *materials* for their future success, so our strategic plans for the future are aligned to create this enduring contribution. We will expand engineering's role to the regional campuses, where engineering/manufacturing technology will soon become the first four-year degrees in those communities. This is CoE's contribution to reversing our state's population loss and associated economic decline that followed the diminution of Ohio's manufacturing base and gave rise to related social challenges such as the opioid addiction epidemic.

A prime example of today's engineering economy is the interface with *medicine,* embodied in our biomolecular, biological, and biomedical engineering disciplines. We will increasingly engineer the human body as well as our physical infrastructure. This interface will only grow as our population ages; it will bring drugs designed for our personal illnesses, better design of the robots that our surgeons and nurses will guide inside our bodies, and the (yet to be discovered) materials and systems that will replace aging body parts or regenerate missing and seriously damaged limbs (figure 18.2).

The increasing dominance of technology and the massive troves of data we generate, analyze, and store will require more and better-educated engineers. Data are ubiquitous: generated by the iPads that travel with Ohio State students; essential for the autonomous vehicles that will transport us on land, sea, and air; required by the artificial intelligence (AI) assistants with whom we communicate daily ("Hi, Siri"); and responsible for the increasing surveillance of each of us through geospatial location technologies (another CoE strength). Thus, each new engineering development brings challenges. We will need to ensure that those who create

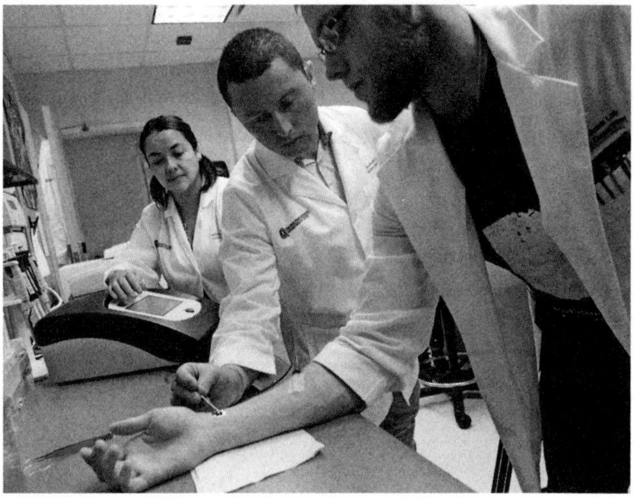

FIGURE 18.2. Gallego-Perez tissue nanotransfection

and build new systems also manage them in an appropriate way, consistent with the ethics we seek to imbue in all students. This is why we now study better ways to educate our students via our new Engineering Education Department (EED), which is an integral part of CoE today. We have created a sound foundation on which to build for the next 150 years.

Engineering for Economic Development

As the college grew in parallel with Ohio industries, we continued to fulfill our land-grant mission to educate the sons and daughters of Ohioans. This mission continues today as we explore and create new degree programs and expand our research areas. No other land-grant engineering colleges in the US have "economic development" in their mission statement, and none reside in an urban area as big as greater Columbus, now exceeding two million in population. We embrace *engineering for economic development.*

There are two preeminent examples of CoE driving Ohio's economy: The Ohio State University Airport (KOSU) at Don Scott Field and the Transportation Research Center (TRC) in East Liberty, Ohio, a university affiliate organization. KOSU and TRC are at the heart of Ohio State's mobility research. These are dedicated engineering campuses, building on our tradition, already noted, of materials and manufacturing for the aerospace and automotive industries and focusing on education, research, community engagement, and hands-on student experience. No other uni-

FIGURE 18.3. Aerial view of Don Scott Field

versity in the world—never mind a single college—is responsible for overseeing and operating a commercial airport and an independent proving ground for the fulfillment of our university role and objectives. It is worth examining these exemplars in more depth.

KOSU

In 1943, during World War II, KOSU (https://osuairport.org) was built at what became Don Scott Field on the (then) outskirts of northwest Columbus. Over the intervening decades, aviation and aerospace activities grew at KOSU. In addition to being an aviation and aerospace education and research campus for Ohio State, our facilities at Don Scott Field are also recognized as one of the finest general aviation airports in the Midwest, where we educate hundreds of pilots and other aviation professionals for an industry that desperately needs them. An appropriately aerial view is shown in figure 18.3.

The Austin E. Knowlton Foundation (http://aekfoundation.org) (which named CoE's Knowlton School of Architecture) has also named the Executive Terminal and Aviation Education Center at KOSU. This gift was appropriate because Knowlton was a pioneer of fractional jet ownership. The largest of such companies, NetJets (https://www.netjets.com/en-us/), is headquartered in Columbus and supports Ohio State aviation-related students, research, and professorships. There are new hangars for fifty small planes, and a corporate hangar campus is under construction to house the jets of local businesses that partner with the university. Some of the 1,400 acres at Don Scott Field is available for economic development, always in partnership with aviation education and research.

At the adjacent Aerospace Research Center (https://arc.osu.edu), engineers test jet turbines for GE Aviation, Honeywell, and Pratt and Whitney. The CoE partners with the US Air Force Research Laboratory (https://www.wpafb.af.mil/afrl/) at Dayton's Wright-Patterson Air Force Base in research ranging from atomic-resolution electron microcopy (https://cemas.osu.edu) of new aerospace materials to hypersonic wind tunnel testing of future ultra-high-speed aircraft. We help the Federal Aviation Administration develop next-generation air-traffic control, minimize the collision of drones and commercial planes, and safely fly drones in civilian-controlled airspace (an integration that is only allowed at KOSU). Such activities contribute more than $150 million per year to Ohio's economy. At KOSU, 90,000 takeoffs and landings occur annually, over 2,000 K–12 students visit the airport, and seven separate colleges perform research and education. In all these dimensions, students play a central role, learning through experience the importance of aviation to our economy, and growing their skills as they contribute to this industry for our state's economic well-being.

Transportation Research Center

In 1967, Governor James A. Rhodes, presciently recognizing CoE's early research in autonomous vehicles, announced the creation of the Transportation Research Center (TRC; http://www.trcpg.com). This center opened in 1972 and operates on 4,500 acres, thirty-five miles northeast of campus along State Route 33 (see figure 18.4). In 1979, Ohio State was contracted to operate TRC Inc., as an affiliate organization, with the engineering dean as board chair. Now Honda's North American headquarters, Honda Research America, and Honda of America Manufacturing all operate adjacent to TRC; 1,400 cars are manufactured daily (https://ohio.honda.com) and 2,500 engineers and scientists research the future of transportation (http://www.hondaresearch.com).

The US Department of Transportation (DoT) also came to TRC. DoT's National Highway Traffic Safety Administration (NHTSA) has its only vehicle research and testing center there (https://www.nhtsa.gov/research-data/vehicle-research-testing), solving the challenges of exploding airbags, non-igniting ignition keys, and tire blowouts that cause rollovers. NHTSA is also responsible for developing policies to regulate self-driving vehicles.

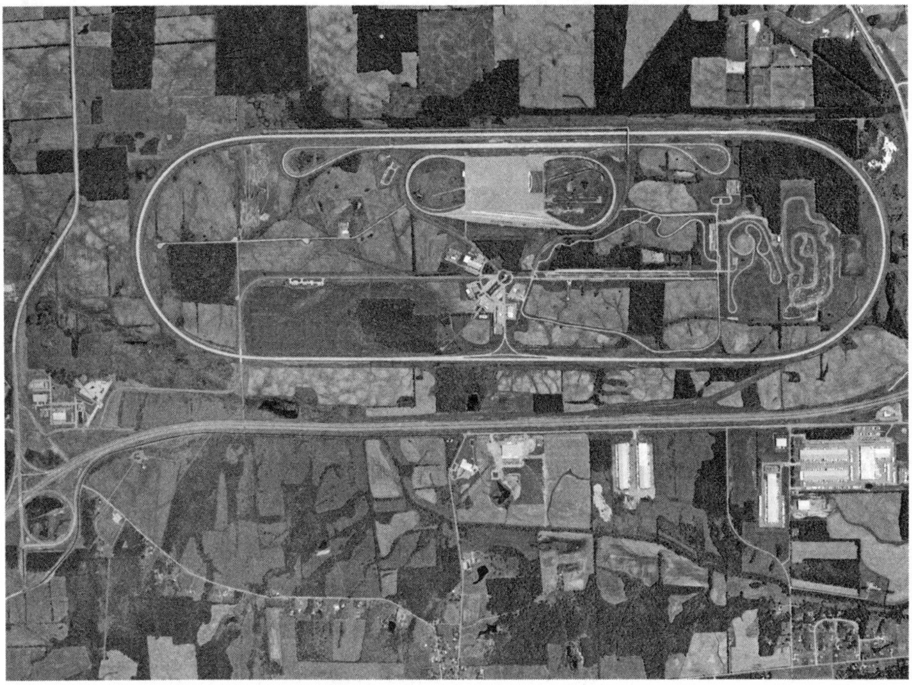

FIGURE 18.4. Transportation Research Center (TRC) aerial view

Engineering students are hired at TRC and NHTSA, expanding their education through hands-on engagement in real-world activities. Honda is a major employer of our graduates and funds capstone design projects involving undergraduates from multiple colleges.

CoE faculty partner with Honda to develop manufacturing methods and help NHTSA design better/smarter "dummies" for TRC's crash test facility. Our ElectroScience Laboratory researchers designed a Honda antenna facility to ensure that vehicle-to-vehicle and vehicle-to-infrastructure communication is secure. We are investing in aero-acoustic research as Honda builds a $140-million wind tunnel at TRC. Economic development, driven by our faculty, staff, and students, in collaboration with Ohio industries, continues apace at both KOSU and TRC.

Impact of Industry Partnerships

All these investments in *mobility* research over seventy-five years ensure a robust future for CoE within the community. The combination of TRC and KOSU has facilitated the creation of the nation's largest integrated autonomous-vehicle infrastructure. The state of Ohio and The Ohio State University are investing $45 million in the Smart Mobility Advanced

FIGURE 18.5. Engineering Expo Career Fair

Research and Testing (SMART) Center at TRC. Covering 500 acres, this is the nation's largest such center. After testing in TRC's controlled space, autonomous vehicles will move onto Route 33, which is now fully invested with hardware and software infrastructure for vehicle-to-vehicle and vehicle-to-infrastructure communication. At the southwest end of Route 33 is Smart Columbus, the DoT's only Smart City (https://www.columbus.gov/smartcity/). Drone technology, developed at KOSU, is also deployed along Route 33 to permit rapid response to accidents and on-site assessment of any injuries, followed by emergency response with appropriate medical treatment. This is just one of many instances where integrated engineering research and education positively impact the citizens and economy of Ohio.

The mobility industries are some of over 2,000 different companies that hire our graduates, support internships and co-ops, and fund capstone courses (figure 18.5). More and more companies are realizing the advantages of tapping into our talent and technology pools to solve their product and process problems. Such partnerships are why we are ranked third among all US engineering colleges in industry-funded research.

Creating New Industries

Economic development in the college is not just about providing an educated workforce. It is also about creating new companies and inspiring entrepreneurs. We educate engineers who think differently about solutions to future problems. We are one of only two public universities to partner with KEEN, a Kern Family Foundation initiative (https://

FIGURE 18.6. Jessica Winter *Cancer Today* cover. Reproduced with permission.

engineeringunleashed.com). KEEN aims to educate future generations of engineers imbued with an entrepreneurial mind-set, focused on entrepreneurship and on entrepreneurial solutions to engineering problems in general. This approach is bearing fruit and in the last five years, twenty-two companies have spun out of CoE, with innovations such as rapid fueling of natural gas vehicles and nanoparticles for drug delivery (figure 18.6). The college accounts for almost one-third of Ohio State start-ups.

Creating intellectual property (IP) and developing it to start viable companies is challenging and complicated. With most CoE faculty engaged in the creation of knowledge, our patent portfolios are matching those of many of our peers. This process has been facilitated by changing the college's promotion and tenure (P&T) guidelines, which explicitly encourage invention disclosures and patents and recognize licensing revenue in the same way we reward funding from federal agencies. So we expect even more IP generation in future.

Patenting IP is the first step in creating a commercial product that can be scaled up for production. Investment is needed at every stage. It is a high-risk process to translate a patent into a start-up company, then into a viable small company (<100 employees) and growing that into a medium-size company (<500 employees). Venture capital in Columbus is greater than in any city between the coasts and is seeding this tech commercialization pipeline. We are confident that good IP will generate investment, investment will generate successful companies, and successful companies will (maybe over decades) reward Ohio State with philanthropic gifts in return.

In 2018, university researchers and staff disclosed 460 inventions, a first step toward possibly patenting and licensing the technology. Simultaneously we were close to the top of the Big Ten with almost $8 million in licensing revenue. In most of the Big Ten, such income is usually less than $5 million. Without a big-hit commercial success (e.g., Warfarin, the anticoagulant drug developed at The University of Wisconsin Research Foundation [WARF]), licensing revenue is a small (less than 1 percent) fraction of research expenditures. At Ohio State, that fraction is $8 million / $850 million. Kathy Ku, the doyen of tech-commercialization leaders at Stanford, noted: "Out of 6,400 inventions in 36 years, only three of them were 'big winners,' defined as having generated $50 million or more in *cumulative* royalty revenue" (Barnett 2016). If you do the math, at Ohio State we are generating more than enough inventions. We need to be patient to find that one—in every 2,000—that might generate millions of dollars.

Economic Outreach

The college is deeply engaged with Ohio's economic development and job-creation organizations such as Ohio Third Frontier, One Columbus (formerly Columbus 2020), and JobsOhio. CoE helps attract companies to Ohio because our more than 2,000 graduates each year constitute a significant part of the high-end workforce essential for tech companies to thrive. CoE's leadership is involved in organizations like the Ohio Aerospace and Aviation Council and the Ohio Aerospace Institute as well as on national university-industry think tanks such as the Business Higher Education Forum and the Council on Competitiveness. In turn, leaders of industry (small and large) and economic-development organizations are a key part of the Dean's External Advisory Council. We are walking the walk!

Summary

Our rapidly changing, technology-based economy continues to be driven by engineering innovations. Therefore, CoE education, research, and outreach continue to be tied inextricably to economic development. We infuse an entrepreneurial mind-set into our students and enable faculty to be entrepreneurial and innovative in their research. We partner with other colleges to stimulate and amplify research at the intersections of Ohio's leadership in materials, manufacturing, mobility, and medicine. The rewards are evident in the growth of industry-funded research, our burgeoning portfolio of new companies, and the increasing demand that industries have for our graduates. The economic future is bright for Ohio, for Ohio State, for the college, and for its faculty, staff, and students.

References

Barnett, Gerald. September 24, 2016. "Has Bayh-Dole Been Successful?" Research Enterprise. Accessed January 13, 2020. https://researchenterprise.org/2016/09/24/has-bayh-dole-been-successful/.

19

Backstage at Ohio State's The Arts Initiative

Defining a World of Arts Enterprise

Valarie Williams

In 2009, our institution continued its search for relevancy in a modern world and brought together the expertise and disciplines of five colleges to create the largest college of Arts and Sciences in the nation that would lead the way to innovation and strategic thinking in all five areas—the arts, the humanities, the social sciences, the biological sciences, and the mathematical and physical sciences. The integration didn't stop with the academic campus; it extended its reach to many nonprofit organizations in the city, around the state, and ultimately, across the nation and world through the support of alumni and donors. One entity that emerged from the newly integrated college was The Arts Initiative.

At first, The Arts Initiative lived in the President's Office with Vice President for Arts and Outreach Karen A. Bell, a forerunner for advancing the arts and creating relationships throughout the city. After Bell's retirement in 2011, The Arts Initiative came to the newly designed College of Arts and Sciences; it expanded to include the award-winning downtown Urban Arts Space, the on-campus Hopkins Hall Gallery, the partnership with the United Kingdom's Royal Shakespeare Company, and the Town and Gown Advisory Committee on the Arts. I took over the strategic planning and academic leadership for what became an era of compelling and critical components for arts students, faculty, staff, alumni, and donors—on and off campus.

Defining the Difference between an A and A+

First up was the creation of a committee between the university faculty and the city's prominent nonprofit leaders in order to discover cross-disciplinary ways we could collaborate and integrate the expertise housed in the disperse disciplines of the college. At meetings of The Arts Initiative's Town and Gown Advisory Committee on the Arts, over twenty partnerships formed. One such collaboration developed between our highly ranked regional opera company, Opera Columbus, and the Vocal Department of Ohio State's School of Music. Through multiple discussions and strategy sessions, a vision for innovative curricular performance and touring experiences emerged for students. Voice majors interested in touring signed up for music credit hours, auditioned with faculty members and the artistic director of Opera Columbus, and began rehearsals during the latter half of the autumn semester. During the spring semester, the ten selected students perfected their music and staging, and headed out early mornings to perform to area school children.

Every spring semester between 2012 and 2018, the ten School of Music voice majors could be found driving across Franklin County warming up and preparing for three back-to-back performances—all before noon. In any one year, the Ohio State students, in collaboration with Opera Columbus's Opera Goes to School! reached over 13,000 and performed familiar arias while interacting with school-age children. The partnership focused on generating and supporting young new talent in our region that directly aligned with part of the mission of Opera Columbus. Funding from The Arts Initiative supported the partnership and laid the groundwork for future collaborations. In an interview with Peggy Kriha Dye, Opera Columbus's artistic director, she stated, "They learned more than the notes on the page, they learned to think quickly and on the spot" (personal communication, February 21, 2019). Students performed in traditional theaters, in gyms, and in classrooms, and sometimes would perform to 800 at one sitting. The students learned by doing, and their negotiation of the different types of settings and large and small audiences informed their talent and ability to excel beyond the typical classroom "A." The students transformed their practice into creative scholarship and engaged with audiences throughout central Ohio.

The partnership allowed Ohio State students to gain real-life experience and academic credit. As well, it afforded them the opportunity to perform in Opera Columbus's chorus in main-stage productions in the

FIGURE 19.1. Department of Dance majors in Opera Columbus's *Madama Butterfly* at the Southern Theatre, Columbus, Ohio, 2018. Photo credit: Randall L. Schieber.

historic Southern Theater in downtown Columbus. The students learned stagecraft and performance practices and studied the art form in a way that can only be achieved by actual participation in fully produced operas. The students excelled as singers in the two divergent experiences, main-stage productions and the educational tour throughout central Ohio performing in the thirty-plus schools.

Opera Columbus soon expanded its involvement with the arts at Ohio State and included faculty and students from the Department of Dance in its main-stage productions (figure 19.1). Internationally noted dance faculty engaged in creating the movement and dances for Opera Columbus's seasonal offerings. The nationally recognized regional opera company drew on the undergraduate student talent of the dance majors for Opera Columbus's productions. Dance majors experienced performing to audiences of over 2,000, worked with elaborate costumes, engaged with hair and wig artists, and learned the skills of application from professional makeup artists. Like the vocal majors, the dance majors earned repertory credit that counted toward their major degree requirements. In interviews, Dye; Destiny Coleman, director of education for Opera Columbus and School of Music alumna; and Patrick Woliver, associate director of the School of Music and Head of the Vocal Department stated the innovative collaboration was a "win-win." Woliver went on to say,

> The synergy that exists brings further depth to whatever [future] experience that comes about because of the partnership. There's a possibility of

> a depth of experience on both sides: on the Town side there is a recognition that there is a vibrancy of activity that's going on, on-campus; and on the Gown side there is a connection to people who have now moved out of an educational environment and into a professional situation. That synergy in itself creates and elevates the human condition (personal communication, February 13, 2019).

Over 100 Ohio State music and dance majors have gone on to put their scholarship into practice beyond the classroom, onto the stage, and throughout the state of Ohio and the nation with Opera Columbus. Those students earned credit hours toward their graduation in an embedded curricular experience that is rivaled by only a few schools in the nation. Our partnership served as the model for Opera Columbus's 2015–2020 young artist program with voice majors of The Juilliard School and as the foundation for the newly developed 2019–2022 performance fellowship program with Capital University.

As our performing arts students were taking the stage on one side of downtown Columbus, our visual arts students were working on the other side of town on a national exhibition entitled *Open This End: Contemporary Art from the Collection of Blake Byrne* in the university's downtown gallery OSU Urban Arts Space and campus's Hopkins Hall Gallery. The exhibition included cooperation with four academic institutions: Duke University, Columbia University, Lewis and Clark University, and The Ohio State University. Kathy Chase, Ohio State's West Coast senior director of advancement, connected several faculty from the Town and Gown Committee on the Arts with donor Blake Byrne. He in turn introduced us to Barbara Schwan, executive director of Byrne's Skylark Foundation, and to Joseph R. Wolin, curator and editor of the exhibition. We discussed the idea Byrne had to celebrate his eightieth birthday—to tour and share seventy-seven of his most important works of art to four universities to which he and his family had personal connections. A top-400 art collector in the world, Byrne was interested in integrating the expertise of faculty and staff with the works of art and in allowing students to have full access to them; the works are from thirty-six different artists, including such notables as Kehinde Wylie, Andy Warhol, Mike Kelley, Cindy Sherman, Agnes Martin, and Mark Bradford.

Byrne has a deep sense of philanthropy and a desire to share his expertise, his home, his art collection, and his passions with students and with the surrounding communities of Ohio State. He talked with me about why he wanted to share the collection with Ohio State, and about his ideas behind the exhibition tour:

FIGURE 19.2. Students from the *Los Angeles Student Experience* with donor and friend Blake Byrne in his Los Angeles, California, home, 2017. Photo courtesy of the author.

> When I started collecting art and got a collection going—well, you realize you're teaching your children, and you're teaching your grandchildren, what art is about. And then you talk with your friends, and they teach you, and you teach them. So when it came time to do something for my eightieth birthday celebration, I thought wouldn't that be great if we could put together an exhibition that traveled to universities where the family has an association, and teach, and use the exhibition as a teaching exhibition (personal communication, March 18, 2015).

The idea of sharing and teaching was the underlying philosophy for this partnership, and before the exhibition could begin its tour, staff at Byrne's Skylark Family Foundation and at all four universities worked together to share information, learn about the works, secure image copyrights, and interact with the Los Angeles Museum of Contemporary Art for loan agreements for those pieces already on permanent loan to the museum. The large-scale project brought together expertise from the East and West Coasts, the Midwest, and the Carolinas, for an unprecedented real-world experience for students and the nation's communities (figure 19.2).

Department of Art chair Sergio Soave and Department of History of Art chair Andrew Shelton engaged in a collaborative plan with faculty and students that focused on activating Byrne's collection throughout the campus and city. This included contributions to the catalogue by history of art professor Kris Paulsen and a graduate student "response exhibition" from the Department of History of Art and Department of Art graduate students. In addition, students from the Department of Art assisted the preparators and handled and hung artwork alongside the professional staff. K–12 art education majors in the Department of Arts Administration, Education and Policy designed lesson plans and tours that met the state standards in Ohio. Senior art education majors planned activities for the noncampus community, and several went on to present their contributions at state and national conferences. The semester before the exhibition arrived, twenty undergraduate students working for The Arts Initiative, from majors across the university, conducted research on artists in the show and created additional information for a gallery guide. In a ten-week period, over 1,000 students engaged in learning outside the classroom, and seven courses in history of art, art education, classics, history, and art built learning modules around exhibition content.

Students, staff, and faculty brainstormed with Byrne on his visits to Ohio State before the exhibition and collaborated on programming that transformed the lives of not only we who lived it, but also of those who visited. Panels focused on four themes from the exhibition: (1) "You don't own the work, you only rent it"—Philanthropy, Ethics, and Art; (2) Where Are We Now?—30 Years of HIV/AIDS Research; (3) The Cultural Politics of Identity; and (4) Video and New Media Art in the Last 50 Years. The panels were sponsored by additional support from the Greater Columbus Arts Council, Ohio Arts Council, Ohio State's Office of Diversity and Inclusion, and Michael Para, MD (one of the first physicians to discover the infectious disease HIV), and his wife, Caroline Whitacre, PhD. The panels highlighted contextual stories and issues surrounding the works of art, the artists' lives, and the issues of their day. The exhibition, panels, and educational components engaged with over 4,000 people from the community and other Columbus-area academic institutions, with the show in two of Ohio State's galleries—the downtown Urban Arts Space and the on-campus Hopkins Hall Gallery.

Attending to the Context of the Land-Grant Mission

The Arts Initiative continued to fulfill its mission of "positioning Ohio State University as a leader through connections with local, national, and international arts organizations" when it entered into an unprecedented partnership between The Ohio State University and Great Britain's Royal Shakespeare Company (RSC) to bring Shakespeare to 15,000 children across the state of Ohio, to train and educate 101 of Ohio's school teachers at the RSC, and to educate and train fifty-one Ohio State students in the Departments of Theatre; Arts Administration, Education and Policy; English; and Teaching and Learning. The seven-year partnership had a profound impact on the educational experience of all entities and in its last year included 800 Ohio State students taking courses in English, education, history, theater, arts administration, and many other disciplines, that culminated in a four day cocurricular experience—interacting directly with the RSC actors and attending the RSC residency at the Brooklyn Academy of Music (BAM) in Brooklyn, New York.

Through sustained collaborative institution-to-institution activities, we transformed the lives of K–12 teachers around the state; enhanced the practices of our faculty, students, and staff; and brought four tours to the US with the Royal Shakespeare Company's *First Encounters with Shakespeare.* In a collaborative spirit, we partnered with the Columbus Association for the Performing Arts (CAPA) to present the US tour of the Royal Shakespeare Company's *Julius Caesar* and collaboratively supported RSC's residency of *King and Country: Shakespeare's Great Cycle of Kings,* the tetralogy of *Richard II*; *Henry IV, Part I*; *Henry IV, Part II*; and *Henry V* at BAM.

We celebrated the first international Town and Gown partnership of its kind between an acclaimed research academic institution and an internationally recognized arts company that was made possible by a lead gift from The Abigail and Les Wexner Family Foundation, with additional support from organizations and individuals in Ohio and New York City. Their vision and support for the university and the state allowed students, faculty, staff, and the citizens of Ohio once-in-a-lifetime experiences and unfettered access to training, behind-the scenes practices, and performances from one of the world's most beloved performing arts companies.

Pondering the Innovation That Is Required to Remain Relevant as Institutions of Higher Learning

When I became the executive director of The Arts Initiative, I brought with me the knowledge of curricular offerings in the college and cocurricular opportunities that our students enjoy on an annual basis. I took this knowledge with me on a first trip to Los Angeles, California, to meet supporters and alumni of the college. While I was there, I was asked over and over, "What are the students like now?" "What do they like to do?" "What are they interested in doing when they graduate?" and "How can we help them?" I was struck by the collective expertise of the alumni and the genuine desire to interact with the current undergraduate students.

Three of my staff and I devised a plan—the *Los Angeles Student Experience.* From 2013 to 2017, faculty and staff from the arts and sciences and I traveled to Los Angeles with students from twenty-five different majors and minors across the arts and sciences for a life-changing experience.

We collaborated with faculty in the College of Arts and Sciences; donors, alumni, and supporters; University Advancement; University Alumni Association; and sixty students with interests in the arts and entertainment industry. Each year of the program, faculty and staff in the arts and sciences selected the top twenty students from a competitive pool of 400 applicants. Students needed to hold a GPA of 3.0 and above, write an essay about their desire to participate, and hold junior or senior rank with interests in the arts and entertainment industry, visual arts, entrepreneurship, or leadership. The bright, inquisitive students paired with donors, alumni, and friends who are known throughout the world as the founders and leaders in their respective fields.

Students signed up for one hour of credit for pre-trip class seminars to prepare for the residency. We spoke about, and put into practice, how to conduct "small-talk" at a reception, how to deliver your "elevator speech" about what you want to do in life, how to dress, how to pack efficiently, and how to draw on each one's own stamina for the whirlwind expedition. Students also spent time learning about each individual they would meet during the activities, and by doing so, learned how to prepare for future interviews and networking meetings.

Throughout the six-day intensive, students interacted with more than ninety donors, alumni, and friends who are business executives, studio executives, executive producers, directors, actors, television and film writers, restaurateurs, and musicians. Some shadowed general counsels of television and film companies. Students watched the shooting of TV shows, participated in conversations and one-on-one mentoring experiences in writer's rooms, casting studios, and directing studios; and were welcomed into individuals' homes and businesses and artists' studios. The first trip in 2013 included twenty experiences; the 2015 trip had twenty-three; and by the time we got to the 2017 trip, we had so many interested alumni and friends who wanted to give back, the students had opportunity to participate in thirty-five different activities. One student from the 2017 class summed it up best: "I can't begin to describe the incredible value of the LA Experience. The LA Experience was the most worthwhile thing I ever did during my time at Ohio State."

Assessing the impact of their engagement with the program, we surveyed the sixty students. By 2018, over 60 percent of graduated student participants found work in one of the industries related to the trip and 20 percent of those moved to Los Angeles. The residency became a success because of the belief in giving back, and because of the dedication of the donors, alumni, and friends. When asked why he participated in hosting students all five years, Don Handfield (1993 OSU alumnus) stated,

> I knew one person when I moved to Los Angeles, a fellow buckeye (Mike Timmons) who let me sleep on his floor when I moved out after college. Without that simple landing pad, I may have never made the leap. It's humbling and extremely rewarding to be able to provide the same for a new generation, who can in turn provide the same opportunity to those who come after them. Go Bucks! (email communication, June 19, 2017)

Those who experience the arts throughout their time at Ohio State develop a deep desire to give back to individuals by sharing their knowledge, expertise, and passions. This learned trait, held dear by the largest alumni body in the world, is what will guide us forward as we continue to excel beyond the A+ and lead the world in engaging with people and solving the issues of a twenty-first-century society.

The Student Experience

20

Ohio State's Second-Year Transformational Experience Program

Enriching Students' Lives in the Modern Land-Grant Era

David Isaacs, Anne McDaniel, Javaune Adams-Gaston, and M. Susie Whittington

The Morrill Act has long been credited with the democratization of higher education. The innovative foundation of the law was the controversial idea that an education should not be limited to the elite, but accessible to all. Congressman Justin Smith Morrill (R-VT), in a floor speech to the US House of Representatives, called it "education of the great mass of the country" (Morrill 1859). More than 150 years later, few programs epitomize the spirit of the Morrill Act more than the Second-year Transformational Experience Program (STEP) at The Ohio State University.

STEP is designed to support both the curricular and cocurricular success of students in their second year of college. Every second-year student, based on their high school graduation year, is automatically enrolled in the program. There are no barriers to access: no additional fees, no need to fill out application forms or write essays, no need to track down how to get into the program, and no grade point requirements. Although students can opt out of the program if they choose, they are part of the program merely by their enrollment at Ohio State. It is not just an open door; students are already, by virtue of acceptance to the university, *through the door.*

STEP adds a modern philosophy to a concept that has existed in the law for more than 150 years. The program provides a pathway that did not previously exist for students of all backgrounds—geographic, cultural, and economic—to have access to an educational experience that includes a relationship with a faculty mentor and resources specifically focused on them and their success. STEP truly levels the playing field for all second-year students.

A student's college experience is a time of sustained development. The first year of college is about discovering the campus and becoming familiar with its resources and opportunities. For many years, Ohio State has had a program for first-year students that encourages their immersion into the university. The university, through research-driven decision-making, recognized the need to continue that attention for students the following year. The second year is about the student discovering their place in the broader campus and global community as part of their self-discovery process. It is a critical time. The so-called sophomore slump is very real for many students, and a time when they may experience academic, developmental, and institutional challenges.

The need for supporting second-year students may be especially acute among first-generation students and those from historically underserved populations. These are among the students who have higher probabilities for not completing their education and are the students who best reflect the modern spirit of deserving the support passed down through the Morrill Act. For Ohio State, thus began the process of developing a program to deliver on that land-grant promise. The foundational premise was rooted in the commitment to providing opportunities for all second-year students to achieve their educational goals. Through academic and proprietary research, Ohio State leaders found that top predictors of student success include living on campus, interacting with faculty, engaging with peers, committing to their institution, and participating in campus events.

Using this information, Ohio State developed a data-driven and student success–focused approach. It was to be called the Second-year Transformational Experience Program, a name that acknowledged the importance of transformational experiences in student development. It began as a pilot program in 2013 with a limited number of students and faculty mentors, then grew to full implementation with the 2016–2017 academic year. Central to the program is increased faculty engagement and mentorship. In addition to providing a variety of educational and developmental programs and support, faculty mentor students through the selection of experiential educational opportunities. These meaningful interactions between students and faculty, both formal and informal, are key to the success of the program. STEP faculty draw on their own expertise and interests to develop distinctive approaches to programming;

these might include a range of discussions, cultural events, outings, or site visits.

Faculty-student interaction is supported and enhanced by cocurricular pursuits offered by units throughout the university, especially the Office of Student Life. This deliberate and comprehensive approach to student growth and development allows Ohio State to put an innovative focus on the student experience, contributing to benefits while at the university and far beyond. STEP was conceived from the very beginning as a collaboration between the Offices of Student Life and Academic Affairs. A faculty committee was formed to develop a plan for the academic component of STEP, including its academic goals and faculty mentors' roles and responsibilities, as well as creating a system of reward and recognition to properly acknowledge and value the contributions of faculty participating in the program. The inclusion of faculty in the earliest stages of development insured faculty involvement and an atmosphere of cooperation across the enterprise. The collaboration allows Ohio State to take a holistic approach to the student experience, from the classroom to the cocurricular and beyond.

While developing the program was an extensive undertaking, there were special challenges in meeting another of the key predictors of second-year success: living on campus. The research at Ohio State found that students who live on campus for two years have higher two-year retention rates and graduation rates than students who did not live on campus for their first two years (retention: 95.7 percent compared to 88.6 percent, respectively, for the 2009 cohort; graduation: 88.2 percent compared to 76.5 percent for the 2005 cohort). Ohio State has technically required second-year students to live on campus for decades but did not enforce the idea due to lack of housing. The second-year live-on requirement led to a major construction project that ultimately saw eight new residence halls, a new recreation center, and a new dining services building. In addition, over 3,750 beds were added or replaced.

A delegation from the Office of Student Life did a significant amount of research into existing programs at other colleges and universities, including a tour of other institutions to obtain firsthand information. They found that while a number of other schools required second-year students to live on campus, none had attempted to fully integrate a program to support their success within the facilities. Consequently, the program became a prime focus for Ohio State. What would become STEP was created first, and the residence halls were designed to accommodate it.

This approach led to a number of design features integral to the core values of STEP. Small and large group meeting spaces were included on the first floor of each of the new residence halls to host meetings between STEP cohorts and faculty mentors. Special-use rooms were included throughout the North District, including dance, art, and music spaces. Extensive green space in the residence areas was designed with locations for outdoor classes and gatherings.

The transformation of the north residential area was complete in time for autumn semester 2016, which allowed STEP to move from a pilot program to full implementation. The pilot in 2013 started with fifty STEP faculty mentors and 1,000 students; by autumn 2017, the program had encompassed 190 faculty members and nearly 3,000 students. In addition, over two-thirds of students in the first year took advantage of a feature that extends the true egalitarian nature of STEP. The program encourages students to take part in a signature project that caps their year of self-discovery. In the spirit of the land-grant mission, STEP not only eliminates barriers to participating in the program but also provides funding to ensure that students have the resources to take advantage of this aspect of the program.

Following the completion of program requirements, students are eligible to write a proposal to receive a fellowship of up to $2,000 to support the STEP signature project they have developed with the help of their STEP faculty mentor. The signature project can be related to any of six unique, educational-enriching categories:

- Creative and Artistic Endeavors
- Internships
- Leadership
- Service Learning and Community Service
- Education Abroad
- Undergraduate Research

Examples of STEP signature projects undertaken by students include hands-on study of individual and group leadership capabilities in the High Sierras and establishing an elementary school after-hours education program in one of the most underachieving schools in the US. In addition, a STEP student wrote, illustrated, and published a book dedicated to the teacher who, as the student shared, "taught me to love science." Students have published music, conducted research in hospital labs, and interned in career-changing social justice agencies in Washington, DC.

From the earliest conceptualization of STEP, the signature project was seen as a key component in the personal and professional growth of students. Equally important, however, was the notion that finances should not be an impediment to taking part in one of these transformational, experiential opportunities. Once again, the guiding principles of the land-grant concept provided a path to eliminating barriers. The fellowship of up to $2,000 removes that potential obstruction and levels the playing field financially for second-year students at Ohio State. It permits students to have experiences that might not have otherwise been available to them, experiences that they might not have thought possible or attainable. The fellowship in effect gives students the opportunity to fulfill a dream about what transformational experience they might have if cash was not a consideration and economic status not a factor. Students have reflected:

> "I was able to gain creative inspiration from multiple sources that have changed my entire outlook as to how I think about design. I was challenged by forcing myself out of my comfort zone . . . in many ways that I did not anticipate. . . . I have developed new perspective into my design works."

> "It was incredible to see concepts I learned at Ohio State get translated into real-life scenarios and testing. After completing and analyzing many different tests, I helped write and publish a research paper."

> "I learned the significance and value of a sustainable infrastructure that is easy to maintain, and I will definitely apply this new perspective and appreciation for sustainability in my future career as a civil engineer."

> "I was able to immerse myself in a culture that was so completely different from everything that I know . . . ranging from religion to transportation. . . . I was able to grow in my understanding and appreciation of tradition, socioeconomic circumstances and opportunities, tolerance, resourcefulness, and religion."

> "By doing preclinical work in this laboratory . . . I realized how important it is to me to work toward finding cures and therapies for illness. Doing research towards these outcomes made me feel valued and important."

> "This STEP project transformed my view of the world."

The signature project could be considered a high-impact practice. National research has shown that high-impact practices of this magnitude are most often reflected in undergraduate curriculum as senior capstone experiences. Providing these high-impact opportunities to second-year students speaks to Ohio State's vision for laying an early foundation on which to build toward even larger impact on student success. Gaining these experiences in students' second year advances their development and allows them to build upon what they have learned, and to be positioned for even greater success when the time for the capstone arrives. It is yet another fulfillment of the land-grant mission to prepare students to become productive members of society upon graduation.

This preparation for life after higher education manifests itself in a number of ways through STEP. Participants are required to attend at least three professional development cocurricular programs in the areas of career preparation, community engagement/global citizenship, information literacy/academic success, wellness, leadership development, and Discovery Themes. In addition, STEP participants are required to complete a two-part financial wellness program.

These requirements align with another of the land-grant precepts: that an education must be practical. In the days of Rep. Morrill, that meant a focus on agricultural and manufacturing skills. Today the mission is expanded to include the life skills that students must possess in order to be successful for the rest of their lives.

A key example is financial wellness. The multi-institutional Study on Collegiate Financial Wellness (2017), led by Ohio State's Center for the Study of Student Life, found that seven out of ten college students are stressed about their finances in general, and their overall financial literacy is low, with students answering 3.3 out of six financial knowledge questions correctly, on average. Students' financial wellness is a complex topic, but financial stress and poor financial decisions are associated with negative academic outcomes.

Meanwhile, Ohio State's Student Life Student Wellness Center has developed a nationally recognized peer-to-peer financial coaching program called Scarlet and Gray Financial (SGF). The program promotes financial literacy and holistic financial wellness free of charge through a variety of mediums, including one-on-one coaching sessions, large group presentations, financial education research, and professional development opportunities.

The backbone of the Scarlet and Gray Financial program is the one-on-one, personal finance, peer-coaching model. During these hour-long coaching sessions, SGF coaches help students develop an awareness of their own financial standing, establish financial goals, and create a financial plan to help achieve those goals. Coaches review fundamental financial concepts during their sessions, including (but not limited to) budgeting, interest rates, loan basics, repayment options, and an overview of personal credit. Coaches (unpaid student volunteers) are trained to use motivational interviewing and other coaching and counseling techniques to ease their clients' financial stress and empower them to achieve life goals through intentional financial planning.

By requiring STEP participants to complete this program, students have the opportunity to acquire critical skills that better prepare them for life during and after college. It is truly a component in a *practical* education as espoused by the spirit of the land-grant mission. STEP is a success story. Compared to students not in the program during the 2017–2018 academic year, students in STEP report statistically significant increases over the course of their second year in their access to campus resources; comfort interacting with faculty; interpersonal communication skills; and academic, leadership, and career confidence.

One of the primary goals of STEP is to improve retention rates among participants. Data from the 2017–2018 academic year show that 99.2 percent of STEP students returned for their third year at Ohio State, compared to 94.7 percent of students who were not part of the program. The numbers are especially dramatic among underrepresented student groups. Among first-generation students, or those without parents who have graduated from college, 99.2 percent of STEP students return for their third year, compared to 92.5 percent of non-STEP students. Among African American and Latinx students, 100 percent of STEP students return for their third year, compared to 87.6 percent and 92.5 percent of non-STEP students, respectively.

While STEP is designed to benefit students, the program is highly rewarding for the faculty mentors as well: 91 percent agree that their role as a STEP mentor gave them a chance to make a difference in students' lives, and 93 percent say they gained a better understanding of second-year students' goals and interests. STEP has been one of Ohio State's greatest and most collaborative successes in recent years. It enriches the educational experience for second-year students, and is additionally rewarding for the faculty members who serve as mentors. It also epitomizes how a modern university can continue to fulfill the vision put forth in the Morrill Act. The land-grant mission is alive and well at The Ohio State University, 150 years after its founding.

References

Morrill, Justin Smith. 1859. Statement regarding land grant universities, February 1859. http://tpscongress.org/critical-thinking/attachments/pdf/section2_morrill_land-grant.pdf.

Study on Collegiate Financial Wellness. 2017. *Key Findings Report.* Columbus, OH: Center for the Study of Student Life, The Ohio State University.

21

I Had No Idea . . . but Now That I Do . . .

Clark Kellogg

I enrolled as a student at The Ohio State University in the fall of 1979. My God-given talent and physical attributes, partnered with parental guidance, excellent coaching influence, and my hard work earned me an athletic scholarship in basketball. While many adults in my sphere of influence impressed upon me the importance and lifelong value of a college degree, my grasping that in a tangible way was limited on several fronts.

First, as the oldest of five children, raised by parents who didn't graduate from college (my dad attended for a semester or so), I was the first in our nuclear family to attend college. The only college graduates I knew personally were a few older cousins and a businessman I met when I was fifteen, who became a mentor and lifelong friend. He also happens to be an Ohio State graduate, as is his wife. While I was the first to attend college in our nuclear family, the oldest of my three sisters would be the first in our immediate family to graduate from college. She and another sister join me in having college degrees.

Second, at eighteen years old, I was incapable of fully grasping the life-altering impact going to college and graduating from college would have on my life. I think that applies to most eighteen-year olds. However, as I was being recruited, many Buckeye alums and fans spoke with great enthusiasm, passion, and even reverence about The Ohio State University.

Their strong feelings of pride about being a Buckeye were palpable, and made a lasting impression on this native Clevelander.

Last, while I enjoyed school and was a good student, the connection I made between education and a productive, successful life was more theoretical than tangible. For all intents and purposes, basketball was the driving force of my life at that time—which worked out quite well for me. Nevertheless, as much as my family, high school academic advisors, and Buckeye alums stressed the quality of education that I'd receive at Ohio State, I was of the mind that I would get a good education wherever I went. Kentucky, Notre Dame, and Michigan were the other schools I seriously considered attending.

That said, my future teammates and coaches, the opportunity to compete at the highest level in basketball, the proximity to my hometown of Cleveland, and the way so many folks throughout the state and region made me feel about joining the Buckeye family (Buckeye Nation) is why I ultimately matriculated to Columbus. And I'm so glad and grateful that I did.

My experience as a scholarship student athlete was fairly myopic. The bulk of my time was occupied by school and basketball. Such is the nature of being a scholarship student athlete. I did engage in a reasonable amount of social activity with my fellow students and teammates, and thoroughly enjoyed meeting new people and learning new things in the classroom, and took a liking to Columbus.

However, in part by choice and necessity, I didn't add much to my plate beyond the aforementioned activities. Doing well in school and on the court, treating others with respect, and representing my family and university well were the things I focused on. That focus served me well, but also lessened my student experience in some ways. Had I the chance for a mulligan (golf talk for a "do-over"), I would engage in a student organization focusing on leadership and service, push myself harder academically, and engage with some of the Olympic sport athletes more.

In the spring of 1982, after three years of solid work (but short of my potential) in the classroom, and a distinguished career on the court, I chose to leave college to pursue my dream of being a professional basketball player in the NBA. My dream was realized as I was a first-round draft pick by the Indiana Pacers.

On track to graduate (needing forty-five credit hours, or three quarters, back then) had I stayed for my senior year, I would eventually get my BS in business administration in December 1996 in St. John Arena. Quite fitting that the place where I spent the most time while a student athlete at Ohio State is also where I received my degree. Receiving that OSU degree is one of the highlights of my life. And graduation day was quite a memory.

By 1996, Rosy and I had been married for thirteen years and our children were ages nine, seven, and five. I had transitioned successfully to my current career as a college and professional basketball television analyst and was working for ESPN and the Indiana Pacers at the time. My promising playing career had ended in the summer of 1987 due to chronic knee damage after just five seasons.

Over a period of fourteen years, I had chipped away at my remaining forty-five credit hours by taking classes in Indianapolis during some of the summers while we lived there, and doing the same at Ohio State when we returned to Columbus in 1993. Not only was I was determined to get my degree from Ohio State, but I wanted to do so in person!

So, after broadcasting a Pacers game in LA the night before commencement, I was on a red-eye flight home. A bit fatigued, but fueled by adrenaline and excitement, I completed my seventeen-year journey to a degree with a handshake and congratulatory smile from President Gordon Gee on December 13, 1996. Two years later, I would have the honor and privilege of serving as the commencement speaker in St. John Arena. And then in 2012, also in St. John Arena, as a university trustee seated on the commencement platform, I was able to present our middle child and oldest son, Alex, with his bachelor's degree. Those experiences were *priceless*!

While that special moment as a trustee will be cherished above many others, the honor, privilege, and responsibility of being a trustee for my alma mater has been one of the most educational, horizon-broadening, and relationship-rich experiences of my life. Along with my fellow trustees, I've experienced the complexity and diversity of challenges and constituencies at Ohio State; the commitment, dedication, and excellence of our leadership, faculty, and employees; the impact and excellence of our students academically, athletically, and in our communities nation and worldwide; and the way Ohio State changes and improves lives daily.

All of which fills me with great pride as an Ohio State alum. And it is my continuing education through service to my alma mater that has opened my eyes to the significance Ohio State holds as a land-grant institution. What an education it has been.

The Morrill Act of 1862 ushered in publicly funded agricultural and technical educational institutions to bring science, technology, agriculture, and the arts to the American people—or, put another way, education that is accessible to "sons and daughters of toil" (Gavazzi and Gee 2018, 4), that is excellent in applied and practical pursuits, and that is outstanding in service to communities. Ohio State is one of almost 300 such colleges and universities in the country. A number of historically black colleges and universities are part of that number as well. As such, land-grants have a distinct responsibility and tremendous opportunity to serve the public good through teaching, learning, research, and service.

It's embarrassing to admit that the term *land-grant* in connection with Ohio State never resonated with me as a student. It was the same even years after leaving for the NBA and then graduating. I recall hearing it occasionally, but I was clueless as to its significance or import.

That started to change during my time as a member of The Ohio State University Alumni Association Board from 2005 to 2009. The "land-grant" mission was spoken about regularly in meetings as we considered how best to serve the university by serving our students, alums, and university friends nation- and worldwide. It was quite enlightening, humbling, and inspiring to witness the dimensions of the impact, importance, influence, and reach that Ohio State has through teaching and learning, research and service.

My greatest learning about the land-grant mission has taken place during my term as a trustee of The Ohio State University. I was appointed to the board by Governor Ted Strickland in 2010, and my term concluded in 2019. I served during the leadership tenures of Gordon Gee, Joe Alutto (interim president), and Michael Drake.

Each of them were and are firmly anchored in espousing and fulfilling the mission of the land-grant. The themes of students first, one university, affordability and access, teaching and learning, academic health care, research and creative expression, collaboration, community engagement, and operational and resource stewardship all are tied to the land-grant mission.

During the last two years of my term as a trustee, I chaired the Academic Affairs and Student Life Committee—continuing education for me in our land-grant mission at Ohio State. Teaching and learning, research and service, and advancing the common good are at the heart of the land-grant mission historically. Being curious and knowledgeable about the work the university is doing in these and other areas in the context of its land-grant mission is something I view as a personal call to action now and going forward. As a former trustee and proud Ohio State alum, I'm compelled to advocate on behalf of my alma mater's land-grant mission in the ways that I can.

Recently, I read the book *Land-Grant Universities for the Future: Higher Education for the Public Good* by Stephen M. Gavazzi and E. Gordon Gee. So much of what I read informed me and resonated with my heart regarding the democratic and pragmatic mission of the land-grant—particularly the premise of land-grant universities being "servant universities" and the "people's universities." Certainly, there are great challenges in higher education, including the current climate of divisiveness, the debate about the value of a college degree, access and affordability for those of low or moderate income, and declining public funding. These challenges are clearly headwinds to the lofty ideal of education for the people, by the people.

However, I agree with Gavazzi, Gee, and others that land-grant universities are uniquely positioned to respond to these challenges. While I had no idea that Ohio State was a land-grant university when I enrolled in the fall of 1979, I do know that my college education and experience changed my life significantly. It also changed the lives of our three children—all college graduates. And there are hundreds of thousands of others who can testify (perhaps with more dramatic stories) to a changed life through education at a land-grant college or university. I am forever grateful for the impact and influence that a land-grant university has had and continues to have in my life, and for the role and capacity land-grant colleges and universities hold to enhance and serve the public good. The mantra of education for citizenship and service to others, if not explicitly stated, was certainly implied across the campus community during my time as a student.

Knowing what I do now about the land-grant mission, as a former trustee and alum of The Ohio State University, inclines me to be more committed to articulating how land-grant institutions can improve communities and to being "fiercely land-grant" in my orientation and advocacy around higher education.

References

Gavazzi, Stephen. M., and Gee, E. Gordon. (2018). *Land-Grant Universities for the Future: Higher Education for the Public Good.* Baltimore, MD: Johns Hopkins University Press.

22

The Abiding Promise of a Land-Grant Education

MATTHEW MAYHEW AND ERIC MCCHESNEY

The unique nature of The Ohio State University is not something that can be gleaned from a quick read of its mission statement. It is not contained in the massy columns of the Thompson library nor captured in the glowing furnaces of our chemical glassworks or the gently effervescing cores of arctic ice in the Byrd Polar Research Center. You will not discover it in the fragments of Assyrian sculpture tucked away in our paleography department, nor in our gurgling hydroponics gardens, nor even in our Ottoman manuscripts, florid and fragile as butterfly wings. Although our nuclear research reactor is one of the last on the continent, it is not what makes our university unique. Our gleaming medical complex, even with its robotic surgical suites, its neuromodulation center, its proton therapy apparatus, and its cutting-edge immunology treatments, does not contain the mystery either. Other universities certainly have championship football teams, dancers who move like molten silver, early music collectives that resurrect melodies from the far reaches of space and time, and materials labs where the laws of chemistry and physics are flexed to the breaking point. Certainly, when the sun sets over Mirror Lake and transforms its burnished surface to a rippling pool of molten brass, or when in the midst of autumn the Oval greets you with a symphony of blazing ochre leaves, or when the bells of Orton Hall toll out sonorous and solemn and mysterious on the first crisp, clear night of winter, one is tempted to say that these are unique to The Ohio State University—but they would be wrong. All these are things that the university has, yet what the university *is* subtends them all, for what it *is* is a promise.

For the past 150 years, this university has whispered its promise to each new generation of students, to the land the university embraces, to the city of which it forms the pulsating heart, to the other bright beacons of knowledge that shine throughout our nation, and to the people who look to its museums and monuments, to its laboratories and libraries, its reactors and religious sanctuaries with longing and hope. It is a promise of two parts: *to teach all who enter its halls with zeal and care,* and *to provide opportunity, knowledge, and power to all who have the skill to pursue them.*

To Teach All Who Enter Its Halls with Zeal and Care

The lecture halls, laboratories, intensive seminars, and scholarly colloquia of The Ohio State University (OSU) employ cutting-edge pedagogical spaces that are supported by advanced technology and informed by the latest research in student development and learning. The University Institute for Teaching and Learning constantly develops, tests, and promotes the use of teaching methods that have been empirically shown to make students question more deeply, work across differences, bring together disparate bodies of knowledge, and more importantly, solve real-world problems. The departments and professors of OSU design curricula that is lithe and flexible, constantly revising it to be suited to the realities of our swiftly changing world and to incorporate new discoveries. Increasingly, our students' learning is enriched by interdisciplinary approaches that make use of a complex nexus of different perspectives, disciplines, and modes of thought. This breadth of learning allows our students to address the challenging and multilayered problems that face modern society, as well as tempering their judgments, increasing their creativity, and making them more adaptable thinkers.

These techniques can, and have, resulted in extraordinary accomplishments. For example, OSU's Chadwick Arboretum is the proud home of the enCORE Solar Decathlon House. This energy-efficient and carbon-neutral edifice was designed by cross-disciplinary teams of undergraduate OSU students spanning ecological science, chemical engineering, architecture, biology, materials science, electrical engineering, interior design, and more. The building now stands as a living model for the future of responsible architecture. Undergraduate students at OSU can expect their burgeoning skills to be put to practical use on diverse teams: Indeed, it is not unusual for them to find themselves developing new bioplastics from algae to reduce the world's consumption of petrochemicals, or using titanium nanotubules and synthetic sapphires to design hardsuits that can withstand the crushing depths of the ocean, or even assisting NASA in inventing ways to make use of inedible plant matter grown aboard the International Space Station. The rigorous curriculum designed for our students enables them to challenge themselves to live up to their fullest potential, and the university assiduously provides them with opportunities to enrich themselves and, through their exertions, to pull their dreams into reality.

The university provides enormous opportunities and challenges, but it also strives to provide students with a stimulating and supportive community and activities that enrich the mind and replenish the spirit. The university regularly hosts luminaries like Ta-Nehisi Coates, Jill Lepore, and Zadie Smith, and invites the public to hear expert panels on everything from the ethics of genetically engineering unborn children to the influence of Beethoven's symphonies on modern hip-hop. The students of OSU may join any of over 1,400 distinct student groups, which provides them with the opportunity to broaden their cultural experiences and enables them to pursue even the most esoteric of interests. A student on our campus may spend their morning scaling the climbing wall at the Adventure Recreation Center, join an interfaith dialogue group for lunch, spend the afternoon viewing a student-run production of Tom Stoppard's *Arcadia,* and join in a Lunar New Year celebration in the evening. Students also benefit from a strong advising system, comprehensive mental and physical wellness centers, and countless athletic clubs to hone their mental and emotional well-being as well as their scholarly abilities.

The Ohio State University is also devoted to ensuring that every student be provided with a diverse cultural as well as intellectual education. In our increasingly diverse and pluralistic society, the ability to work across differences, read cultures, and critically reflect upon one's own beliefs and lifestyle are necessary skills. When exercised to explore other cultures, religions, and traditions, these skills can provide great wonder and joy, as well as leading one to become deeper and more thoughtful about their own culture. The OSU Multicultural Center regularly provides workshops and immersive experiences that help students to experience other modes of life and thought, while simultaneously establishing safe and brave spaces that facilitate encounters with the unknown. Neither does this commitment to establishing culturally aware and ethically thoughtful students end with the establishment of a university center—rather, these principles are woven throughout the curriculum, environments, and first-year experiences of our students. In this way, the university maintains its adamant commitment to providing a robust marketplace of ideas that teems with possibilities, and that allows the students of this rich and varied land to better weave the fabric of our nation out of the threads of numberless peoples and traditions.

As our nation transitions ever more firmly to an interconnected knowledge economy, The Ohio State University strives to provide our students with the tools they will need to navigate the research laboratories and workplaces of the twenty-first century. To do this, our university provides cutting-edge technology to our students—for example, every single first-year student admitted in 2018 was given an iPad, will learn and work online, and will make use of university-designed course management systems to access digital readings, submit assignments, and conduct research. Yet that is the very least manner in which technology is integrated into our students' learning experiences: In physiology courses, students can expect to use virtual reality to examine the complex interplay of breath and blood that sustains the human form; aerospace engineering students use augmented reality to overlay systems schematics upon turbojet engines so that they can view their mechanisms in operation; surgical residents at the university's Wexner Medical Center may use the DaVinci robotic surgery system to perform lifesaving procedures on patients half a world away, and may do so with a precision and dexterity that no human hand can match.

These technological affordances are used to support the teaching of some of the most renowned professors in the nation. The faculty of The Ohio State University are carefully chosen—not simply because they are the best in their fields, but because they are willing to serve as true teachers, supportive role models for their students and colleagues. *Expressed through hiring practices to reward structures, President Drake's unequivocal commitment to good teaching is and remains unparalleled, especially among comprehensive research universities.* In this university, classrooms are experiments in progress, and professors are dedicated to teaching the bright and far-darting minds of the next generation in ways that are more rigorous, more practical, and more empowering. Professors regularly incorporate student feedback into their pedagogical practices by using real data to enhance the depth of student learning and better prepare the leaders of tomorrow. Additionally, the university has consistently made strides to establish faculty diversity as one of the cornerstones of the educational experiences of our students. Faculty racial diversity has increased every single year for the past fifteen years, as the composition of our professors rapidly approaches the composition of our state and of the city of Columbus. In addition to bringing diverse perspectives into university departments, the faculty of OSU are deeply committed to transformative inquiry, guided by moral probity and sober judgment, while attendant to compassion and conviction. Augmenting this endeavor is the powerful and far-reaching research directed by the faculty of OSU, which devoted $864 million last year alone to developing new medicines, enriching our arts and culture, refining our collective understanding of the universe, and crafting a more just society for all.

As expressions of these values, The Ohio State University has long placed at the very core of our identity what past president William Oxley Thompson termed "the refining of the human spirit." The habit of mind most deserving of cultivation is a deep and abiding concern for the just treatment of one's fellow human beings. To this end, the university strives to instill into its students the essential values of benevolence, ethical conduct, hard work, and concern for justice. Nor does the university simply espouse these principles in word, but rather enacts them within and around our campus. To single out just a few programs, the annual BuckeyeThon raised over $1.7 million this year to fund cancer research and treatment in children; the Buckeye Food Alliance provides sound and reliable nutrition to the food-insecure on campus; and a broad array of service-learning courses allow students to spend significant time contributing to the development of the local community. In this way, the university and the students who attend it commit themselves to the construction of a more just, more inclusive, and more tolerant world.

This, then, forms the first of the promises this university has striven to uphold over the past fifteen decades: the special covenant it forms with each new student to provide them the resources and training that will enable them to be authors of their own identity, and masters of their own fate. The university works to ensure that no student shall leave its campus without becoming more sound in mind and spirit, more open-minded and generous-hearted, and both more thoughtful regarding the challenges they face and more resolute when facing them. Through a curriculum calculated to empower, through classrooms illumined by the brilliance of insightful and caring professors, through technology that prepares students for the workplaces of the future, and through a context that builds a spirit of civic service, The Ohio State University upholds its pledge to provide the best public education in our state.

To Provide Opportunity, Knowledge, and Power to All Who Have the Skill to Pursue Them

The Morrill Act of 1862 established land-grant universities for the explicit purpose of supporting the people of each state. In a time when institutes of higher education were frequently the retreats of the wealthy elite, land-grant universities held forth the promise that higher education would one day be the just right of all who possessed the talent and tenacity to pursue it. The Ohio State University was one such institution and has unyieldingly shattered barriers to college access for its students. This land-grant ethos is made manifest in the university's commitment to inclusivity, affordability, flexibility, and sustainability. Every year for the past five years, the OSU student body has become more diverse and is increasingly reflective of our true national character. A plethora of different funds and initiatives focus on increasing the diverse perspectives of our school and on making it easier for minoritized groups, like people of color and single parents, to fulfill their educational potential. For example, the Morrill Scholarship Program provides free tuition to diverse student applicants who demonstrate leadership in civic service and social justice activities, and the ACCESS Collaborative Program provides single parents with unique scholarships, childcare, mentoring, and housing assistance. Due to efforts like these, the Education Trust has ranked OSU as one of the top five schools in the nation for improving the graduation rates of minoritized students, most especially members of the LGBTQI community. These efforts are buttressed by the fellowship provided by community support groups and student groups like Buckeyes for Appalachia and the First-Generation Student Association that ensure our students feel the welcome and sense of belonging in our community that they deserve.

The Ohio State University also actively cultivates the next generation for college success and civic leadership. The Make College Happen Initiative works with students from fourth through tenth grade and provides them with the guidance, inspiration, and resources they need to become successful applicants to the greatest college in the state of Ohio. Every year, dozens of our undergraduates participate in the College Mentors for Kids program, where they inspire students to believe in themselves and to viscerally comprehend that, no matter their background, they too can attend and graduate from college. The university takes fierce pride in its mission to transform our society through providing opportunities for social mobility, most especially to capable students who are the first in their family to attend college, or who are from economically disadvantaged backgrounds. To accomplish this, OSU has joined the American Talent Initiative, which has resulted in the university enrolling 7 percent more financially disadvantaged students last year than the year prior. When first-generation students arrive, they can receive specialized mentorship through the Young Scholars Program, participate in the Upward Bound Summer Institute to ease their transition to college life, and when disaster strikes, they can even apply for free grants of up to $500 for things like car repairs or medical costs through the First-Generation Student Emergency Fund.

It is a core value of the university that one's intellectual prowess and dedication should be the determinants of their entrance to the school—not their financial situation, or that of their immediate family. To this end, The Ohio State University ensures that those with the talent can attend, succeed, and thrive. Last year alone, the university distributed over $370 million in financial aid and is currently ranked by *The Chronicle of Higher Education* as the *best school* in the nation for providing affordable in-state tuition. In 2015, OSU instituted a freeze on tuition, fees, and housing and dining costs that will remain until the year 2021—and even as tuition has flatlined, the university has sought to reduce the cost of attendance for students by eliminating 70 percent of course fees and saving students nearly $2 million every single year.

Furthermore, our university has committed to providing in-state tuition to veterans and active military members, their spouses, and their children, no matter where in the nation they reside, and making it easy for them to transfer credits into and out of the OSU system so their educational accomplishments can be justly recognized. Finally, the university recognizes the unique financial difficulties faced by some families that can make sending a student to college unusually difficult.

For example, even with a Pell Grant and the fullest possible funding from state and federal financial aid, students with powerful financial need may still face a gap of up to $3,500 in the cost of attendance each year. Therefore, President Drake has provided over $100 million to the Buckeye Opportunity Program that will fill that funding gap for every single student who needs it, and he has doubled the yearly allocation of Land-grant Opportunity Scholarships that provide bright students from impoverished families with free room, board, and fees. Finally, the university now provides $1,000 Completion Grants for those who have nearly completed their degree, but whose sudden financial need might prevent them from graduating.

The Ohio State University is also committed to providing a quality education to brilliant students no matter where they are. Our five regional campuses in Lima, Mansfield, Marion, Newark, and Wooster enroll over 7,000 students and act as community and education centers that intertwine our university with the cultures and concerns of many other parts of the state. Furthermore, as the state's digital flagship university, OSU provides some of the best distance education in the nation. Offering twenty-four self-paced programs that can be completed almost entirely online, The Ohio State University ensures that nontraditional students have the flexibility to learn what they need, when they need it, no matter how far they are from a campus. As part of our commitment to these students, the university waives all campus fees for them; has worked with industry partners to increasingly offer inexpensive, high-quality, open-source textbooks; and offers them in-state tuition, even if they live in another state. As a result of these efforts, *U.S. News and World Report* lists OSU as third in the nation for providing quality online undergraduate education.

Conclusion

The Ohio State University encompasses more than its constituent parts; it is more than a place, more than a center of research, more than a community—it is a promise. For 150 years and counting, The Ohio State University has been a proclamation of enduring possibility: a bold assertion that within our halls, you shall not be defined by what you have previously been, but rather, by what you have it in you to become. It is a solemn pledge vowing that our professors and staff shall pour the mighty torrents of their intellect and energies into the mental cultivation of the ready student, no matter their background. It is a covenant that we shall not hold ourselves separate from our people, that we shall not hoard our knowledge in the inaccessible vaults of an ivory tower, but rather, that we shall work hand in hand to build an ivory city, and ivory nation, and ivory world.

This is our singular nature and the unique promise that makes us who we are. Just as they always have, the doors of the university remain open to its people, its hands eternally outstretched to future generations, and should you decide to enter our halls, to become a Buckeye, to join this mighty endeavor, then the promise of The Ohio State University shall abide in you as well.

Insider Observations

23

The State of Ohio Leadership Institute

TREVOR L. BROWN

As an adolescent in the late 1930s, John Glenn sat transfixed in a high school civics classroom. His teacher, Hartford Steele, educated the sons and daughters of New Concord, Ohio, on the virtues of democracy, the basic structure and operation of the American system of representative government, and the duties of citizenship. A few years later, with the world still reeling from a global financial crisis and in the throes of a multicontinent war, Glenn answered the call to serve his country. Thus began a life of service in which Glenn became a decorated Marine fighter pilot in World War II and Korea, the first American to orbit the earth, a four-term US senator, and the oldest human being to travel in space. When asked what had inspired him to serve and ultimately lead, Glenn pointed straight back to Steele and his civics classes.

By exposing students to new information and equipping them with skills to perform tasks they were unable to undertake when left to their own devices, formal education can be a transformative experience. But can formal education grow civically oriented leaders like Senator Glenn? Can professional development and training prepare public officials for today's highly divided political environment? Glenn believed it could. In the final chapter of his life, after he retired from the Senate in 1999, Glenn devoted his eighties and nineties to building an institution of higher education that could, in his words, "inspire citizenship and develop leadership" for public service. His efforts resulted in the creation of the John Glenn College of Public Affairs at The Ohio State University in 2015; in his name, the college offers an array of formal educational programs to help prepare the next generation of public servants and elected leaders. In 2017, the Glenn College expanded its offerings by receiving funds from the state of Ohio legislature to create the State of Ohio Leadership Institute, a resource designed to prepare the next generation of Ohio's state and local elected officials through training programs and the provision of information to inform public decision-making.

This essay provides an overview of the impetus and the need for the State of Ohio Leadership Institute, identifies the audiences it is to serve, describes the principles used in program design, and details its component programs. Taken together, this discussion shows how a public land-grant institution can design and deliver programs to serve an important constituency—state and local elected officials and the citizenry they serve. The Ohio State University embraced the opportunity to build the State of Ohio Leadership Institute because of its fundamental alignment with the university's motto, "disciplina en civitatem," or "education for citizenship."

The Need and the Impetus for the State of Ohio Leadership Institute

On November 3, 1992, a majority of Ohio voters approved amendments limiting the terms of state elected officials. Issues 3 and 4 limited state senators to two successive four-year terms, state representatives to four successive two-year terms, and the lieutenant governor, secretary of state, treasurer of state, attorney general, and auditor to two successive four-year terms. The impetus of the term-limit movement in Ohio (and nationally) was to provide opportunities for more "citizen" legislators to bring new and innovative ideas to government and increase the accountability of elected officials to voters.

As expected, turnover in state elected offices has increased. In the last decade, Ohio's elected officials have served in their roles for shorter periods of time than in the past. An unintended consequence of term limits has been the loss of institutional knowledge among elected officials about Ohio's government, the major policy issues facing the state, and the ethical requirements of representing the public. While each election brings a new collection of Ohio citizens into office, it also ushers out many officials who have gained expertise about how Ohio's government functions and the important details about what policy approaches have worked and what approaches have not. With less time in office, state legislators have a shorter time horizon for the policy and fiscal changes they consider.

The turnover at the state level has also had cascading impacts at lower levels. With state-level term limits opening up elected positions more frequently, local elected officials—city council members, mayors, county officials—have left their offices to run for state office. The same loss of institutional knowledge and short time horizon among state elected officials now exists at the county and local levels as well.

The character of elections and policy making has also changed. Elections are designed to provide citizens a choice between candidates competing for office with different sets of public priorities and alternative solutions to address those priorities. In recent elections, political discourse has gone from objective debates about alternative policy proposals to a more negative portrayal of candidates, parties, and constituents. Newly elected representatives face less electoral pressure to make decisions that take different constituent perspectives into account. Incivility is on the rise and collaboration across party lines is rare.

The result is that every two years, scores of newly elected officials take state and local offices in Ohio fresh from victory in sometimes combative campaigns; with limited knowledge about the structure, operation, and financing of Ohio government; and with short time horizons for Ohio's future.

In the winter of 2019, the Glenn College conducted a series of focus groups with Ohio state and local elected officials and civil servants about their need for leadership training to prepare for service in democratic institutions—city councils, county commissions, the state legislature, publicly accountable police departments, and government agencies. The focus group participants uniformly reported a need for leadership development in a partisan context. One respondent highlighted the pressure of serving in a highly divided time: "It's a strange feeling after getting elected. You realize that half of your constituents don't like you because of your party affiliation." This insight aligns with national findings; a November 2018 Pew survey found that 44 percent of Americans expect relations between Republicans and Democrats in Washington will get worse in the coming year. This is up from only 28 percent in November 2010.

Another focus group respondent articulated the burden of public leadership by feeling the pressure to serve all those in their community, regardless of their political affiliation: "Balancing what I want to accomplish with what we can realistically do is a challenge. I think I know what we need to do, but it's impossible to satisfy everyone." Another chimed in,

"I feel strongly about being a public servant. I have a lot to learn. I don't want to let people down."

In 2018 the Volcker Alliance, a national nonprofit named after former Federal Reserve chairman Alan Greenspan and devoted to advancing effective management in government, conducted an extensive survey of public servants across levels of government in the US and found similar results. Over half of all respondents across levels of government (and 72 percent of state respondents) indicated that they needed professional development for leading in a democratic context.

Partisan competition makes leading in a democracy difficult—diverse political constituencies often want policies that pursue competing values (e.g., equality of outcome versus equality of opportunity). This poses vexing challenges for many newly elected or appointed leaders. One focus group respondent revealed, "After four years [in elected office], I feel like I am finally beginning to know what's going on, but I have so much more to learn. People think they know democracy. I don't know democracy!"

The Vision of The State of Ohio Leadership Institute

Ohio is America. Ohio is home to the seventh largest population in the country, is fourteenth among states in agricultural production, and has three of the US's forty largest metropolitan areas (only Texas and California have more major metro areas). Ohio's demographic makeup mirrors the demography of the country. Ohio is the consummate political swing state—the last candidate to win the US presidency without carrying Ohio was John F. Kennedy in 1960.

Ohio needs value-driven elected officials that are knowledgeable about the structure, operation, and financing of state and local government. For elected officials to create innovative and effective solutions to the economic development, education, criminal justice, and health care challenges that face the state and its communities, they need analytical, financial, and managerial skills. They also need to be ethical, civil, and collaborative. They need to be leaders capable of long-term thinking in a world of term limits.

The vision of the State of Ohio Leadership Institute is to prepare and develop Ohio's elected and appointed officials as ethical leaders driven to deliver value to the constituents, customers, and citizens of Ohio over the long term. The State of Ohio Leadership Institute's target audience includes elected and appointed officials at the state and local levels:

- Executive and legislative elected officials
- High-ranking policy staffers (e.g., chiefs of staff and policy directors)
- Agency heads and principal staff
- County commissioners
- Auditors
- Treasurers
- Elected county council members (Cuyahoga and Summit)
- Elected city council members
- Mayors and city managers
- Township trustees and administrators

By delivering programming across levels, the State of Ohio Leadership Institute contributes to institutional continuity across elected and appointed offices—a common grounding in elected leadership training will ensure that as officials leave one office, those replacing them will be equipped with the knowledge, skills, and values needed to deliver value to Ohio's citizens over the long term.

The State of Ohio Leadership Institute offers leadership training to state and local elected officials through a variety of short-term and long-term educational programs. The training programs are intended to complement rather than duplicate existing training for newly elected and appointed officials (e.g., the governor's LEAD Ohio program, the Legislative Service Commission's New Member Orientation). The institute's leadership programs offer coursework in the following areas:

- Knowledge and understanding of the basic structure and operation of state and local government in Ohio.
- Knowledge and understanding of state and local public finance (e.g., bonding, contracting, general revenue funds), fiscal analysis and dynamic financial modeling, positional fiscal authority, and ultimately fiduciary responsibility for serving as an elected or appointed official.
- Knowledge and understanding of key policy areas that impact the state and Ohio's localities (e.g., K–12 education, regulation and privatization, workforce development, regional and community development, transportation, energy, utilities, health care, criminal justice).
- Public sector leadership skills and competencies (public policy analysis, public administration and management, team building and motivation, political and managerial communication, economics and public budgeting and finance).

- Cultivation and development of core public values (service, equity, justice, fairness, accountability, transparency).

The institute relies on four basic means through which it trains the next generation of Ohio's state and local elected officials:

- The Public Leadership Academy
- Short-term workshops on leadership skills and knowledge areas
- Student internships in state and local offices
- Leadership symposia and conferences

Public Leadership Academy

The core institute program—the Public Leadership Academy—provides cohorts of recently elected and appointed state and local officials knowledge, skills, and values for leadership through one-week and two-week residential programs. Graduates of the Public Leadership Academy will receive a certificate signifying successful completion of study. Each year, the academy welcomes a new cohort of participants to receive an intensive residential course of study and practice in leadership development for public service. Prospective participants apply to the academy, and a selection committee composed of important internal and external stakeholders reviews applications to build a cohort for each year. The competitive and objective review process includes input from current elected and appointed leaders, who are also welcome to nominate potential participants. The goal is to create cohorts that mix elected and appointed officials across levels of government and parties. Having diverse participants helps build a culture of trust and civility that will carry forward after the training program is complete.

The academy course of study integrates four component parts.

Part I—Values

Each academy cohort program starts with an orientation to build connections among the cohort and embrace the values that drive ethical elected leaders. By starting with team building and value immersion, participants are immediately connected to their peers and create the norms and standards that will guide their course of study.

Part II—Knowledge

The next step is to build the knowledge base of Ohio's system of state and local governance and finance. Participants work with local, state, and national leaders and experts to learn the basic structure and operation of state and local government, administration, and finance. Each participant receives an understanding of not only their office or position but also how their office or position fits into the larger system of governance in Ohio.

Part III—Skills

The third phase of training is to equip participants with the core set of skills required to be an effective leader. Training includes hands-on sessions in strategic communication, policy analysis, forecasting, and budgeting, to name a few. The combination of values, knowledge, and skills positions participants to put solutions into action. In particular, skill development focuses on crafting policies to address pressing issues facing the state and then moving proposed policies through the legislative process and into implementation.

Part IV—Application

The final phase of the program is to apply the knowledge and skills. Each cohort is broken into teams to focus on a major challenge facing the state. Teams work together (note again that each team will be composed of participants from different levels of government and different parties) to craft a solution and plan for implementation.

Short-Term Workshops on Leadership Skills and Knowledge Areas

The institute also offers leadership training in shorter increments (e.g., one week at night or a full-day workshop) on specific content and skills. Newly elected officials who were not selected for the academy or who are unable to commit to the full course of study can take these shorter courses to build their leadership skills. For example, in the fall of 2018, the Leadership Institute partnered with the Ohio Legislative Services Commission to offer new member training for all the newly elected members of the Ohio House and Senate. The institute also worked with the political leadership of the Ohio House to offer professional development training for staff members.

Student Internships in State and Local Offices

In an effort to attract young people to public service, the institute also coordinates internships in state and local offices for college and high school students. The purpose is to create a positive work experience that inspires students to pursue public service and elected office in the state. The State of Ohio Leadership Institute also launched the Ohio Public Service Internship Network to serve as a clearinghouse of best practices and an information-sharing network for other public and private universities across the state that offer public sector internship programs. In this way, the Leadership Institute serves as a hub for connecting other universities in promoting public service.

Leadership Symposia and Conferences

Throughout the year, the Leadership Institute also participates in or sponsors symposia and conferences open to a broad audience of elected and appointed state and local officials on leadership issues in the public sector. These symposia and conferences showcase national leadership experts and innovative public leaders throughout the state and across the nation who are making change in their organizations and their communities.

Conclusion

The requirement for institutions of higher education, at least in Ohio, to invest in training and preparation for today's public leaders appears clear. In an effort to create an informed and engaged citizenry, public land-grant institutions have a duty to serve more than the residential undergraduate and graduate students who enroll in the formal degree programs. The Ohio State University is committed to serving the breadth of the state's "students," including state and local elected and appointed officials. Senator Glenn's experience as a student of civics convinced him—one of the few people to serve in combat, navigate the stars, and represent his constituents—that the need to invest in public leadership was as important now as it was when he signed up to serve the cause of liberty almost a century ago.

References

Pew Research Center. 2018. "More Americans Expect Partisan Relations to Get Worse Than Did So after Three Prior Midterms." https://www.people-press.org/2018/11/15/public-expects-gridlock-deeper-divisions-with-changed-political-landscape/g2_new/.

The Volcker Alliance. 2018. *Preparing Tomorrow's Public Service: What the Next Generation Needs.* https://www.volckeralliance.org/publications/preparing-tomorrows-public-service.

24

Why We Count

Using Data to Be Our Best Selves

Julia W. Carpenter-Hubin

Information collections about education have existed for as long as there have been teachers and students. The gleam in Plato's eye and reasoned questions he asked as Socrates discussed a problem served as evidence of understanding—the same informal, yet reassuring evidence that faculty collect today in classroom discussions. More formal data collections and research are ages old as well. According to noted Stanford and former Ohio State psychology professor W. H. Cowley, Yale University engaged in such research in 1701, the year in which that institution was founded: "The founders of Yale, after reviewing the single governing board structures of Scottish universities and the University of Dublin, had adopted a similar structure, which differed from the dual governing board structures of Harvard and William and Mary, the only two American colleges then in existence" (Reichard 2012, 4). This analysis, with roughly a dozen data points, may well be, as Cowley notes, the very first example of an "institutional research" study.

As The Ohio State University reaches its sesquicentennial, so too does the formal collection of student data in the US. In 1869–1870, the federal Office of Education began collecting education data, including information on college and university enrollments and degrees conferred (Snyder 1993). At that time, enrollments across all higher education institutions for which data was gathered (there was no central list of all institutions of higher education) totaled 63,000, or less than the current combined enrollment of the six Ohio State campuses.

Today, American colleges and universities, including Ohio State, participate in a variety of data and information collections. Nearly all take part in the federal Integrated Postsecondary Education Data System (IPEDS) collection. Public universities share data with state education officials. National associations facilitate data sharing between institutional members. The number of collections by media outlets and private organizations has grown over the years, with each collection differing enough to claim a unique perspective. And of course, data and information are collected for internal use to support institutional improvement and strategic decision-making. These data collections have had, and continue to have, both positive and negative impacts on higher education. This chapter will look at the impacts of various data and information collections through the lens of The Ohio State University and its land-grant mission.

Federal collection of higher education data has grown tremendously both in scope and in scale since that initial collection in 1879. Today's IPEDS data collection evolved from the Higher Education General Information Surveys (HEGIS), administered between 1966–1967 and 1986–1987. IPEDS was phased in between 1985–1986 and 1988–1989, and initially included "all institutions whose primary purpose was providing postsecondary education programs and that were open to the general public" (Fuller 2011, 6). Under the National Center for Education Statistics, IPEDS amasses data from over 6,700 institutions of higher education in the US, ranging in scope and size from career schools enrolling as few as two postsecondary students to the University of Phoenix, with well over 100,000 students. The data collection includes the original HEGIS information on institutional characteristics, enrollments, degrees granted, and finance. It has also expanded to include data on student retention and graduation rates, financial aid, numbers of employees and salary outlays by job type, and information on library collections, as well as more detailed information on numbers of degrees granted by level and by discipline, and revenue and expenditures. In 2000–2001, IPEDS moved to a fully web-based system, both for data collection and for publication (Burns and Wang 2011), providing easier access to higher education data for colleges and universities themselves, but also to government entities, the media, and the general population.

In 1966, the same year that HEGIS was initiated, the Ohio Board of Regents (OBOR) developed its Uniform Information System. Reports included information on enrollments, staffing, finances, and physical facilities, and these data were submitted using punch cards or magnetic tapes. Over time, this has evolved into the OBOR Higher Education Information System, a comprehensive relational database that includes student enrollment, course, financial aid, personnel, facilities, and finance data submitted by Ohio's public colleges and universities. Both systems were developed in consultation with participating institutions, including Ohio State, and the data are used both by OBOR and by participating institutions for a variety of purposes that include reporting on higher education outcomes, funding formula and financial aid program support, policy analysis, and strategic planning.

The state and federal data collections allowed colleges and universities to do comparative analyses, which inevitably led to more questions that then required more data and information. Ohio State and the other research-intensive institutions that make up the Association of American Universities (AAU) began a private data exchange in 1974 of faculty teaching load and salary information to support comparative analyses and benchmarking. Represented initially by Madison Scott and Sherrill Cloud, Ohio State joined the exchange in April of 1974, and has participated ever since. The number of information items exchanged quickly grew, and by 1979, members of AAU Data Exchange (AAUDE) were also sharing data on compensation for teaching assistants, administrative salaries and job descriptions, and fall term credit enrollment. Like the IPEDS data, the shared information was first exchanged via paper reports; today member institutions upload data on an ever-growing number of topics to a sophisticated data warehouse located at the Massachusetts Institute of Technology, an AAUDE member institution.

These data collections have proven invaluable to Ohio State, as they allow us to compare our performance in specific areas to that of other universities like us. Comparative compensation data help us attract and retain the best faculty, staff, and graduate associates. Doctoral completion rates and time to degree by discipline at similar institutions tell us where we need to invest and improve. The most useful AAUDE information exchange is perhaps the ad hoc query, which allows member institutions to pose questions to the entire group. AAUDE ad hoc queries have informed OSU policies on graduate fellowship, faculty workload, and childcare programs, to name but a few. The federal and state exchanges support accountability both to the public and to the governmental or other structures that support them, and they provide data to multiple public audiences, including higher education researchers and the general public.

Data are only useful to those who can translate numbers into accurate information and then take the time to do so. While all the aforementioned data collections are valuable within the higher education community and to various government entities, they do not directly address the needs of most of the general public. Data on graduation rates, for example, could appear to provide a student success measure; if the desired outcome for college students is a completed degree within four years, it could seem reasonable that the four-year graduation rate would be a useful student success metric. Comparing the four-year graduation rates of two institutions, however, one with a rate of 60 percent and another with a rate of 80 percent, tells you nothing about the likelihood of an individual student's success unless you combine it with information about the qualifications and predicted likelihood of success for each institution's first-year students. Prospective students, their families, and the general public need an unbiased and easy-to-understand source of useful information on higher education. In the 1980s, entrepreneurial magazine publishers saw an opportunity to expand their audience and stepped forward to assist.

Among the publications to first take up this opportunity was *U.S. News and World Report* (*USNWR*), which first published college rankings in 1983. Based entirely on survey responses from college presidents, these early *USNWR* rankings were published every other year, with the survey findings first published as a stand-alone guidebook in 1987. In 1988, *USNWR* incorporated objective information, including data on school selectivity and resources. Not only did the magazine pull together information about colleges and universities in a much friendlier format than had previously existed, but it created rankings so that students and parents could rely on a single number calculated through what appeared to be a thoughtful approach to evaluating higher education. The *USNWR* rankings proved tremendously popular. While they no longer publish data about their website traffic, the release of their 2014 Best Colleges rankings resulted in "2.6 million unique visitors and 18.9 million page views in a single day" (*U.S. News & World Report* 2013). Not surprisingly, a host of additional national and international rankings have been developed over the past several decades. *Forbes Top Colleges,* the *Wall Street Journal/Times Higher Ed College Rankings,* the *QS University Rankings, Washington Monthly,* and *Niche Best Colleges in*

America are but a few additional sources for undergraduate institutional or program rankings; several of these provide similar rankings for graduate programs as well. Other rankings, such as the Academic Rankings of World Universities, focus primarily on the accomplishments of an institution's faculty. Ohio State's Office of Institutional Research and Planning currently tracks seventeen different college and university rankings from eleven different publishers, and many of these produce additional rankings at the disciplinary level.

In the early days of rankings, many of the data used were in fact the same data that institutions provided for federal reporting. Retention and graduation rates, numbers of faculty, and cost of attendance were among the common data points requested by rankings producers, and these remain important in today's rankings. But as more media outlets and consulting companies made ranking higher education institutions their business, each had to find a way to differentiate their rankings product. More and more of the data that any one rankings company or media outlet requires must now be provided specifically for them by colleges and universities, so that each ranking organization can publish a unique perspective.

By complying with the demands of these publishers, colleges and universities have allowed themselves to be evaluated and graded through their rankings, which are more numerous than ever. We have ceded evaluation of our work to entities that have little interaction with us, and whose primary motivation is profit rather than student success. We have allowed them to grade our work without determining first whether they have any qualifications to evaluate us, or whether their metrics are aligned with our purpose. Colleges and universities across the full range of missions saw Harvard, Princeton, and Yale at the top of a list and felt both subtle and not-so-subtle pressures to compete for prestige and accolades with these elite institutions. Such competition can be healthy and lead to positive change when the rules are clear, fair, and appropriately support the desired goals. A significant problem with rankings, however, is that they primarily define performance by the outcomes, rather than the value added. This is an issue worthy of further examination.

Few, if any, rankings pay heed to mission, ranking land-grant and Ivy League universities together on outcomes, and not on the contribution of the institution. Many of the rankings producers compare graduation rates and postgraduation salaries across universities. These are important metrics, and they provide information that is important to students and their families. But if we do not consider the starting point for these students—what high school they came from, the average math and English ACT scores for students from those schools, and the average income for their families—then our analyses begin with a false equivalency that is really quite problematic. Consider the possibility of ranking investment firms on the total wealth of their clients rather than on their increase in wealth due to smart and well-informed investments. We can imagine two firms. The first has a client with $100,000 to invest, and after five years, that client's investment has grown to $101,000. Another has a client with $25,000 to invest, and after five years, that client's investment has grown to $50,000. If we calculate outcomes for the investment firms the way we primarily calculate higher education outcomes today, the $100,000 client had a better investment firm because they have ended the measurement period with more total wealth.

And that is exactly what we do with colleges and universities. The highly selective colleges and universities accept only those high school graduates who scored the highest on standardized tests, had exceptional grades, and participated in an amazing range of activities. When these institutions do well by those students, propelling 95 percent of them on to academic and then career success, they absolutely deserve a top ranking. But we ought not accept the perspective that such a university is a better institution than one that accepts students who have struggled to overcome financial, educational, or personal obstacles, and then helps 75 percent of them to reach their potential. The starting point matters. Ohio State and other land-grant institutions cannot turn away from their mission to serve the populace in order to choose only those members of the populace that best serve the institution's rankings. To their credit, *USNWR* has included a metric based on the predicted and actual graduation rates since 1998, and that attempts to include the institution's contribution to student success. This measure, however, counts for less than 10 percent of the overall ranking.

Rankings generally measure what is easily measured and ignore the work that is difficult to quantify. It is fairly straightforward to calculate retention and graduation rates for students, or to count the number of articles published in prestigious journals and the citations associated with those articles at a national level and to make comparisons across institutions and individual researchers. Comprehensive universities, and land-grant universities in particular, bring complexity to any attempts to evaluate and compare outcomes, however. It is more challenging to determine, across institutions, states, and even countries, which dance or musical performances are highly prestigious and then determine a ranking. And while the Association of Public and Land-grant Universities (APLU) Council on Engagement and Outreach and the Committee on Institutional Cooperation (CIC) Committee on Engagement both initiated efforts to develop agreed-upon metrics to evaluate and compare the outcomes of institutional outreach and engagement activities and programs, these efforts waned, largely due to the variety of programs across institutions (Bargerstock and Fitzgerald 2011). As a land-grant institution, Ohio State has a commitment to outreach to and engagement with the community. We can evaluate the success and value of each of our outreach activities, but it is problematic, and almost certainly counterproductive, to apply metrics that score those activities against each other. It is difficult to see the value in developing a scoring mechanism that pits, for example, a program focused on alleviating poverty through entrepreneurship against one that teaches parents how to cook healthy, kid-friendly meals while helping children to learn kitchen skills.

In his address to the university in 2014, President Michael Drake stated, "Our vision to continue our ascendancy among leading land-grant universities will require our very best selves." As Ohio State moves beyond its first 150 years, we must continue to follow our own path to excellence without falling prey to the siren song of popular but vapid rankings. We will no doubt continue to pay attention to these external metrics, but we must prioritize our performance measures based on what we know matters most to our students, faculty, and staff, as well as to the larger community we serve as a land-grant institution.

References

Bargerstock, Burton A., and Hiram E. Fitzgerald. 2011. *Aligning a Research Intensive University with an Engagement Mission: Measures and Metrics.* http://ncsue.msu.edu/files/AligningMeasuresandMetrics10222011.pdf.

Burns, Shelley K., and Xiaolei Wang. 2011. *NCES Handbook of Survey Methods.* https://nces.ed.gov/statprog/handbook/ipeds.asp.

Drake, Michael V. 2014. "The Heart of Innovation: Our 21st-Century Land-Grant Mission." University address, October 30, 2014. https://president.osu.edu/21st-century-land-grant-mission.

Fuller, C. 2011. *The History and Origins of Survey Items for the Integrated Postsecondary Education Data System.* Washington, DC: US Department of Education, National Postsecondary Education Cooperative. https://nces.ed.gov/pubs2012/2012833.pdf.

Reichard, Donald J. (2012). *The History of Institutional Research.* In *The Handbook of Institutional Research,* edited by Richard D. Howard, Gerald W. McLaughlin, William E. Knight, and Associates, 3–21. San Francisco, CA: Jossey-Bass.

Snyder, Thomas D., ed. 1993. *120 Years of American Education: A Statistical Portrait.* Washington, DC: US Department of Education, Office of Educational Research and Improvement, National Center for Education Statistics. https://nces.ed.gov/pubs93/93442.pdf.

U.S. News & World Report. 2013. "U.S. News Breaks Online Traffic Record." September 12, 2013. https://www.usnews.com/info/blogs/press-room/2013/09/12/us-news-breaks-online-traffic-record.

25

The Model Land-Grant Library at Ohio State

DAMON E. JAGGARS

Central to fulfilling the promise of the nation's public land-grant universities, often described as "the people's universities," is an active, progressive commitment to the core missions that drove their founding and subsequent development: broadened access to affordable higher education and the dissemination of research for community benefit. An essential element enabling the teaching, research, and public outreach missions that motivate land-grant universities is the academic research library, the entity entrusted with providing the information services needed to educate an ever-changing student body and fuel knowledge creation across the academic disciplines, as they respond to the challenges that confront local communities and the wider society and culture.

The most successful libraries are those that strive to effectively align with and integrate their efforts into the priorities and activities of their parent institutions. Within the land-grant context, success for a library should be measured not only by traditional markers of quality, such as collection size, but by how well it advances core land-grant values and missions as expressed through initiatives guided by university-level priorities. Land-grant academic research libraries are not in the "library" business in isolation; rather, they exist to further the objectives of their sponsoring institutions and, in doing so, must continuously adjust and transform as the tools and methods for realizing teaching, research, and outreach missions evolve.

The Ohio State University Libraries aspires to be the leading library elevating the values and missions of a flagship public land-grant university. As its overarching mission, the Libraries "promotes innovative research and creative expression, advances effective teaching, curates and preserves information essential for scholarship and learning at Ohio State, and shares knowledge and culture with the people of Ohio, the nation, and the world" (The Ohio State University University Libraries 2018). This work requires purposeful alignment with the university's strategic priorities and deep integration with institutional activities that support enterprise-level goals and objectives. For the University Libraries, the lion's share of this work is framed within three broadly conceived areas of endeavor:

- Equipping students for lifelong success
- Empowering knowledge creators
- Engaging for broader impact

The initiatives and projects upholding these thematic pillars are reinforced by activities focused on the iterative, ongoing development of the organization and the faculty, staff, and student employees who sustain it. All of this is done with the goals of increasing efficacy and shaping innovative approaches for meeting the institution's educational, research, and outreach objectives—to model the activities of a modern, agile, and effectual academic research library and how it should operate for maximum impact.

Equipping Students for Lifelong Success

To activate the university's broad student success agenda, the Libraries strives to promote equitable learning outcomes through the support of transformational teaching in the classroom and progressive services furthering student learning and college affordability. Activities sustaining student success begin with the Libraries' long-standing commitment to the university's First Year Experience and Second-Year Transformational Experience Program initiatives, both aimed at raising retention and completion rates by enhancing the student experience for early career undergraduates. The Libraries also partners with the Office of Undergraduate Research each year to fund multiple undergraduate research fellowships designed to expose students to how scholarship is created, communicated, and disseminated through work with library collections and with guidance from librarian mentors.

The Libraries' support for teaching and learning effectiveness includes a strategic partnership with the University Institute for Teaching and Learning, the campus body charged with enriching teaching and improving the learning experience for students at Ohio State. This maturing partnership entails locating the institute within Thompson Library, the iconic main library facility on the Oval—the heart of campus—as well as a growing slate of co-investments in teaching enrichment. These involve the creation of several teaching-enhancement trainings designed and taught by Ohio State librarians, including a self-paced, interactive online workshop that prepares instructors to purposefully integrate information literacy and critical thinking concepts into their courses, and a five-part workshop series that introduces instructors to equitable and inclusive pedagogical practices for incorporating information literacy and critical inquiry into research and writing assignments.

The Libraries is also focused on advancing twenty-first-century literacies to help better prepare students for a rapidly changing society, including boosting competencies in using data and evaluating media with cross-cultural and ethical fluency. A highlight in this area is the Designing for Meaningful Inquiry grant program, created, in partnership with the Center for the Study and Teaching of Writing, to incentivize instructors to design or revise course assignments with the goal of expanding information literacy and critical reading skills by engaging students' identities and interests through well-constructed research-based writing assignments.

To further the university's aggressive affordability agenda, the Libraries invests as a strategic partner in the Affordable Learning Exchange (ALX), an initiative designed to encourage and assist faculty in reducing the overall cost of a college education by lowering the cost of course materials. ALX partners, led by the Office of Distance Education and eLearning, work with instructors to cut costs for students utilizing a "one size does *not* fit all" approach. With an emphasis on maintaining or improving the student learning experience, solutions range from the adoption of lower-cost textbooks to free open educational resources, which can include materials accessible from Ohio State's library collections to content authored by the instructor to online readings found in the public domain.

Librarians from Ohio State also participate in the Ohio Open Ed Collaborative, a statewide effort to reduce the cost of textbooks and other course materials for students through the development of open educational resources. Working on project teams with faculty from across the state, Ohio State librarians have contributed to the creation of course content in various disciplines, most significantly in mathematics, as well as serving on the planning and assessment teams for the initiative. These and related initiatives have resulted in millions of dollars of savings for students—savings that will only increase as additional courses transition to more affordable options in the coming years.

Empowering Knowledge Creators

The Libraries catalyzes innovative research and creative expression at Ohio State by fostering, preserving, and sharing knowledge and scholarship. Librarians and curators build robust collections—world-class in some areas—to support both research and teaching. Areas of particular strength include the Jerome Lawrence and Robert E. Lee Theatre Research Institute performing arts collections; the Hilandar Research Library, the largest collection of medieval Slavic manuscripts on microform in the world; the distinctive collections housed in the Rare Books and Manuscripts Library, which includes the renowned William Charvat Collection of American Fiction; and the Billy Ireland Cartoon Library & Museum, the world's largest collection of materials related to cartoons and comics. In addition to the University Archives, which serves as the official memory of Ohio State, having collected more than 30,000 linear feet of manuscript material and more than two million photographs documenting Buckeye history, the Libraries houses the Byrd Polar Archives, chronicling the history of polar exploration, and the Ohio Congressional Archives, anchored by the archives of Ohio politician and astronaut John Glenn. The Libraries also holds significant international collections supporting Chinese and Korean, East European and Slavic, Japanese, Jewish, Latin American, and Middle Eastern studies.

Though the collection of scholarly and cultural heritage materials is critical for future research, employing new methods to acquire, preserve, and ultimately use collections is equally important for bolstering new, emerging research and educational methodologies across the scholarly disciplines. Complicating the playing field, the explosion of available published and archival information over the last quarter century, driven by the rapid adoption of computer, network, and media technologies, has, by necessity, pushed academic libraries into collaborative relationships with the goal of utilizing collective scale to build and provide access to collections.

For Ohio State, the Libraries maintains long-standing strategic partnerships for volume purchasing at the state and regional levels through OhioLINK and the Big Ten Academic Alliance (BTAA), which have resulted in the twin goods of vastly expanded content (articles, e-books, digitized archives, etc.) at greatly discounted costs owing to volume pricing. These same economies of scale are used to drive down costs through the relatively seamless sharing of books and other resources across OhioLINK and BTAA partners, reducing the need for member colleges and universities to purchase lesser-used materials or duplicate copies to fill short-term needs. Ohio State, stewarding the largest overall collection within Ohio and one of the largest within the BTAA, is currently the sixth largest lender of books and other materials within the global resource-sharing network. Through these collaborative endeavors, among others, the Libraries ensures that scholars around the world have access to Ohio State's collections, and in return, Ohio State faculty and students have access to hundreds of millions of books and other important research materials not held locally.

Similarly, the Libraries leverages multiple strategic partnerships to better and more efficiently store and preserve both print and electronic collections. Within Ohio, the Libraries operates the largest and busiest high-density storage and preservation facility within the statewide print repository network. Looking toward a future where the use of electronic books and other texts grows and the use of print continues to diminish, the Libraries is planning a program to secure and preserve unique copies of books with research value from across the state, the Ohio Last Copy Project, as partner colleges and universities look to de-emphasize lesser-used print collections and recapture space for other uses on their campuses. At the regional level, the Libraries is an active participant in the BTAA Shared Print Repository initiative, in which partners co-fund and maintain a shared collection of print journal backfile volumes, obviating the need for all to store duplicative content on each campus and freeing space in local facilities.

As usage of electronic content continues to surge, the Libraries looks to exploit economies found in building and utilizing shared infrastructures to store, preserve, and access digital books and other content. For instance, the Libraries is a member of the HathiTrust Digital Library, a digital preservation repository and access platform on which members store and provide access to books and other materials digitized locally and through large-scale efforts, such as the Google Books Library Project. As an OhioLINK partner, the Libraries also utilizes the Electronic Thesis and Dissertation Center platform to preserve and access all of the undergraduate and master's theses and doctoral dissertations produced at Ohio State. Both are examples of the Libraries partnering in collective efforts to deliver higher quality and more cost-effective solutions than isolated and duplicative local efforts could afford.

Apart from the provision and management of collections, the Libraries actively promotes knowledge creation through the Research Commons, both a space and a suite of services that scaffolds faculty and students in the learning and application of emerging, often computationally driven, methods and tools in their research. Created in partnership with the university's offices of Research and the Chief Information Officer, among others, the Research Commons offers expert assistance in finding, managing, and visualizing data; geographic information systems; digital humanities; and measuring research impact in a dynamic physical environment designed to nurture and celebrate collaborative, multidisciplinary work.

The Libraries' Copyright Services unit provides the Ohio State scholarly community expert guidance on the application of copyright law to facilitate teaching, research, and scholarship. This work entails consultations on everything from registering copyrights to navigating the use of copyrighted material for teaching to the intellectual property considerations involved in publishing research results. All of this is buttressed by a team of dedicated, subject specialist librarians—each expert in navigating the literature and research practices of their academic discipline—working diligently to ensure that the information necessary to fuel research and teaching is available and accessible to faculty and students.

The publishing of research results within the scholarly literature in many ways drives the academy, and the Libraries' Publishing Program works with faculty and students to publish their scholarly work in a variety of formats, with an emphasis on broadening free or low-cost publication as an alternative to more expensive commercial options. With the goal of promoting open access to Ohio State scholarship, the Libraries offers publishing and hosting services for academic journals and conference proceedings, as well as assistance to faculty who wish to teach academic publishing to their students through hands-on experience with writing, peer review, editing, and publication design. Projects range from publishing and hosting partnerships with journals such as *Disability Studies Quarterly* and *Empirical Musicology Review* to "new model" interactive, multimedia ventures like *Latinx Talk.*

As the costs of commercial scholarly publishing continue to rise, the Libraries participates in collaborative projects at the regional and national levels intended to disrupt untenable business practices and build more sustainable models for scholarly publishing. The Libraries is a leader in efforts within the BTAA and OhioLINK to change the business relationships between commercial scholarly publishers and university customers from one of ever-increasing subscription costs for content held behind paywalls to a model that funds the open access publication and reading of journal articles under more predictable and sustainable pricing structures. Relatedly, the Libraries invests in a series of initiatives, along with several partners within the Association of Research Libraries, to incentivize academic journals to move from high-cost commercial publishers to platforms owned or controlled by academic institutions, with the goals of reducing or eliminating subscription costs, providing open access to scholarship, and maintaining intellectual property for authors.

The Libraries also participates in the *TOME (Toward an Open Monograph Ecosystem)* initiative, a partnership between the American Association of Universities, the Association of Research Libraries, and the Association of University Presses, which seeks to broaden the dissemination of scholarship in the humanities and humanistic social sciences through the publication of digital open access editions of peer-reviewed and professionally edited monographs. Through *TOME,* the Libraries is investing $250,000 over five years to support Ohio State faculty members in publishing digital open access books that will be freely accessible worldwide for teaching, learning, and future research.

Engaging for Broader Impact

A defining feature of land-grant universities is their outreach to and engagement with the communities they serve. For the libraries at Ohio State, this manifests in the pursuit of initiatives aligned with university priorities that promote a more connected and better-informed society within Ohio and beyond. This work is often propelled by dynamic cross-campus and external partnerships, taking many different forms, that enable impact much greater than any one entity could deliver.

In this vein, the Libraries partners with multiple community-based organizations to aid underserved and at-risk communities throughout Central Ohio. These include an ongoing relationship with the Mid-Ohio Foodbank, an organization that helps over 500,000 people each year who struggle with food insecurity, for which Libraries' faculty and staff provide assistance through numerous volunteer and fund-raising projects. The Libraries also contributes ongoing support for Project Mentor, a mentoring program for primary and middle school students facilitated by Big Brothers, Big Sisters of Central Ohio. Through this program, Libraries faculty and staff present a positive role model and a caring ear to vulnerable children grappling with difficult academic, interpersonal, and home life issues.

Similarly, the Libraries advances an ongoing partnership with the Expanding Visions Foundation, a Columbus-based nonprofit that works with at-risk youth to provide career development and leadership training. Through this partnership, students from local high schools come to Ohio State to take part in a career institute designed to cultivate work and life skills while exposing them to a college campus, often for the first time. After completing the institute, students are encouraged to apply for a paid summer internship at the Libraries, working alongside professionals, receiving additional mentorship, and learning what work life is really like. The internship program is proving highly successful, resulting in several returning interns and some future Buckeyes, as students realize that attending college is achievable and Ohio State is home.

Through a robust calendar of public programming, including a wide range of exhibitions with accompanying speakers and panels, the Libraries promotes vigorous dialog on issues important to society. The Libraries' exhibition program aims to spur public engagement with thought-provoking topics reflected through professionally curated exhibits of materials from Ohio State's collections. Recent standout examples include *Front Line: Editorial Cartoonists and the First Amendment* and *Looking Forward, Looking Backward: U. S. Immigration in Cartoons and Comics* at the Billy Ireland Cartoon Library & Museum, and *Creative Responses to the Cold War* at the Thompson Library Gallery. Another highlight was the Libraries' participation in the citywide, yearlong celebration of Columbus native son James Thurber with local partners, including Thurber House and the Columbus Museum of Art in 2019. *Thurber's Columbus,* an exhibition focusing on his early years and pulling extensively from Ohio State's impressive collection of Thurber drawings, documented how his hometown shaped his imagination and offered a source of inspiration throughout his career.

Modeling Excellence

The people who embody the University Libraries, its faculty and staff, live a set of "land-grant" values in all that they do. Those values—discovery, connection, equity, integrity, and stewardship—permeate decision-making about what the organization will do and how it will allocate and deploy its effort. To fully meet its aspirations to be the model library serving a land-grant institution, the Libraries has set out a bold program, guided by these values, to prepare the organization and the people who compose it to operate and work differently.

Through extensive workforce development and organizational learning investments designed to build and strengthen a culture of leadership, risk-taking, and accountability, the Libraries strives to increase its strategic and operational effectiveness by developing the full potential of its faculty, staff, and student employees. A new agile planning and operations framework has been implemented that aims to facilitate an iterative, ongoing organizational conversation about the Libraries' strategic intent and how it will prioritize resources and effort to achieve its objectives. This ambitious new approach seeks to enable enhanced flexibility and responsiveness to unforeseen opportunities, as well as to effectively measure and communicate the Libraries' impact on fulfilling the university's land-grant missions and, ultimately, its promise as the people's university.

References

The Ohio State University University Libraries. 2018. "Strategic Directions." https://library.osu.edu/strategic-directions.

26

Ohio State Leadership

Rick Martin and Tayo Switzer

Leadership within an institution of higher education, particularly at The Ohio State University (OSU), follows many of the same principles that govern leadership in other kinds of organizations. Leadership must establish direction, must generate alignment and garner the commitment of people, and often involves leaders and followers. Followership, though, within a university often entails following a passion, a curiosity, an idea, a promising lead, an ideal, or a singular vision more than it entails following a person. Followership in this environment is different, because the institution is driven by the prototypical knowledge worker—faculty.

In order to fully appreciate what it takes to lead at a university, and in particular OSU, it is useful to illuminate further what it means to be a faculty member and that value to the institution. Faculty members exist to create and disseminate new knowledge. In a pedestrian way, they take the important accumulated knowledge on a given topic and translate that into a class that ideally helps students better understand their world and be successful in it—that is, they teach. They are also charged with creating, discovering, and inventing new ideas through research and creative expression. Last, they are expected to provide some service to the university or outreach to the community.

Excellence in these ventures looks like carving out a niche for oneself and becoming the world's expert in that niche. Sometimes it is referred to as creating extreme expertise that is an inch wide and a mile deep.

While perhaps something of a cliché, this points to how new knowledge, new thinking, and new discoveries are made—by committing oneself wholly to an endeavor, scouring the existing research, reading exhaustively what others have written on similar topics, and thinking long and hard. It involves coming up with novel approaches to things and failing your way to success. In some disciplines, this is a solitary undertaking; in other disciplines, it is a team sport. But the point here is that faculty are expected to become extremely knowledgeable about some things in order to (1) simplify and teach that something, without making it simplistic, and (2) discover the edges of what is known, tackle unsolvable problems, and follow their curiosity to new places.

Tenure is typically awarded to a junior faculty member after six or seven years of keeping their nose to the grindstone of research. Tenure, in part, is intended to free faculty from some of the tides of organizational life and allow them to freely follow their interests in the pursuit of new knowledge. The ranking of institutions is directly tied to how good faculty members do these things, especially the research part. While teaching is becoming more important, research and the funding that accompanies it are interconnected with high-quality graduate programs and intimately tied to departmental rankings and subsequently university rankings. Publishing, in most fields, is critical to those rankings and driven by the research and creative expression activities of faculty. So, yes, faculty members "report" to department chairs, who "report" to college deans, who "report" to the provost, who "reports" to the president. Yet, direction (or directions) from any one of these leaders doesn't ensure that most people will follow.

The leadership author Wilfred Drath, in his seminal book on leadership called *The Deep Blue Sea* (2001), talks about leadership as a sum of individuals and what is evident rather than pointing to individuals who are identified as the leaders. Leadership is evident if there is a perceived sense of direction, alignment, and commitment. The student, faculty, administrator, and legislator are the primary components of leadership of the university. Their combined efforts produce leadership. This has always been the way of Ohio State and is the only way in which to fulfill the land-grant mission and attend to the needs of the citizens of today.

At Ohio State, a foundational element of the leadership is a university senate, composed of 50 percent faculty, 30 percent students, and 20 percent staff administrators, which is a unique structure for shared governance among universities and intends to set a national example for what shared governance can be within a university. Established in its current form in 1972, the committees of the senate connect to all administrative offices within the university and work together with university administrators to develop and advise on policies, processes, and solutions for issues facing the university. As a consequence of this unique governance structure, leaders at Ohio State operate in a more interdependent fashion than most leaders in corporations and even in other institutions of higher education.

In their book *Engaging the Six Cultures of the Academy* (2008), William Bergquist and Kenneth Pawlak discuss six distinct subcultures that exist within many universities: collegial, managerial, developmental, advocacy, virtual, and tangible. While this chapter won't go into detail about these cultures, there are four worth noting when beginning to discuss leadership at Ohio State: collegial, managerial, virtual, and tangible. One expression of collegial culture that exists in most institutions of higher education is some sort of faculty council or faculty senate. This is typically a governing body exerting strong influence over all things academic and, as the name implies, populated with faculty.

As it has in many other universities, managerial culture has risen in influence in the past two decades. With increasing economic pressures, greater demands for fiscal accountability (and more predictable tuition), and trends to "professionalize" the management of universities, more people without higher education experience are entering universities as managers, administrators, and leaders.

The managerial culture and mind-set will likely be familiar to the reader. This way of thinking and the ethos and financial objectives that come along with it are common in our society. While the volume may be turned up on the managerial frame at OSU in the past decade, this culture has always been present at OSU. Now, however, university leaders must be stronger financial stewards and managers, while navigating the (often misunderstood) pushback they get from faculty about the commercialization of the university.

These pressures and the influx of leaders with experience in the corporate world can bring or heighten tensions between the traditional values of the academy and the managerial mind-set. One way to think about leadership at Ohio State is to look at the ways in which it has led as a result of the creative tension that the increase of the managerial mind-set has brought. Ohio State was the first university of its scale, and the first state university to lease its parking rights.

The emergence of a meaningful university-wide strategic plan now guides much of the spend of that differential influx of money. The other two cultures described by Bergquist and Pawlak in *Engaging the Six Cultures of the Academy* that are of note in the discussion of leadership at Ohio State are the virtual culture and the tangible culture. Virtual culture represents the advent of the digital revolution—online education, the proliferation of electronic communication and computing devices, the rise of social media, and higher education's collateral ethos with the responsive, open, and collaborative cultures that have come with technology companies. Ohio State's institutional leadership has led to a unique collaboration with Apple, known as the Digital Flagship University—a university-wide digital learning initiative aimed at supporting educational innovation for students and economic development opportunities for the community. What this means for deans and chairs in particular is a more acute set of technological and social media demands on teaching methods, classroom experiences, communication between faculty and students, and communication between students and university leaders.

Leaders in the university, especially academic leaders, must create environments that foster dialogue across multiple communications platforms and help bridge the gaps between digital native students and sometimes digital dinosaur faculty. The tangible culture is tied to the physicality of the place. It values face-to-face education and physical space, with implications for pedagogy, architecture, urban planning, geography, and transportation. Approximately ten years ago, the university embarked on a comprehensive physical infrastructure assessment and future needs assessment. Called the University Framework, it articulated the philosophy, assumptions, and parameters that would guide the university's space and physical planning for decades. It has already been updated once.

For a leader within the university, this framework both guides and constrains what one might do. But with one of the world's largest student populations on one campus, and with five regional campuses as well as hundreds of properties around the state of Ohio, a set of guiding principles only makes sense. For university leaders, engaging this aspect of the university and its communities requires a comprehensive thinker.

Recent Efforts

There are countless examples of the university bringing support and new thinking and resources to each of Ohio's eighty-eight counties. But the university in the last decade has strengthened its capacity to add value to the state as an economic engine and flagship through worthy initiatives and novel ways of adding value.

The authors of this chapter are those students and those Ohio citizens who benefited from the leadership of Ohio State and are products of the land-grant mission. One was raised in New Carlisle, Ohio; the other was raised in Newark, Ohio. Each journeyed to Columbus, Ohio, to new and life-shaping experiences. Each calls Ohio home and contributes to the state by being a good citizen and by working at their alma mater to support the next generation of land-grant students.

Ohio State has already made great strides to establish what it means to be a land-grant institution in the twenty-first century. Visionary leaders such as Les and Abigail Wexner and university president Gordon Gee had the foresight to see the possibility of what Ohio State could be and needed to be for the state of Ohio and its citizens. They realized that the university could be a gateway to the world.

University leadership at the time established new international partnerships in China and Brazil. These new partnerships were to attract and bring to Ohio State a greater representation of international students. Gordon Gee and Joe Alutto sought out top-tier academic leaders in Dave Williams, dean of the College of Engineering; Cheryl Achterberg, dean of the College of Education and Human Ecology; and Bruce McPheron, dean of the College of Food, Agriculture, and Environmental Sciences, who would go on to become the provost of the University.

These moves followed the first wave of reinvention to the university that had been initiated when Gordon Gee was president of the university in the 1990s. This is when the university's research agenda became more prominent and the designation of being an R1 institution was established. The shift to prioritizing research started to change the practices of the university. Increasing the quality and incorporation of research into faculty practices meant academic leadership had to be more judicious about the attraction and allocation of resources. Securing grant dollars, establishing space for research, attracting graduate students, and elevating access to research resources became the pursuit of the board and administration.

These changes at the end of the last century and the beginning of the new one set the stage for further reinvention of the university. The beginnings of an infrastructure that could leverage and harness the university's scope and scale began to emerge, manifested in the form of the Discovery

Themes—a set of critical initiatives meant to address global issues such as hunger, energy, and health. These efforts attracted top researchers, such as world-renowned neuroscientist and surgeon Ali Rezi, as well as provided support, funding, and autonomy for The James Cancer center to elevate its national profile under the leadership of Michael Caliguiri.

Efforts of leadership showed themselves in the building of a new and impressive student union, the building of a new nationally ranked cancer hospital, the complete overhaul and remodeling of the heart of the main campus library building, and the establishment of a framework for laying out and connecting the main campus in a more unified and coordinated layout for the next 100 years. These leadership efforts also began to sharpen the focus on an institution-wide agenda. Funding was looked at more holistically, and a substantive institutional strategic plan got created. Highly qualified nonacademic professionals came to the university to build the managerial infrastructure needed to advance Ohio State to a top-tier research institution and a top-ten land-grant institution. Individuals such a Geoff Chatas, chief financial officer, who came from the energy and banking sector, spearheaded groundbreaking efforts in academia, establishing the first 100-year bond in higher education, the leasing of parking operations, and a one-of-a-kind energy-management partnership.

In early 2009, the governor's office, through the chancellor of the board of regents, saw clearly that Ohio State was key to Ohio's future economic prosperity, which meant becoming an attractor and driver of economic growth and development for the state. The recruitment of Dave Williams as dean of the College of Engineering is an example of the creation of significant public-private partnerships with business such as Honda, NetJets, Boeing, and Battelle. These and other partnerships provide research opportunities for faculty and students and help attract new researchers as well as donors, business partners, and students. The growth and stature of the college is recognized by numerous faculty hires that have occurred since Williams stepped into that leadership role.

These steps may be viewed as ways to expose Ohio State students to the world and at the same time expose the world to Ohio. While it is good and useful to expose the world to Ohio—to its people, resources, and unique contributions—it is a twenty-first-century expression of the land-grant mission to bring the world to Ohio. This idea—bring the world to Ohio—is the mission of Ohio State as a twenty-first-century land-grant, and it is the responsibility of leadership to fulfill that mission.

Ohio State as a Twenty-First-Century Land-Grant Institution

In 1873, the first students of the Ohio State traveled from various regions of the state to Columbus, Ohio, and onto the campus, then known as Ohio Agricultural and Mechanical College. That first cohort of twenty-four individuals—twenty-one men and three women—would become the first to benefit from the mission associated with the Morrill Act in Ohio, as articulated by Justin Smith Morrill. Morrill saw advancements in agriculture happening in Europe due to the promotion of agricultural education. He used this as a stimulus for the bill to address the competitiveness of the country with European nations agriculturally and to infuse an opportunity for a better life for the masses.

Governor Rutherford B. Hayes took advantage of the bill exactly as envisioned by Morrill, to uplift the state of Ohio, and established the college in the state capital. Recognizing the need for greater access to funds and political decision-making, and to benefit all congressional districts in the state, Hayes's plan featured the inclusion of a representative of each congressional district on the college board of trustees. These early acts of leadership established the purpose and mission of the institution in a unique way.

The responsibility of university leadership has always been to benefit the lives of the citizens of Ohio. Since day one, when the first cohort of students stepped into the classroom with the founding faculty members, the same purpose has existed: to create a learning environment in which the practical and pragmatic necessities of life can be learned, examined, explored, and challenged, and for those experiences to be created, crafted, and guided safely and responsibly by those shaping that experience.

Leaping to the twenty-first century, Ohio youth have access to an inconceivable amount of content through the internet. Yet, discernment comes from where? The twenty-first-century land-grant university provides a place to separate the wheat from the chaff as far as content is concerned. The university is also able to shape experiences and oversee those experiences as a responsible entity in the lives of Ohioans. A gateway to the world meant bringing the world to Ohio. University leadership must be capable of continually expanding the entry point of the portal to include both emerging and ancient ideas, and ways of life both incredibly foreign and incredibly familiar.

Now, in the twenty-first century, the need for the university to benefit the lives of its citizens remains. For example, there is an urgent and substantive need to recognize the destructive consequences of the opioid epidemic and the high rates of infant and fetal mortality in our state. A modern expression of the Morrill Act now needs to align with the challenges that come from the rapid advances of technology (which often make jobs obsolete in less than twenty years), access to social media (which exposes citizens to new ideas and thinking and cultures without discrimination), and the ease of travel. Population shifts to greater urbanization bring their own challenges, such as a disconnect from the land and a loss of understanding of where food comes from. The specialization of professions and the shift of social and political groups to increased insular activity creates new levels of disconnection, fear, and misunderstanding of differences.

The ability of the university to harness and capitalize on its own resources, in partnership with other state entities, local governments, and business partners, is challenging. Although the university should never mandate faculty to abandon their scholarship for an organizational cause, it must continue to seek a way for a greater whole of the university to participate in a meaningful response to the challenges facing Ohio citizens. These are enduring challenges facing Ohio State leaders.

The main campus of Columbus, with almost 7,000 faculty, is an urban campus with its own culture and dynamic. And yet, there are more than 400 faculty who work in the hundreds of other places around Ohio that are also Ohio State. When considering a new initiative or changing a process or policy, the implications can be enormous, yet leaders can't let themselves be paralyzed. This level of geographic and "tangible" complexity breeds leadership qualities perhaps more common to international companies.

To this point, we have provided some dimension to the scope and scale of The Ohio State University and shed a little light on the implications for leadership within the institution. Successful leaders at OSU must be comprehensive systems thinkers with a long view of the future and the patience and determination to pursue it. They must influence across geographic and disciplinary boundaries, advance an agenda in a shared governance environment, and account for a unique blend of autonomy and common cause. The uniqueness of Ohio State's leadership and its leaders is, of course, due to these factors as well as many others. And there is a grounding, a foundation to this institution that is both unique in Ohio and shared among all states—the land-grant mission. It is instructive to revisit this foundation amidst the waves of accelerated societal and technological change and political, environmental, and economic uncertainty.

Justin Smith Morrill is best known for sponsoring the Morrill Act, also known as the Land-Grant College Act. This act was signed into law by Abraham Lincoln in 1862 and established federal funding for higher education in every state in the country. In Morrill's own words:

> This bill proposes to establish at least one college in every State upon a sure and perpetual foundation, accessible to all, but especially to the sons of toil, where all of needful science for the practical avocations of life shall be taught, where neither the higher graces of classical studies nor that military drill our country now so greatly appreciates will be entirely ignored, and where agriculture, the foundation of all present and future prosperity, may look for troops of earnest friends, studying its familiar and recondite economies, and at last elevating it to that higher level where it may fearlessly invoke comparison with the most advanced standards of the world. (quoted in Parker 1924, 273)

Certainly, there is much unique and special about The Ohio State University that calls its leaders to be remarkable, that makes its leadership significant, and that enables the institution itself to lead and be viewed as a leader. Deep roots are what allow trees to grow tall. The land-grant roots, now some 150 years old, remain as a foundation. Ohio State's leaders today and tomorrow will be well served to reground themselves here, and allow their intelligence, curiosity and creativity, and commitment to transform themselves as leaders transform the institution into a beacon for the state and its people. We hope that the reader has gained some insight into the difficulty, challenges, unique character, and exceptional nature of The Ohio State University leadership.

References

Bergquist, William H., and Kenneth Pawlak. 2008. *Engaging the Six Cultures of the Academy.* San Francisco: Jossey-Bass.

Drath, Wilfred. 2001. *The Deep Blue Sea: Rethinking the Source of Leadership.* San Francisco: Jossey-Bass.

Parker, William B. 1924. *The Life and Public Services of Justin Smith Morrill.* New York: Da Capo Press.

27

The Ethos of the Engaged Institution

Roger A. Rennekamp

We as individuals have distinct personalities. Those personalities are shaped in part by genetics, but also by various life experiences. We also hold deep assumptions about how we as individuals should engage with the world around us. Academic institutions are no different. They, too, operate from a set of assumptions that influence how they view themselves, how they behave, and how they are viewed by others. These assumptions shape what is called the organization's ethos, or way of being.

Think of the universities with which you are familiar. It is likely that you have shaped different impressions of these institutions based on your experience with them as a student, a parent, an alumnus, an employee, or a private citizen. In this essay, I identify a unique set of attributes that, through my experience, are typically associated with "engaged" institutions. These include humility, an outward-facing orientation, a willingness to listen and learn, a desire to serve others, respect for partners, and accessibility. The six attributes are distilled from more than forty years of professional experience at three land-grant institutions. I also will advance the notion that institutions that possess these attributes have a competitive advantage over their counterparts in communicating their value proposition to a public that has become increasingly skeptical of the relevance of the nation's colleges and universities.

Humility

As faculty of one of the nation's most highly regarded academic institutions, we have each gone to great lengths to master our respective disciplines and become experts in our fields. Similarly, our colleagues are also experts in their own areas of work. Together, we are a community of scholars hard at work to solve some of the world's most pressing problems. The problem is, many outside of academia don't care much for experts, particularly those who act as though they are. Gifford Pichot, the first head of the US Forest Service, once said to his team of foresters, "Get rid of the attitude of personal arrogance or pride of attainment of superior knowledge" (United States Forest Service 2016). His message may be as important today as it was a century ago.

The 2016 presidential election was a referendum on elitism. It represented a societal pushback against the economically elite, the politically elite, and even the academic elite. Both sides of the aisle are dissatisfied with public higher education, but for different reasons. Some dissatisfaction stems from issues with access and affordability. Others believe that America's land-grant universities are no longer relevant to the "sons and daughters of toil" that they were charged to serve. Still others categorize the academically elite as individuals of privilege. So, being able to occasionally step back from our role as experts may serve us well at this point in history.

Certainly, we as members of the academy possess great knowledge, and we are experts in certain things. But we may not always be aware of what we don't know. We must recognize that members of the varied communities we serve are experts too, even if they lack advanced formal education. They possess lived experience that we may never have. In areas where they are experts, we are the students. We endear ourselves to others through humility, not condescension. Engaged institutions know that and behave accordingly.

Outward-Facing Orientation

Engaged institutions view themselves not as islands, but as being inextricably intertwined with the world in which they exist. Their success is dependent on the success of their surrounding communities and vice versa. Outward-facing institutions have many mechanisms by which they engage with their respective communities. They typically have positive working relationships with representatives of state, county, and city governments. Plans for growth and expansion are developed in partnership with these various units of governments as well as with neighborhood groups. They are cognizant of the impacts that faculty, staff, and students have on traffic, services, and infrastructure and work to ensure that their actions do not have negative impacts on the livability of surrounding neighborhoods.

On a more global scale, outward-facing institutions are actively engaged in applied research that has a direct relationship to the issues of today's world. Their research focuses on issues such as cancer, climate change, food insecurity, and antimicrobial resistance. Additionally, engaged institutions go the extra mile to translate new knowledge into a form that can be easily consumed by the public. That extra mile means going beyond sharing the knowledge with peers and professional presentations to sharing it in a form that can inform policy, best practices, or individual behaviors.

Inward-facing activity of colleges and universities focuses on things like faculty governance, ensuring academic freedom, promotion and tenure processes, office space, and committee work. We must guard against internal processes being an end unto themselves. Communications from colleges and universities to their relevant constituent groups often speak volumes about the degree to which they are outward facing. Communications that focus on how the institution is helping to solve the grant challenges of today's society are characteristic of engaged institutions. In my experience, communications from those that focus on the resources they attract, the awards they have won, the quality of students they attract, or where they rank among their peers tend to be more inward facing.

A Willingness to Listen and Learn

It may seem strange to suggest that institutions initially created to teach should display a willingness to learn. But the most successful organizations are those that have developed the ability to listen and learn. These are typically referred to as "learning organizations."

When railroads first began transecting our nations, people would put an ear to the tracks to hear whether a train was coming. That way, they could determine whether or not a train was near well before it came into view. Businesses spend countless dollars to track changing consumer preferences to make sure that they produce products that people will want to purchase. They have employees charged with listening to the public so the company can gain insights into what customers will need and want in the future. Businesses that are steadfastly committed to delivering an outdated product that people no longer need and want eventually go out of business.

Not only do businesses need to be aware of what is coming down the tracks, but they also need to know how they are currently performing. Just think of the number of times in the last month that you were prompted to go to a website listed at the bottom of a receipt you received at a checkout counter to evaluate your shopping experience. Information received from customers allows the business to tweak its operations in ways that improve service.

Engaged institutions also keep their metaphorical "ears to the tracks" to inform research priorities, redesign degree programs, and prioritize outreach activities. Information gained from students, alumni, employers, and the public helps those institutions remain relevant to contemporary needs. Even at institutions where curricular decisions are at the discretion of the faculty, making decisions about what students need to learn without consulting relevant stakeholders carries with it huge risk.

A Desire to Serve Others

Engaged institutions have a commitment to serve. We even refer to entire groups of institutions by the segments of society to which they uniquely provide "service." For example, urban-serving universities offer degrees and other programs that specifically benefit the needs of the nation's cities and urban communities. Hispanic-serving institutions focus on addressing the unique needs and interests of those of Hispanic origin or culture.

But the notion that education should serve the needs of the nation is not new. Thomas Jefferson and many of our founding fathers believed that an educated populace was critical to the survival of the new nation they fought hard to establish. They believed that the public needed to be educated as to the ways of the world if they are to be able to actively engage as citizens in a democratic society. But it wasn't until Abraham Lincoln signed the first Morrill Act in 1862 (which created land-grant universities) that the availability of public higher education for the masses became more than a dream.

While many believe that the Morrill Act focused exclusively on agriculture and the mechanical arts (now engineering), the act also included a clause that ensured that the liberal and classical studies would not be neglected in these newly created institutions. Still today, students attending these institutions are expected to fulfill general education requirements that go beyond simply preparing students for gainful employment in a chosen field, but prepare them for life as members of families, communities, and broader society. The growth of service learning as an important dimension of the education of students is an example of how engaged institutions are helping students be ready for this broader role in society.

But the reach and impact of these institutions goes far beyond what occurs on campus. Engaged institutions have continual connection with the broader populace through programs that reach into cities and towns as well as the more rural parts of the nation that help them live richer and fuller lives. Extension programs of these institutions reach into communities with information that helps them make healthy choices, manage their finances, and improve the communities in which they live. Engaged institutions know they exist because of what they do for others, not what they do for themselves.

Respect for Partners

Across public higher education, there are few institutions that possess all the resources they need to accomplish their varied goals. Consequently, they are establishing partnerships with business and industry, government agencies, and even other educational institutions to jointly accomplish mutually agreed-upon goals. Successful partnerships, however, are built on mutual respect, meaningful engagement, and reciprocity.

Mutual respect is based on the notion that each partner possesses something that has value to the other. But partners must also act in ways that communicate the respect they have for each other. For example, the locations selected for meetings of the partners might rotate between the facilities of various partners. Roles and responsibilities of partners are agreed upon in advance and each partner honors their commitments. Language used in the partnership is inclusive rather than proprietary. Credit is shared among members of the partnership.

Potential partnerships disintegrate quickly when one partner behaves badly. For example, it is not uncommon for an organization to request letters of support for a grant application they are submitting. All too often, however, authors of the support letters never hear the outcome of the submission. That tends to be a quick way to lose the respect of potential partners.

Partners are not always institutions. They can also be individuals who have agreed to participate in our research. But the language we use to describe these partners is not always complimentary. For example, participants in research projects are often referred to as "subjects" who will receive "treatments" administered by the researcher. Members of the audiences we want to reach with our outreach programs are sometimes referred to as the "target" audience. Consequently, we may want to think about how our language communicates the nature of our relationship with the people we wish to engage.

Meaningful engagement occurs when partners have input into the design, implementation, and evaluation of a joint venture. Community-based participatory research (CBPR) involves members of a community in the formulation of research questions, collection of data, interpretation of findings, and sharing of results. Nonformal education programs involve learners in determining what they want to learn, how they want to learn it, and how they give meaning to what is learned.

Reciprocity refers to the exchange of things for mutual benefit. For example, a community-based organization may have an existing relationship with a group of individuals that another organization or educational institution wants to engage. The community-based organization lacks curricula, tools, and technologies that the community needs. The other party is unknown to the community and has not developed a necessary level of trust to gain access to the community. A partnership based on reciprocity can help both parties obtain something of value from the other.

Accessibility

Colleges and universities are complex social structures. For outsiders, navigating such structures can be difficult. Engaged institutions, however, are continually looking for ways to make it easier for the public to navigate those complicated structures. One example of how engaged institutions make public access easier is through their websites. Their websites are organized by what visitors to the page are looking for. The websites of inward-facing universities are typically organized in a way that mirrors their organizational structure. That means that visitors to the site need to know where a particular function or expertise resides to find what they are looking for.

Engaged universities tend to have an easy-to-access front door. That front door might be a visitor center with ample parking for guests, staffed by individuals who can help visitors find their way to the part of campus they are trying to access. Parking staff are focused on helping visitors find appropriate places to park, not on telling them where they can't park. Self-service parking kiosks are available for visitors. Some universities, unfortunately, still require that visitors begin their campus visit with a stop at the campus police headquarters to pick up a parking pass. That might not generate the best first impression of the university. Engaged universities also tend to make their facilities available to the community in which they reside. At a small liberal arts college in Oregon, recreational facilities for students are shared with the community as a result of a joint development agreement with the city government.

Restoring Support for Public Higher Education

Support for public higher education has declined significantly over the past several decades. As discussed earlier in this essay, there are a number of reasons for this decline, all of which stem from a growing belief that higher education is no longer relevant to a large percentage of the American population. The list of companies that no longer require college degrees for high-paying jobs is continuing to grow. Companies like Apple and Google are looking more at skills and experience as they evaluate applicants for employment.

Is public higher education still relevant? I believe it is and that a case can certainly be made for the contributions it makes to society, our economy, and the health of our planet. But are we engaged enough with the public for them to feel that America's colleges and universities are of benefit to them? I suspect we can do better at that.

The six attributes of engaged institutions introduced in this essay can go far in building a sense of connectedness between higher education institutions and their relevant constituencies. Accessible institutions with an outward-facing orientation, a willingness to listen and learn, a desire to serve others, and a respect for partners have a competitive advantage over their counterparts in communicating their value proposition to a public.

The sesquicentennial of the founding of the university is an appropriate time to ask ourselves whether or not we are fully engaged. There is significant evidence to show the ethos of engagement is fully developed in many parts of the university. There is also evidence that several characteristics of engaged institutions are broadly evident across the entire university.

But becoming a fully engaged university means that the characteristics of engaged universities are universally evident across *all* our campuses and varied units. Achieving that goal will require that faculty, staff, alumni, and students engage in continual self-evaluation of our "way of being" to ensure that Ohio State remains a relevant and vital force in improving our world.

References

United States Forest Service. 2016. "Pinchot's Guide to the Behavior of Foresters in Public Office." Milford, PA: United States Department of Agriculture. https://www.fs.usda.gov/Internet/FSE_DOCUMENTS/fseprd547191.pdf.

28

Responding to Student and Community Change through Academic Program Reviews

Ryan J. Schmiesing

Former Harvard University administrator Henry Rosovsky referred to the academic department of a university as a favorite whipping boy. He pointed out that departments have been considered by some as "inherently conservative structures that prevent interdisciplinary approaches and the appointment of mavericks" (Rosovsky 1990, 208). While higher education continues to be criticized for not being accessible, for being too expensive, and for not properly preparing its students for postgraduation employment, the academic department often is where much of this criticism is directed, especially in the preparation of students.

Some critics go so far as to refer to anything outside the boundaries of the university property or postgraduation as "the real world." The university, in fact, does not function in some alternative universe and is regularly engaged in the real world. If a department and its faculty, staff, and students remained so isolated and never interacted with anyone outside the halls of the institution, then the argument that it is not the real world would be true. However, we know that successful, highly respected departments do interact with, and are a part of, the community, regardless of how one defines community. In this case, it is the cities, towns, and villages of the state; the business community; professional organizations and associations; public funding agencies; alumni groups; and private and public financial supporters.

How do we know if the academic program is successful or meeting the current and future needs of students? While a relatively straightforward question, the answer is sometimes elusive and can be, at times, controversial. Yes, there are rankings for departments and programs offered by a variety of outlets; some carry more "weight" than others. Popular rankings are the *U.S. News and World Report College and University Rankings, Times Higher Education World University Rankings, Forbes College Rankings,* and *Money's Best Colleges,* to name a few. In the academy, administrators, faculty, and others like the rankings when they highlight what are believed to be excellent programs and decry them when individuals feel they have missed highlighting excellence, or when it is felt others are relying on them too heavily. While some may dismiss rankings, others value them—faculty, students, donors, alumni, employers.

Each stakeholder group likely has their own reason for placing some degree of value in the rankings, and those reasons are certainly valid. When there are programs that are not ranked because publications or outlets do not rank them, it is not uncommon to rely on emphatic assertion to get the point across about excellence in the discipline. Alternatively, anecdotal stories are relied upon that have been repeated, sometimes for many years, that support the notion that the program is, in fact, in the top ten of the discipline or focus area. Rankings are one measure of success or reputation, but they do not really reveal how well the department is responding to changes in society, new program opportunities, and changes in faculty, staff, and student demographics and expectations. Universities must employ different strategies to measure success or progress, and the academic program review is one such strategy. There are many different models for academic program reviews and each university determines their focus, depending on needs, such as resource management, increased efficiency, or long-term central planning.

The Ohio State University has long implemented academic program reviews as a strategy to engage in continuous improvement and evaluate effectiveness and success. For the purpose of this essay, the department is the academic program. The review is based on a number of measures that include, but are not limited to, faculty research, quality of teaching, student outcomes, staff satisfaction, and alumni or advisory committee engagement. At the heart of the process are three key questions that all external review teams are asked to address: (1) What are the strengths of the department? (2) What opportunities exist for improvement? and (3) What are the recommendations from the team? Key to answering these questions are two important components of the review: (1) department or unit self-study and (2) the site visit by the external reviews. Follow-up, based upon the review, is initiated through a plan of action written by the department and presented to the provost.

Self-Study

The self-study is oftentimes the piece of the review process that takes the most time and is most valuable when completed with active engagement and input from department faculty and staff. The self-study reflects the current state of the department, driven by data and reflective of progress or changes from the last external review. Additionally, many departments will provide a summary of actions taken or changes in the department since the last review. The department is provided a comprehensive list of potential topics to address in the self-study; however, the final content is left to the discretion of the authors so that they may best reflect their department. Key elements of the self-study include the following:

- a description of the department faculty, including trends, diversity, mentoring, and retention;
- research agenda and foci, including funding and interdisciplinary efforts;
- educational programs and students, including undergraduate and graduate and their recruitment, diversity, time to degree, curriculum, and student outcomes;
- outreach and engagement, including current efforts and future activity;
- infrastructure and resources, including staffing, academic support, and space; and
- governance, including leadership and succession planning.

The self-study is evidence based and should be produced through the active engagement of the faculty and staff in the department. A quality self-study represents the collective input from the academic unit and relies on data that the unit collects as part of ongoing quality improvement processes or data provided by a centralized office or unit, including the Office of Institutional Research and Planning, the Office of Student Academic Success, the graduate school, or similar entities. The data allow reviewers to see trends and potentially investigate reasons for increases, decreases, or no movement of key metrics. Finally, the self-study provides a great opportunity for the academic program to share insights into future plans or potential areas being considered; the external review team is in a position to provide feedback and test ideas with faculty, staff, students, administrators, and alumni they meet with during their visit.

External Reviewers

External reviewers are at the heart of any review, as they provide the critical feedback to validate the data-driven self-study and identify key aspects that deserve additional attention by department faculty and staff, college leadership, or university administrators. When identifying external reviewers, chairs or directors generally consult their faculty in order to develop a list of reviewers for the college administration to consider. Suggested reviewers typically have one or more of the following characteristics: national and international reputation, current or former department chair or head, funded researcher, appreciation for interdisciplinary work, and experience teaching at the undergraduate or graduate level. The overwhelming majority of reviewers have current experience at a major public research university, although it is not uncommon to have a reviewer with current or past experience with a related entity such as a national lab, national foundation, and so on. The experience of public university faculty and administrators gives them the current knowledge of the university's tripartite mission of teaching, research, and outreach, as is critical to understanding the comprehensive nature and mission of a public, land-grant institution.

Review Feedback

Immediate feedback offered during the review exit session provides department, college, and university leaders a first glimpse of how the team is considering the three original questions of what is working, what the opportunities are, and related recommendations. Additionally, as part of the written report provided to the department, college, and university, it is not uncommon to hear about the strengths of the academic program, how pleased undergraduates are with the curriculum and teaching, graduate students praising the mentoring they receive, or about the strength of the staff in the unit. However, constructive criticism is also offered by the review team focused on a range of issues from time to degree, advising, physical infrastructure, and relationships internal and external to the university community. Recommendations range across the board and generally address one or more of the areas that the external review team feels strongly about, based upon their interactions with students, faculty, staff, and administrators.

Themes do emerge across the reviews conducted at the university and could be classified as follows:

Faculty hiring—review teams are specifically told to not simply report that the department or unit needs to hire additional faculty. Rather, the most helpful recommendation is to offer insight into the current makeup of the faculty, its expertise, and future trends in the discipline. The review team will often provide feedback on potential areas of need based upon impending, known retirements or gaps that have emerged for various reasons. Finally, if the department or unit has a strategic hiring plan, review teams offer insight into this plan to validate it, or suggest alternative approaches based upon their knowledge of the discipline, needs in the profession, or gaps across the country.

Curriculum—broadly, review teams provide feedback on the content of the curriculum, including the number of courses in a particular sequence or the overall number of hours required, especially for graduate programs. It is not uncommon for departments to have already identified curriculum reform as a priority and begun work on the process. In those cases, the review team may confirm the trajectory the department is on or provide input into how they might approach this important process. Within the curriculum discussion, time to degree, especially at the graduate level, is often discussed, and when too lengthy, commented on. Finally, student placement is discussed at the undergraduate and graduate ranks and is especially germane to the national conversation on the value of higher education. In those cases, especially at the graduate level, where placements are low, departments are challenged to address the subject.

Facilities—this component of the conversation is as varied as the diversity of disciplines found at large public universities. Setting aside the amount of space needed, the quality of the space from labs, offices, conference rooms, classrooms, lounges, and student meeting options are all part of the review. The importance of this can't be overstated as faculty need quality space to teach, conduct research, and meet with students; staff must have space that allows them to accomplish their work; and students must have the type of space that is conducive to learning, group activities, and other engaged learning.

Research foci—central to the review are the questions "Does the department have research foci?," "What are they?," and "Are they appropriate?" While review teams comment on all these questions, the focus of the conversation generally turns to the number of research foci first. If a department has nine different subgroups and a smaller faculty, review teams may critically analyze the outputs from those groups and provide feedback on their overall values. At the same time, a department that has three very distinct focus areas may have created such silos that there is not a sense of faculty cohesion. Offering input as to how departments or units may break down silos, especially using a curriculum review process (or something similar), are often shared.

Outreach and engagement—depending on the makeup of the review team, feedback on the efforts of the department vary, as does the intentional focus of the department on this critical component of the university mission. Although limited, review teams do comment on the connections and interactions with K–12, business, and other discipline-specific communities. Departmental or unit advisory committees are important strategies being used to gain input and build relationships with the community, especially those partners that ultimately hire graduates.

Service—depending on the size of the department, the amount of service that faculty engage in may be problematic. Smaller departments with a significant number of committees may result in faculty being overburdened due to the small number of tenure-track faculty. Feedback from review teams rarely solves this problem, but it does highlight the issue for department leaders.

Diversity—nearly every department or unit reviews the diversity of their faculty and students (undergraduate and graduate) in their self-study and includes this in conversation with reviewers, and ultimately in the plan of action. Acknowledgment of the lack of racial diversity in faculty is common, and strategies are discussed that hopefully lead to improvement. Diversity within the student body may show brighter signs, though opportunities for improvement are evident and oftentimes highlighted by review teams.

Plan of Action

Developing a plan of action is the final formal step to be completed by department leaders for the academic program review. This is not a defensive or corrective response to the external review report that is submitted by the reviewers; rather, it is a plan, submitted to the provost, that outlines the steps the department intends to take, based upon the review findings and recommendations. The plan of action, like the self-study, should reflect the collective thoughts and input of the faculty and staff of the department and not be solely authored by any one individual. In the plan-of-action meeting, the department chair outlines their intended actions. An important outcome of the plan-of-action meeting is the connections made for the department chair to existing resources, programs, or activities that relate to their potential plans.

Departments at The Ohio State University serve a critical organizing function for the creation and dissemination of knowledge through research, teaching, and outreach and engagement functions. Now, more than ever, it seems there continues to be criticism for being out of touch with the real world and not properly preparing students for employment. Holistic reviews of these departments, though, reveals that they do, in fact, undergo continuous quality improvement exercises and continue to identify strategies that enhance the research, teaching, outreach and engagement, and service missions that result in setting a standard of a modern land-grant university.

References

Hanover Research. 2012. *Best Practices in Academic Program Review.* Washington, DC: Author. http://www.asanet.org/sites/default/files/hanoverresearch_bestpractices_programreview.pdf.

The Ohio State University Office of Academic Affairs. 2017. *An Introduction and Guide to Academic Unit Review: For Departments and Schools.* Columbus, OH: Author. https://oaa.osu.edu/sites/default/files/uploads/strategic-planning/academic-unit-review/AUR-Guide_Depts-Schools_2017-04.pdf.

Rosovsky, Henry. 1990. *The University: An Owners Manual.* New York: Norton and Company.

29

Building Generations of Leaders at The Ohio State University

Donald A. Stenta

I have taught courses at The Ohio State University for nearly two decades, and practically every course has referenced or studied the idea that Ohio State was founded as a land-grant university. Most people know this and have a basic understanding of federal lands that were granted to states to start these institutions. Most students have understood that there was a focus to educate more Americans. And it's been clear to most that the commitment to be made was to ready a workforce. What's less clear is the intentional role that land-grant schools had in training and developing leaders. Our motto, "Education for Citizenship," puts much into perspective. My take on this motto is that "citizenship," then, is what we call "leadership" today. That's how I'd like to frame this essay. What's the role of a land-grant school in creating, developing, and training leaders?

Most courses I have taught have a leadership focus to them. Every time I teach, I explain that I teach leadership courses for five reasons. First, I believe in the inherent capacity that people have to be effective leaders, and that leadership can be taught and learned. I think people in leadership roles crave the ability to be great leaders and want to make important differences. I think leaders want to improve and get better. This inherent capacity that exists as potential in people should be tapped and released.

The second reason I teach leadership classes is that I believe it is critically important that we *teach* people how to lead. I wouldn't go to a dentist who didn't have a DDS degree and was not certified by the state of

Ohio. So why would I be OK with someone leading my team or organization with no leadership credential or preparation? Why do leaders move into critically important roles without having preparation, experience, or knowledge? We allow this to happen because we have limited expectations that well-trained leaders are around us. In fact, most conversations early in my career where "leadership" was being taught asked me to think of the worst leader I had ever had at work, and then directed that I should do the opposite of that person. That was my training! I want The Ohio State University to feel a mandate that the institution must *teach* people *how* to lead, over their life-span.

The third reason I teach leadership courses is that I want to make it my mission to stop having leadership referred to as a *soft* skill. Why are the skills that are visible in day-to-day work known as "hard" skills, but the skills necessary to lead others in teams commonly referred to as "soft" skills? I reject this. If anything, these interpersonal skills are the most challenging aspects of success in organizations. A study from the Center for Creative Leadership (CCL) illustrates this. Since 1983, CCL has studied the causes around career derailments of leaders who were thought of as having high potential for success.

> The most common reason for career derailment is an inability to relate to people in meaningful ways. Executives who are unable to establish strong interpersonal relationships are described by their bosses, peers, and direct reports as insensitive, competitive with others, self-isolating, dictatorial, overly critical, over demanding, easily angered, arrogant, emotionally explosive, manipulative, and/or aloof. (Chappelow and Leslie 1983, 14)

We must prioritize leadership development in our organizations so that we avoid these failures in how team members are treated.

The fourth reason I teach leadership courses is that we have but only scratched the surface of uncovering who claims leader self-efficacy. Paglis and Green (2002) state that "an individual's judgment of self-efficacy influences the initiation, intensity, and persistence of behavior. People get involved in activities that they judge themselves capable of handling; once engaged, their efficacy beliefs influence how much effort they devote to the task and how long they persist in the face of obstacles." (216). When describing how to leverage leader self-efficacy, Kodama and Dugan (2013) cited other studies that found leader self-efficacy "to be a positive, significant predictor of socially responsible leadership capacity that explained more variance statistically than educational interventions associated with the collegiate environment" (184). What Ohio State offers to enrolled students is often geared at students who already see themselves as leaders. What about the other students who aren't in that position? What do we offer students to make them see themselves as having leadership potential? There is much work to do here.

Finally, I teach leadership courses because I believe it is in line with the transformational component of a land-grant university and thus should be taught at a land-grant school. Leaders should work to transform others and the organizations to which they are connected. The land-grant idea was to train workers to not only be successful at work, but to have them participate in active ways as leaders in their communities. The strongest impact one can have in the community is serving as a leader to make that community a better place to live.

I have used space in the essay outlining my motivation to teach enrolled students about being an effective leader. So what happens when these students graduate? Who is responsible for this continued engagement over the life-span? Our alumni association!

Why do people elevate to leadership roles without proper education, preparation, or training? In most cases, we don't have a say in who leads us—in our families, organizations, or jobs. Sometimes we can vote for our leaders or being involved in a selection process. But because leadership is still so thought of as a top-down, positional role, the person "in charge" of us is selected by someone other than us. Since we can't influence that, maybe that's why we remain detached on expecting our leaders to learn to be great leaders. Perhaps it's because leadership is a true experiential enterprise. We need to know and understand theories and frameworks in order to practice this well.

What's needed is to change the paradigm of who a leader is. If we move from positional roles and think about leadership in relational terms, this may cause the disruption necessary in our organizations today. I'd like to see Buckeye alums pick up the label of relational leader and create new ways to lead their organizations and communities.

A relational leader at work can work hard to explore ways to make sure colleagues and coworkers get to know one another, beyond icebreakers and teambuilders. Knowing about your colleagues' work styles and lives add depth to one's own work life. Knowing why a coworker thinks and behaves in a particular way results in meaningful engagement that builds trust. This trust allows deeper grounding in relationships, which then leads to deeper trust, a critical perspective in relationship building.

University of Maryland, College Park emerita faculty member Susan Komives reframed ideas about leadership in this context. She and her colleagues wrote that “leadership is a relational process of people together attempting to accomplish change or make a difference to benefit the common good” (Komives et al. 1998, 21). This definition serves as the foundation for her work, *Exploring Leadership,* the first book that focused on building leadership capacity with college students. I believe Komives’s work, in collaboration with that of dozens of colleagues, helped begin the process of understanding how a land-grant university can stay focused on building leadership capacity for college students. That Dr. Komives spent her entire career dedicated to research focused on college student leaders and at a land-grant university (and now fellow Big Ten institution) makes this discussion really special and relevant.

This idea of relational leadership is how we can connect alums to alma mater. The alumni association can serve as the place that facilitates lifelong learning around leadership development. There are many exciting possibilities about how this can happen.

We can offer a leadership education pathway that provides continuing education and personal development for alums to build on their leadership potential. Alums can learn techniques to explore their leader self-efficacy and work toward identifying coworkers and members of their communities who could benefit from great leadership education.

I’d frame this leadership education pathway by connecting to four high-impact practices about leadership development that are a result of a long-standing research study called the Multi-Institutional Study of Leadership (MSL). I encourage readers to learn more about the study (see www.leadershipstudy.net) to see the hundreds of colleges and universities listed as participants. Ohio State has been involved with the study, now conducted every three years, in 2010, 2012, 2015, and 2018. While the study has focused on college student leadership development, there is an opportunity for us to lead the effort to explore leadership development with college and university alumni.

Over the course of years of surveys, the MSL outlined four high-impact practices that help teach college students about leadership. These practices include peer-led sociocultural conversations, mentorship programs, community service, and membership in off-campus organizations. The Ohio State University Alumni Association can use these practices in our work by organizing similar experiences with our alums.

The primary way that this can happen is with the 130-plus alumni clubs located all over the US and in about ten locations around the world, and with the nearly fifty alumni societies, organized by college, special interests, or constituency. Thousands of alums engage with clubs and societies by serving in leadership roles or attending events with these groups. With training and support, the leaders of these clubs could serve as facilitators of the peer-led sociocultural conversations. The conversations could include activities that would allow alumni to share information about their backgrounds, their beliefs, and how to build on this learning. In addition to serving as a vehicle for social engagement, asking clubs and societies to build in moments of acquaintanceship can help elevate what it means to be a Buckeye alum for life.

The alumni association has hosted a Young Alumni Academy for five years in Columbus. This twelve-month-long program brings together forty to fifty young alumni for a cohort-based professional development experience. The young alumni are each paired with a mentor who helps with job- and career-related advice and counsel, along with teaching about the practice of how to get work done in organizations today. We are in discussions to expand this program by offering daylong institutes to focus on personal and professional development and cohort-based experiences in cities beyond Columbus for more young alumni participation. A major reason for the expansion of the program is to build the mentorship effort. Recruiting seasoned alumni to serve as mentors adds value to their alumni experience as well.

The MSL finding that community service experiences help develop leadership capacity makes great sense. When we serve our communities as volunteers, we benefit by learning about the social justice issues at hand during that service experience. The service-learning principles of good practice offer "learning strategies that will complement and reinforce the civic lessons from the community experience" (Howard 2001, 19). The alumni association can help offer learning topics when the association's groups plan community service projects. These topics can get to the core social justice issues that can leave the alumni participants with more information about what they can do to support the agency or organization beyond the one actual service activity. For example, in addition to volunteer experiences at a food pantry, the planners can engage faculty members or policy makers to explore the complex array of issues that lead people to need services offered at a food pantry.

The fourth high-impact practice for the student audience is some level of engagement with off-campus organizations. This is easily translated to the alumni community. The alumni association can encourage more involvement in our clubs and societies, along with other community organizations that need help from our talented and loyal Buckeye alums.

I believe that if we can implement these evidence-based high-impact practices for an alumni audience, we can then begin testing the effectiveness of how our alums can become more focused on relational leader ideas. At the core of relational leadership is people working toward making our communities better places to live, work, and learn. This is an important way to elevate the land-grant status of our dear institution. It also brings to life our current social media hashtag #BuckeyeForLife.

What does it mean to be a Buckeye for life? And what difference does being a land-grant university make? What must happen is a shift of the culture of what it means to be an alumnus. Every alumnus must know how important individual and collective contributions on behalf of alma mater have in our communities. Every alumnus must understand that it takes long and sustained efforts to stay connected in meaningful ways so that we can activate the power of Buckeye Nation. Every alumnus needs to have resources available to help design and structure a lifelong journey of engagement. The association's board of directors and staff members will be working to develop an alumni pathway plan in conjunction with the sesquicentennial. The plan will outline ways to stay engaged over the lifespan, so that the engagement builds meaningful experiences for the alum and on behalf of the institution.

We must help create a leadership development pathway for all alumni to help improve work experiences and our communities. A leadership development pathway for all alumni would have ongoing learning experiences so alumni would continue to learn about what it means to be a leader—and how to be an outstanding leader. The most significant impact that can happen is that we deeply integrate and infuse the concept of integrity into what it means to be a leader today. Buckeyes who sharpen their leadership skills after graduation, with a focus on integrity, can honor our land-grant tradition and help change our communities for the better.

One would think that with the mandate we have as a land-grant university, we would be fully fixated on and obsessed with our leadership efforts across campus and have a strategic, integrated leadership development effort. Leadership programs and services on our campus are thriving and contributing deeply to the lives of students and their mentors, mainly focused on top students who come to our campus already believing they have deep capacity for leadership growth. While these individual programs are wonderful, the efforts are not integrated with a common strategy to effect local, state, national, and international change. This is counter to the relational leadership idea—that it's about people working together to better our communities.

Why is it that we can't coordinate these efforts better? I make no claim that we need to have one voice or only one leadership perspective for all students. The effort should absolutely include the richness of multiple disciplines and experiential moments.

I'd like to challenge Ohio State to take this moment, as we celebrate our 150th anniversary, to elevate the scholarship of leadership literature regarding college students so that The Ohio State University becomes the premier institution in the world that teaches all college students how to be an effective and transformational leader after graduation. The history of the land-grant university requires us to step up and demonstrate how we honor the commitment in our motto—let's take the discipline of leadership to the communities in our eighty-eight counties and beyond to develop and grow citizens to be leaders.

References

Chappelow, Craig, and Jean Brittain Leslie. 1983. *Keeping Your Career on Track: Twenty Success Strategies.* Greensboro, NC: Center for Creative Leadership.

Howard, Jeffrey. 2001. "Principles of Good Practice for Service-Learning Pedagogy." In *Michigan Journal of Community Service Learning: Service-Learning Course Design Workbook,* edited by Jeffrey Howard, 16–19. Ann Arbor, MI: OCSL Press.

Kodama, Corinne M., and John P. Dugan. 2013. "Leveraging Leadership Efficacy for College Students: Disaggregating Data to Examine Unique Predictors by Race." *Equity & Excellence in Education* 4, no. 2: 184–201.

Komives, Susan R., Nance Lucas, and Timothy R. McMahon. 1998. *Exploring Leadership: For College Students Who Want to Make a Difference.* San Francisco: Jossey-Bass.

Paglis, Laura L., and Stephen G. Green. 2002. "Leadership Self-Efficacy and Managers' Motivation for Leading Change." *Journal of Organizational Behavior* 23, no. 2 (March): 215–23.

Outsider Observations

30

Adventures of Being a University President

E. Gordon Gee

I often get asked what recommendations I would give people who wish to become a university president. My first answer is to have higher aspirations. And it is only partially tongue in cheek because, although I have had thirty-nine years of a remarkable career at five different institutions, two of them twice, I still think that the university presidency is something you should ponder carefully before taking the jump.

The reason is that a university presidency is very challenging in terms of being able to balance your personal and your professional lives. I became a university president when my daughter, Rebekah, was three years of age. At the time, I was thirty-six and West Virginia University made the consummate mistake of naming me as president when I could hardly spell *university.* But it commenced a journey of nearly forty years. The issue of balancing personal life, professional life, and spousal commitments was truly challenging. My wife, Elizabeth, was finishing her PhD, which she did complete at West Virginia University. I was very proud, as was she, of that achievement while being the dedicated first spouse in terms of her presence at university events, entertaining, and being engaged with the overall life of the university. When I look back, I realize that was a time in which we were just barely keeping our heads above water. And I had not fully understood the strain of personal and professional life until 1991, when Elizabeth died of breast cancer and left me as mother and father of a sixteen-year-old. During Elizabeth's battle with cancer, I asked the question, "Should I step down, take a leave of absence, or just plow on?" At her urging, I continued, but I can assure you that I have regretted that decision almost every day because, in many ways, she battled cancer bravely on her own. I still remember with immense regret the night before she died, I gave a speech in Dayton, Ohio, to an alumni group of Ohio State supporters. I should have been at home at her bedside, maintaining a vigil of love and support. The reason I start this essay in such a maudlin fashion is that every opportunity is a bright, shiny penny until the opportunity is yours. Then one realizes the parameters of strain and loneliness that come with that responsibility.

Do I regret becoming a university president? Absolutely not. It has given me a life full of purpose, full of opportunity and, certainly, a group of friends that I otherwise would never have been able to make or meet. So, now, I ferry on at age seventy-five, still in the left seat, trying to determine when the right time is to step down and what I can do to ease the pain of doing so for myself. When one has lived such a structured life for forty years, it is a challenge to even go on a vacation without having a near–nervous breakdown. On the other hand, living a structured life has allowed for remarkable opportunities that few, if any, would have the privilege to enjoy. So, obviously, at this moment in my own life, this is a time of reflection and decision-making.

With that as a preface, let us talk about the difference between public universities and private institutions and the particular opportunities presented by the land-grant universities. Of the five universities that I have served (West Virginia University, the University of Colorado, The Ohio State University, Brown University, and Vanderbilt University), two of them are land-grant universities and I have been privileged to have been president of both of them twice. West Virginia University and The Ohio State University have many similarities in that they are large, comprehensive, and a combination of a liberal arts university, research university, and mission-centered land-grant institution. The University of Colorado is a wonderful research-centered university, but the land-grant institution in Colorado is Colorado State University. There is a clear division of the role of those two institutions. I often comment that both Ohio State and West Virginia University are a combination of the University of Colorado and Colorado State, Iowa and Iowa State, Indiana and Purdue, or Michigan and Michigan State. On the other hand, Brown and Vanderbilt are highly selective private institutions with substantial resources and wealth, both among their alumni and friends, as well as their parents and other supporters. Because of their wealth, they also can have substantially higher tuition without fear of losing market share. That, of course, is a wonderful advantage not enjoyed by many institutions. In the end, I truly enjoyed both of those institutions, although I was at Brown for only three years.

But what I appreciated about the private institutions was the fact that the external politics were minimal. By that I mean one did not have to deal with legislators, governors, newspapers, and Freedom of Information Acts. However, the internal politics were much the same. In fact, in many ways they were more brutal because the smaller institution does not provide the president as much protection as a larger organization. I tell the story about when I came to Brown, I called my first faculty meeting expecting that Brown would have a university senate where a few senators would show up, we would have a pleasant discussion, and they would leave. Instead, the whole faculty showed up and it was hand-to-hand combat from the very beginning. Although Vanderbilt had more of a sense of Southern civility, it was still challenging in terms of its size and internal politics.

I should also note that there is a profound difference between the structures of private university boards and public boards in that public boards are smaller and generally appointed politically. Private boards are much larger and are more focused on fund-raising. For example, Brown had sixty-one board members, while Vanderbilt had forty-one. The Brown board would meet twice a year and the Vanderbilt board would meet three times a year. Interestingly enough, I attempted to increase the number of meetings, without much avail. But, at both institutions, I was able to institute a term-limit policy that, as you can imagine, was extremely unpopular among the older trustees. The two private institutions each had an executive committee, but the power of the presidency at both institutions was significant and board relations were focused more on giving rather than governing.

On the other hand, the public universities are about total transparency and public exposure. There is very little that is private, and even more, there is very little for which there are not rumors abounding. There are continued requests, requirements, and bureaucratic responses from legislators and government officials. And, there is the omnipresent nature of the public press, which makes it difficult for a university president to really have candid discussions about pressing issues because one cannot talk in relative quiet about the challenges confronting the university. The net result has been that university presidents have become increasingly "gray" and try to be as noncontroversial and nonoffensive as possible. I really do believe that public university presidents, in the main, are now chosen from individuals who have offended the fewest number of people over the longest period of time. I know we can always talk about the golden era of higher education in which university presidents roamed the earth. Whether or not that ever was the case, it is clear that that is not the era in which we live.

But, for all the political, social, and cultural challenges of a public university, it, in my view, is far and away the most exciting opportunity confronting someone wishing to be engaged in academic leadership. The reason is that when, as president, I wake up in the morning, I know my exact responsibility, which is to the people of the state I am serving and to work nonstop to make their lives better.

That brings me to the land-grant university, because these universities have a very special mission. They were established by Abraham Lincoln at the height of the Civil War to bring healing to the nation and to open the doors of opportunity for every citizen of the country. They were the people's university. And, without a doubt, the Morrill Land-Grant Act, in my view, was the greatest single act passed by Congress because it made education available to the masses. One can argue about the GI Bill, the Civil Rights Act, and other landmark legislation, but none had a more profound effect on our democracy than the growth of the land-grant university.

As we now slide into the modern era, Steve Gavazzi and I have argued in our book, *Land-Grant Universities for the Future* (2018), that the land-grant universities have lost their way. In many ways, they have turned from helping hands into ivory towers and have lost that sense of being a beacon for all and now attempt to be like those non-land-grant universities always struggling for greater recognition. As an aside, I believe that the greatest destructive force to modern higher education is mainly due to these incessant public rankings. It all started with *U.S. News and World Report,* which was going out of business, but saved itself by creating this arbitrary and capricious university and college ranking system.

To lead a land-grant university is not a job, it is a ministry—a calling to a higher order. And I do not say that lightly. If one is truly devoted to the mission of a land-grant university, one is devoted to dealing directly with the lives of the citizens of the state you serve and those citizens that are beyond the boundaries but can be affected by the role of a land-grant institution. In our own instance, at West Virginia University, we run the largest youth program in the state, 4-H; we are the largest employer in the state; and we have extended offices in every county of our state, using this capacity to lead and inspire our citizens. The land-grant universities that remain fiercely land-grant are those that focus entirely on their purpose. Those that wander from that purpose to public accolades are clearly institutions that have failed to understand the special mission of the land-grant university.

That is the landscape of higher education as seen from my particular perch. So, what have I learned from these extraordinary experiences? Let me just start by noting that there is no presidential manual, secret or otherwise, about how to run universities. There are 4,500 universities and colleges in this country, each of them unique, with particular cultures, opportunities, and challenges. Although I have been urged on several occasions to write a manual about the university presidency, there is not a manual to write. Rather, there are observations that I think can be applicable in a more global context.

These observations apply particularly to the public land-grant universities because of their importance and unique calling. The first of those observations is that university presidents need to learn to exercise humility. One of the truths that I have seen in people in my profession is that the higher the calling, the more arrogant the response. There is no collective wisdom in the senior administration of a university. Rather, there is an absolute requirement that university leaders should lead from in front and with a great listening ear. Humility and the desire to listen and learn are incredibly important.

A university president needs to learn to accept that your friends will come and go but your enemies will accumulate. At some point, that accumulation of barnacles will tip the scales against you. Now, the caveat of that is *if* you are making decisions, because there are no decisions made in a university, particularly in today's raucous world, in which you do not make equal friends and enemies. So, eventually, in universities, you will have offended almost everyone. Always be prepared to pack your bags.

Develop a very thick skin. If you cannot stand criticism, then *please* do not enter the public arena. Everyone has an opinion, most of them ill-informed, about how you are to do your job, and when you do not do it exactly how *they* expect, then you are public fodder for criticism. Sometimes I believe the real name of the university president should not be *president,* but rather, *piñata.*

To go along with your thick skin, you must have a good sense of humor. By that I mean you have to learn to laugh at yourself and to find joy in the mistakes you make and in the silly things that happen. But it cannot be at the expense of others—only, rather, at your expense. Today is a world of single-issue politics and almost everyone will be offended on a given day. But humor is a common bond that binds people together in a humane and, most often, civilized way.

Then, once you have thickened your skin and honed your sense of humor, make certain that you never, ever lose that sense of humor, even when people want you to become bland. In my own instance, my humor has gotten me into trouble more than once, but it also has saved me from many painful days. And it is who I am. Genuineness is a mark of leadership, in my view.

In the end, the issue for any university president is to display courage when courage in universities is in short supply. Particularly in today's world of gender and identity politics and challenges to free inquiry, it becomes easier for a president to go along and get along than to draw lines. First, it is absolutely imperative for a president of a public university to clearly draw lines that the university will not cross. My most immediate example is the denial of invited speakers on the campus due to fear of offending someone or the fear of causing a confrontation. The fundamental underpinning of a university is the protection of ideas and the expectation that all ideas will be appropriately welcome, whether they are good, bad, offensive, or inescapably stupid. Universities are a marketplace of ideas and the marketplace will prevail. Once that line is breached, the legitimacy of the university can never be regained.

The other part of this notion of courage really goes to the university president being willing to say that the emperor has no clothes. There is, unfortunately, increasing intellectual nonsense that occurs on the university campus, and a university president should exercise his or her First Amendment rights to so state. And, once you make a decision, stand by that decision, remembering that you understand the parameters of the decision more than anyone. Those critics who want you to change your mind generally only have access to part of the facts and even less access to your reasoning. Life in a university requires certitude.

That brings me to the notion of culture and the dynamic of saying no. I believe the most powerful word in the university administrative lexicon is *no.* For too long, university presidents have said "yes" and "maybe" and therefore spread resources and consequences of those decisions across the university like marmalade. The real issue is to say "no" in order to mean "yes" when a "yes" is needed. In today's world of unlimited appetites and limited resources, we know that there are inevitably going to be winners and losers. If everyone wins, then no one wins. That is the harsh reality of resource constraints and resource allocation.

As a consequence of courage and saying *no when appropriate,* a university leader will then be able to focus on that intricate dance between talent and culture. Clearly, universities are places of very talented and educated people. Whether it be faculty, staff, or students, there is an unusual level of bright people in any given room. However, what is lacking in universities, in general, is a culture that empowers that talent to grow intellectually and socially within the university. We have a tyranny of departments, colleges, and gerontocracy. We need to break that tyranny in order to have a culture that really nurtures talent and enables talent to clearly flourish. My favorite analogy is that we treat everyone in the university like McDonald's hamburgers, not recognizing their differences and the power that comes from those differences. The net result is that we create winners and losers instead of winners and more winners. Very often, the culture of a university is brutal to its faculty and staff and very unforgiving when someone tries to break out of the norm. Our culture and our ability to inspire is limited by that reality.

I could continue about lessons of leadership, learned from my time in universities, particularly in the land-grant institutions. That said, I want to make one final plea to all who will read this: that the future of the US university is differentiation, not amalgamation. Let us not strive to be Harvard or Stanford; let us strive to be the very best institution we can be, which I believe is a much higher aspiration. And let us realize, in the best biblical sense, that there are multiple roads to salvation in terms of recognizing and rewarding our faculty and staff and there is a much more thoughtful way to encourage and nurture our students by creating curricular structures that are free-flowing and not limited by requirements that, in the end, make no sense.

The US university for a century has been the most powerful instrument for intellectual growth in the world. Now, however, I fear that we are quickly losing our place in that world, not through overcompetition but through massive missteps in our own body politic. Let us return to being places of curiosity. Let us get back to being instruments of creativity rather than conformity. And let us be the front door to the American Dream, which was the promise of Lincoln in 1862 when he signed the Land-Grant Act.

References

Gavazzi, Stephen M., and E. Gordon Gee. 2018. *Land-Grant Universities for the Future: Higher Education for the Common Good.* Baltimore: Johns Hopkins University Press.

31

America's Education Crisis

Can Land-Grant Values Be Our Salvation?

William E. Kirwan

The Morrill Land-grant Act, passed in 1862 at the height of the Civil War, was intended to provide to the then so-called industrial segment of the population, access to a "practical education" that had direct relevance for their daily lives. Up until this time, higher education was only for the elite. This act was expanded in 1890 to create such institutions in the segregated South and in 1992 to create "tribal Colleges" on Indian reservations.

Many, I among them, say that the Morrill Act and its companion pieces of legislation, the Hatch and Smith-Lever Acts, together with the GI Bill and the Pell Grant, are the three most important pieces of federal higher education legislation ever enacted. I have had the privilege and honor of serving as president of two of our nation's leading land-grant institutions, the University of Maryland and The Ohio State University. Like other land-grant universities, these two institutions have had a transformative impact on their states and the nation. Often the largest institutions in their states, land-grant universities have historically provided broad access to educational opportunities, most especially to students of limited economic means.

In addition, they have been engines of innovation for their states and the nation through the high volume of research they conduct as part of their mission. Collectively, our nation's land-grant universities receive more than $40 billion in externally funded research annually, much of which is from the federal government and directed to issues of national interest. But that's not all. Our land-grant universities have widely dispersed "extension" offices, disseminating relevant information to advance the economy and quality of life throughout the states they serve. Simply put, land-grant universities have contributed immeasurably to advancing educational opportunities and the economy and quality of life in the US. Their creation is truly a phenomenal success story.

And, yet, despite the contributions of land-grant and other higher education institutions, we have reached a point of crisis with higher education in the US. What is this crisis? Simply put, as a nation, our higher education institutions are not educating nearly enough people at a level of quality to sustain our economy and to provide the equality of opportunity that is such a fundamental aspect of our nation's founding values. I believe this is the greatest long-term problem facing our nation.

There are two major interrelated aspects of our education crisis. The first is the dire need for higher education to serve many more underserved students, especially low-income students and students of color. The second is the declining public investment in higher education and the resulting rising cost of achieving a high-quality higher education degree. Failure to satisfactorily address these twin issues places our nation at great risk of losing two of its most valued and fundamental qualities: the vitality and competitiveness of our economy, and our *founding ethos* as the land of opportunity, the quintessential upwardly mobile society.

As has been well documented, over the past three or four decades, the essence of our nation's economy has changed, irreversibly, from high reliance on physical labor to an ever-growing dependence on a well-educated and highly skilled workforce. There are many reports, such as a recent one from Anthony Carnevale and Georgetown University's Center on Education and the Workforce (CEW), pointing to the growing demand for college grads in the workforce. According to CEW's analysis, the US economy will grow twenty-five million new jobs by 2020, and 65 percent of these will require a two- or four-year college degree. At current degree production rates, CEW estimates the US will fall short by up to ten million workers with a postsecondary degree.

The problem is compounded for the US in the highly competitive global economy because other industrialized nations are ramping up their rates of college completion in response to the demand for a more highly educated workforce. In the span of a few decades, we've dropped from the top rank in possessing the most educated adult population, as measured by the percentage of adults with at least a bachelor's degree, to second-tier status in this regard. According to Bureau of Labor Statistics data, in

1990—just thirty years ago—the US had the world's highest proportion of adults with a bachelor's degree (Organization for Economic Cooperation and Development).

Fast-forward to today. The US is tied for tenth in the proportion of twenty-five- to sixty-four-year-olds with a four-year degree and tied for fourteenth with in the proportion of twenty-five- to thirty-four-year-olds (Organization for Economic Cooperation and Development).

The data on twenty-five- to thirty-four-year-olds is especially alarming. It shows other nations are rapidly passing us by and strongly suggests that our standing in college degree completion is not likely to reverse in coming years, but instead will continue to fall. Most economists agree that a major reason the US has had the largest and most successful economy over the past fifty to sixty years is that we had the most highly educated workforce, triggered by the GI Bill following World War II. Clearly, we are on the verge of losing that competitive advantage, which places our nation at grave risk, especially in an economy dependent on brainpower and a well-educated and highly skilled workforce.

But, our failure to graduate more students, especially low-income and underrepresented minority students, is of such grave concern for another reason. In the era of the "knowledge economy," it poses a threat to the nation's core values and social stability. From its inception, our nation has been seen around the world as the shining city on a hill, the "land of opportunity." Perhaps the most basic element of our national identity is the proposition that the economic stratum of a person's birth does not determine his or her station at the end of life. Fundamental to our national values is the ingrained belief that ability and hard work are all that are needed in the US to enjoy a successful career and a high quality of life. In today's economy, however, with such a demand for a well-educated workforce, achieving the American Dream most often requires a college degree.

So, how well are we doing in ensuring low-income students have equitable, or even somewhat equitable, access to college degrees? The short answer is, not well at all. The Pell Institute's 2018 report on equity of education opportunities tells us that a child born into the top quartile of family income is six times more likely to earn a college degree than a child growing up in a family in the bottom quartile and three times more likely than a child in the second quartile of family income.

Disturbingly, the proportion of lowest quartile income students earning a college degree within six years of high school graduation has hardly moved over the past forty years and is still in the 10 percent range, whereas at the top quartile of income, the proportion has almost doubled during these years. Data also show that, tragically, a high-ability, low-income student today has about the same chance of earning a college degree as a low-ability, high-income student.

The sharp difference in college attainment based on income helps explain the rapidly growing income disparity in the US. At the root of these disparities is the "education premium," or the added boost education provides to income generation, as our economy has shifted from one relying on manual labor to one requiring knowledge, skill, and innovation. A child growing up in poverty fifty years ago without a college degree could find meaningful work and an income relatively in bounds with that of the more educated population. That is simply not possible, or at least highly unlikely, today. In a recent column, Nicholas Kristof of the *New York Times* captured our present circumstances well. He wrote, "More children in America live in poverty now (22 percent at last count) than at the start of the financial crisis in 2008 (18 percent). They grow up not in a 'land of opportunity,' but in the kind of socially rigid hierarchies that our ancestors fled, the kind of society in which your outcome is largely determined by your beginning" (Kristof 2015).

A recent study of income disparities in thirty-two countries around the world ranked the US with the fourth greatest disparity, topped only by Turkey, Chile, and Mexico. And, we had the second highest proportion of people living in poverty. This surely doesn't describe the country we like to think we live in. Given the need to increase the pool of educated talent for our workforce and given the imperative for much greater social equity in the "land of opportunity," the conclusion seems inescapable: As a nation, we simply must significantly increase access to higher education for underserved populations, including most especially low-income students, a responsibility that is at the heart of the land-grant mission.

In attempting to meet this responsibility, a question naturally arises: Are there significant numbers of low-income students graduating from high school equipped with the academic preparation necessary to gain admission to our more selective institutions? Indeed, there are! Georgetown's Center on Education and the Workforce reports that fewer than half of the Pell recipients with an SAT score above 1120, the median SAT for students attending the nation's selective institutions, actually attend these institutions.

Several important points about this data: A low-income student capable of achieving a 1120 on the SAT in all probability has the intelligence to score significantly higher were he or she raised in a middle-class family with access to out-of-class educational experiences, tutoring, and test-prep courses. Second, convincing research shows that controlling for income and test scores, low-income students have a much higher graduation rate at selective institutions than at open-admission colleges and universities. And, finally, the need to serve many more low-income students must be seen as an "all hands on deck" imperative, including for our most selective institutions. The bottom line is that low-income students who can succeed at even our most selective institutions exist in substantial numbers, and these institutions simply must do a much better job of serving them.

Institutions committed to this goal will, of course, have to change many things. Among them are developing more targeted recruitment practices aimed at identifying high-ability, low-income students, including working adults. They must also change the way financial aid is distributed. Much more aid will have to go to admitted students based on need rather than institutions "buying" more affluent students with high test scores.

This means these institutions will also have to pay less attention to the "beauty contest" rankings, such as those in *U.S. News and World Report*. Honestly, if a foreign power had wanted to diminish the US and its role in the world, to create the dire education crisis we now face, they could hardly have done better than invent the *U.S. News* rankings. These rankings reward selectivity at a time when our nation needs greater access to higher education. And they reward high levels of expenditures at a time when higher education needs to find efficiencies that do not compromise quality.

We need a new ranking system, one that measures institutions' success in addressing the higher education needs of our nation. One candidate for this purpose is the *Equality of Opportunity Project,* led by Raj Chetty, a distinguished economist at Stanford. Through this project, Chetty's group ranks universities by their success in promoting social mobility through access for low-income students. Incidentally, Washington University in St. Louis was ranked at the bottom in these rankings when they first came out. To its credit, the institution immediately launched a new effort to recruit more high-ability, low-income students, which shows Raj Chetty's work is having an impact. This step required institutional leadership because the admission of more low-income but qualified students will almost certainly result in lower SAT and ACT scores for the university's admitted students.

Another example of courageous leadership recently occurred at the University of Kentucky (UK), a land-grant university. A few years ago, roughly 1,200 undergraduate students left UK without a degree. When he learned this, Eli Capilouto, the president, asked his staff a simple question: "Why did they leave?" Everyone naturally assumed these students were struggling academically and either got discouraged or were academically dismissed. What they learned was a surprise: 30 percent of them had a 3.0 GPA. However, these students had something else in common, too. They all had $6,000 or more of unmet need. When the university looked at the rest of the institution's 3.0 students, they found most had little or no unmet need. In fact, quite a few had been allocated grant funds in excess of their cost of attendance.

To his great credit, President Capilouto said that this was unacceptable and immediately instituted a new need-based aid program. Previously, UK had allocated 90 percent of its institutional student aid based on merit, trying, as so many institutions do, to "buy" students with high SAT scores. Going forward, 70 percent of aid will be allocated based on need. President Capilouto acknowledges that UK's *U.S. News* ranking will probably drop because of this move, but he's willing to do it anyway. I can only hope that UK's action will catalyze a movement and many other institutions will have the courage to follow his lead and respond similarly to what I see as a "higher calling": namely, our nation's needs, not superficial rankings.

But, a redistribution of institutional financial aid, important though it is, can only partially address a primary reason for our educational crisis, namely, the rising cost to the student of obtaining a college degree. Tuition has risen so dramatically in large measure because there has been a precipitous decline in state support for higher education. The actual expenditures per student have hardly changed at all—roughly a 3 percent increase over the past fifteen years. What has changed significantly during this period is the sources of revenues to support these expenditures. In constant dollars, state investment on a per-student basis has declined about 20 percent and tuition has risen well over 40 percent since 2005.

As a result of the significant rise in tuition, student debt levels have soared, now reaching $1.4 trillion, which exceeds total outstanding credit card debt and is topped only by outstanding home mortgage debt. As we've all observed, after years of dramatic increases, tuition has become a "third rail" issue with the public. In state after state, tuition is either capped or increased at very moderate levels. This reality raises an extraordinarily difficult challenge for higher education and our nation. If we need an increase of between 20 and 30 percent in the annual production of bachelor's degrees, where will the resources to do so come from?

Obviously, tuition increases aren't going to pay for the needed growth. I think we can all agree on that. While we must continue to press states for greater investment in our colleges and universities, that is not likely to occur, at least in the intermediate term. Quite the contrary. Most economists say that if anything, the new tax laws and rising health care costs will put additional pressure on state investment in education. In fact, a year or so ago, Moody's issued a negative warning on higher ed finances.

The inescapable conclusion is that we can address this aspect of our nation's education crisis only if we can find *lower-cost means of delivering high-quality higher education degrees,* which sounds blasphemous to those of us in higher education. We have it within our DNA to equate higher quality with higher levels of expenditures. As I noted, that view is at the heart of the *U.S. News* rankings.

With so much at stake for our nation, I fault those of us in higher education for not taking more seriously the responsibility for exploring new means, doing more research, and investing more effort in developing new strategies for delivering high-quality higher education at lower costs. Ironically, for all but a relatively few institutions, the need to be doing so should be apparent because the traditional financial model for higher education is breaking down and is certainly not capable of educating the millions of additional students we need to reach for the future well-being of our nation.

There are things we can and should be doing much more aggressively: expanding early college opportunities in our schools and providing more seamless transfer from our two-year colleges to our universities, both of which bring down the cost to the student of earning a four-year degree and increase capacity at our universities to serve more students. But the gains here will be marginal. Meeting the full need will require newer and bolder strategies.

In most other sectors, technology has been used as one tool to flatten or drive down the cost of operations. Is this possible in higher education without diminishing the quality of education delivered? This latter point, "without diminishing quality," must be a given, a sine qua non of any strategy we explore. That said, I am one who believes technology properly utilized holds real promise. Let me cite just a few examples.

As I'm sure many of you are aware, a few years ago Georgia Tech, a land-grant institution, introduced an MS degree in computer science taught through the medium of massive open online courses, or MOOCs. Georgia Tech's full-time faculty teach the cyberspace students with a high degree of interactivity. The cost of the degree is $10,000, versus $46,000 for students who reside on the campus. Over 4,000 students are now enrolled in the program, and its revenue is positive for the institution. Moreover, there has been no drop in applications for the on-campus version, which suggests this effort is expanding, not drawing from, the residential program. In fact, it's so successful that Georgia Tech is developing a second low-cost MS program for this delivery system.

Of course, lots of schools offer online degree programs, but they almost always do so at the same or even higher cost than the on-campus face-to-face degree. What makes Georgia Tech's effort so special is the conscious effort to offer the degree at a much lower cost. Bud Peterson, the Georgia Tech president, tells me he is convinced that, keeping faith with land-grant values, the institution will be offering lower-cost undergraduate degrees through this medium within five years.

I am also intrigued by an initiative at Arizona State University (ASU). ASU has developed a set of MOOCs covering the institution's general education requirements. In partnership with EdX, the MOOC platform developed at MIT, another land-grant institution, ASU offers the option for an entering student to take his or her first year of courses through MOOCs at a greatly reduced cost. The students then come to campus for their final three years, potentially saving, in effect, one-fourth of their college costs, while enabling Arizona State to expand capacity to serve more students.

Interestingly, Anant Agarwal, president of EdX, thinks what ASU is doing could become a much more common model in higher education. President Agarwal predicts that in the future, many students will take their first year of work at home, perhaps while still in high school, through MOOCs, like those offered at ASU; come to a residential campus for two years; and then spend their senior year away from campus, studying abroad or holding an internship and completing whatever formal course work remains online. Who knows if this will come to pass. What's very encouraging to me, however, is the innovative thinking about course delivery a few universities are engaging in to make high-quality degrees available to more students at reduced costs.

Let me sum up my thoughts on our nation's education crisis. While I think higher education has been too slow to respond to the crisis we face resulting from the undereducation of our population, especially our low-income citizens, I am an incorrigible optimist. I remain hopeful that through collective efforts, we can mount a successful response. I'm pleased to see how much of the efforts to date have been led by land-grant universities, which is not surprising since the challenges that must be addressed strike at the core values of these remarkable institutions.

A satisfactory response to our education crisis, however, won't be easy, and it surely won't come from a single silver bullet. It will only happen if governing boards come to understand the consequences for our nation if our colleges and universities don't respond to this crisis, and in response provide the crucial support and guidance for the needed policy and priority changes. It will only happen if we have a growing number of university leaders with the courage to respond to this need. It will only happen if we can encourage more of our extraordinarily creative faculty and staff to explore and develop strategies for delivering high-quality degrees at lower cost to the student and the institution. It will only happen if our university communities become open to new ways of doing things, to supporting innovation, and to scaling up successful strategies, even if they go against some of our long-held traditions and practices. And, finally, it will only happen if we can find more effective ways to explain to the general public the existential consequences our nation will face if we do not provide far greater equity in access to high-quality higher education degrees in the US. Our nation's *future* requires it; our nation's *values* demand it.

References

Carnevale, Anthony P., Nicole Smith, and Jeff Strohl. 2010. "Help Wanted: Projections of Jobs and Education Requirements through 2018." Washington, DC: Georgetown University Center on Education and the Workforce.

Indicators of Higher Education Inequality in the United States: 2019 Historical Trend Report. The Pell Institute. Accessed January 10, 2020. http://pellinstitute.org/downloads/publications-Indicators_of_Higher_Education_Equity_in_the_US_2019_Historical_Trend_Report.pdf.

Kristof, Nicholas. 2015. "U. S. A., Land of Limitations?" *New York Times,* August 8, 2015. https://www.nytimes.com/2015/08/09/opinion/sunday/nicholas-kristof-usa-land-of-limitations.html.

Organization for Economic Cooperation and Development. 2002. *Education at a Glance 2001,* and unpublished tabulations.

32

Leadership Lessons from The Ohio State University

Ed Ray

The land-grant mission is to provide service to others, bringing college education, the development of advanced skills, and cutting-edge research into the daily lives of people from ordinary circumstances to promote economic growth and social progress throughout the nation. When President Lincoln signed the Morrill Act in 1862, he referred to the land-grants as the "people's schools." I was the first in my family to graduate from college, Queens College of the City University of New York. The people of New York City funded the system. So, in a way, the land-grant philosophy of the people of New York made it possible for me to go to college. I have great affection for the land-grant mission.

At The Ohio State University, I learned many leadership lessons and discovered the supportive community and culture of learning, service, and innovation characteristic of every land-grant university. When I arrived at Oregon State University sixteen years ago to assume the presidency of another land-grant university, I brought lessons learned and my passion for the land-grant mission, and I felt very much at home. I met alumni who told me proudly that they are fifth-generation Beavers. I understood exactly what they meant. So, I quickly implemented two major initiatives rooted in land-grant thinking.

First, I learned that the university created a degree partnership program with our local community college partner, Linn-Benton Community College, that simultaneously enrolled students in the college and the university, virtually eliminating the so-called transfer problem. We moved quickly to establish partnerships with all seventeen community colleges in Oregon. A student can begin higher education studies in any community college and earn a degree from Oregon State.

In 1993, I became the first chief information officer (CIO) in the history of Ohio State, tasked to combine the separate academic and administrative information systems into one organization, which I did. So, when I arrived in Corvallis and the university CIO asked me if I was interested in expanding our fledgling online education program, I told him that given our mission to bring higher education to the people, I think of online education as a twenty-first-century adaptation of the land-grant mission. Today we have the sixth-ranked online undergraduate degree programs according to *U.S. News and World Report.* Our undergraduate programs in the humanities have been ranked number one in the country. We have 6,500 students taking all their coursework online to earn their degrees. Each commencement we have a reception for online graduates, where many wonderful and tearful life stories are shared. This year, we opened our OSU Portland Center in an iconic building in the heart of downtown Portland, Oregon. We teach hybrid courses there for adult learners who can best benefit from a combination of online and in-person instruction and support services.

My ability to write about leadership lessons learned at The Ohio State University derives from the fact that I served the university in various roles from 1970 to 2003, beginning as an assistant professor of economics and finishing up as executive vice president and provost. I believe I was the youngest chairperson in the history of the university at age thirty-one and the youngest tenured full professor at the university at age thirty-two. All of which is to say that I had a lot to learn given my complete lack of actual leadership experience. I served as the chair of the department of economics for sixteen years and then in central administration for eleven years at Ohio State before becoming president of Oregon State University for the last sixteen years.

The Ohio State University has produced many leaders who became presidents at other colleges and universities. So, I am hardly unique. My peer group included Kermit Hall, who was president of Utah State University; Judy Genshaft, president of the University of South Florida; Greg Williams, president of the City College of New York and later chancellor at the University of Cincinnati; Jim Garland, president of Miami University of Ohio; Nancy Zimpher, president at the University of Wisconsin–Milwaukee, chancellor at the University of Cincinnati, and later chancellor of the SUNY System; and Joe Alutto, who served twice as interim president at The Ohio State University. Also, Barbara Snyder, who served as one of my vice provosts, is now president of Case Western University. Most of the bad examples of leadership I observed were associated with people who were typical products of their times rather than flawed individuals.

My bride of one year, Beth, and I arrived on campus at the beginning of fall quarter 1970 following the Kent State University tragedy that closed down many college campuses, including The Ohio State University. In fact, at our first faculty meeting, one of my senior colleagues recommended that faculty carry guns to class. Another suggested that if demonstrations broke out, we should use our influence with the rest of the class to set upon the troublemakers. Fortunately, neither policy was adopted.

In addition to its other developments, 1970 was a watershed year in economics; the profession was becoming more mathematical and analytical and less about institutional history and political economy. So, there was a genuine old guard versus young guard feel throughout the department. The department chair and senior faculty had very little interaction with the junior faculty, most of whom were not expected to earn tenure and therefore would have to leave within five years. The year I was hired, our department of about thirty-seven faculty hired eleven new assistant professors. The department chair and a few "chosen" colleagues were the only ones aware of what was going on in the department. Rumors were common and information scarce. Finally, the young faculty and a few senior colleagues staged a revolt, insisting the dean hold a vote to appoint a new department chair, and in July 1976 the assignment fell to me.

Not liking the culture of the department and having no positive role model for my new position as department chair, I decided on my own golden rule of leadership: Become the leader you would be proud to have as a boss and that you could admire and respect. That meant I had to be open, transparent, and accountable in all things and to deal directly with each faculty member on the most important matters to them: teaching schedules, office assignments, salary increases, and tenure and promotion decisions. I met with each colleague annually to explain what I recommended to the dean for salary increases, and I talked to each colleague about preferred teaching schedules. I circulated a complete draft of the teaching schedule for the next year and a month later gave everyone the final schedule. When we moved from Hagerty Hall to Arps Hall in 1983, I asked faculty for their office preferences and I made individual assignments.

In my second year as chairperson, I explained to a colleague old enough to be my father that I could not give him much of a raise because he was not doing any research and his teaching was rated poorly by students. As he got up to leave, I turned to shuffling the papers on my desk, feeling bad about what I had to say. I heard him say: "Thank you." I asked why he was thanking me, and he said that he did not want to hear what I said but he appreciated that I respected him enough to be honest with him, and that was not how he had been treated in the past. That was a powerful lesson to me that I always need to respect others enough to be honest with them when I have to deliver bad news.

Since I wanted time to prepare for my classes and to do research, I decided to bring my brown-bag lunch to the conference room every day and share any information I had with anyone who asked. I discussed tenure and promotion matters with affected faculty directly, and when I disagreed with the tenured faculty recommendations, I called a faculty meeting to explain my decision. Not everyone bought into my approach to department leadership. For example, the graduate students asked for permission to evaluate graduate courses through a quarterly survey. After my sixteen years as department chair ended, the department immediately eliminated the graduate course survey.

In 1980, the university was faced with state budget cuts. The university president announced that we were facing difficult times and that he was stepping down as president. At the time, another university was trying to get me to leave Ohio State to be chair of their economics program, and I was so appalled that the Ohio State president would announce a crisis and resign at the same time that I decided I could not leave. I told that story to President Gordon Gee during his first term as president at The Ohio State University and he told me the former president did not intend to resign until he met with the board the day of his announcement. So, presidents do not always step down at a time and place of their own choosing.

I have benefitted from the wise counsel of many deans at The Ohio State University. In the early 1980s, Justin Davidson, dean of the college of business, had a health scare that landed him in the hospital, where I visited him. He asked me what I like to do in my spare time and asked if I scheduled time for such activities. He observed that scheduled time crowds out unscheduled time, so we need to schedule time for relaxation. I share this advice with others but fail to follow it.

Joan Huber became dean of the college of social and behavioral sciences in 1983, and I benefited greatly from her counsel and leadership.

She observed once that it took her many years to realize that mother does not always know best. Her mother told her that anything worth doing deserves your best effort. But she told the department chairs that a recent task the provost set for the deans and department chairs was not worth a best effort. At another point, the president and provost were not communicating effectively with each other, so Joan told the chairs to send any requests to each of them separately. I asked her if it was a good time for the peasants to keep their heads down and she said yes.

Ed Jennings became president of The Ohio State University in 1981. He was young, smart, and very charismatic. I got to know the president quickly thanks to Madison Scott, the director of human resources (HR), who befriended me after I helped HR design a gender equity compensation assessment program. Also, the president's field was finance, which is a close academic cousin to economics. Ed Jennings left an important imprint on the university and taught me the importance of legacy. He raised faculty salaries substantially in the face of the budget crisis, noting that the faculty are the heart and soul of the university. He also worked with state government to begin to invest in university research, graduate education, and technology initiatives. Finally, he moved the university away from open enrollments and set universal standards for admissions to the university. Those actions set the groundwork for the Ohio State University of today.

I adopted that same focus on primary objectives by asking my direct reports to inform me in two pages or less at the beginning of each year of the three or four things they needed to accomplish during the coming academic year, and in the spring to provide me with two pages or less on what they had accomplished for the sake of evaluations. I provide my bosses with the same basic material to this day.

In 1992, Joan Huber became executive vice president and provost at The Ohio State University and asked me to join her staff to manage budgets and strategic planning. Ironically, when I was asked to apply for a similar position in 1987 by then provost Myles Brand, Joan told me that such positions are career killers. This was a time of university-wide budget cuts and Joan told the associate provosts on the first day that we would be part of the solution to university problems for the first six months and that after that we would be viewed as part of the problem. As we adjourned, she called after us to note that not everyone gets six months.

Joan also told us that any requests of the president should be one page or less. Several weeks later, she asked me how I was doing and I told her that I had a recurring nightmare that I had died and stood outside the gates of Heaven. St. Peter told me that I actually had a chance of getting in if I could write a compelling statement justifying my life. As I trudged away to do my homework, St. Peter called after me to observe that the statement had to be one page or less.

Given that I had been at the university for twenty-two years before joining central administration and the times were tough, friends and colleagues kept asking me how I was doing. The answer I settled on was that I felt like the priest who had died and gone to Hell. This was not at all what I expected, but I saw unlimited opportunities to do good works.

Fortunately, I found an ally with whom I worked closely for the next eleven years, Bill Shkurti, who was the vice president for finance and administration. He had been the state budget director serving Governor Celeste during the 1980s. Apparently, people find me very direct and easy to read, which does not always serve me well. By contrast, Bill has a great poker face, and when someone says something ridiculous, he gets very intense and quiet, while I am rolling my eyes. I have tried to copy him and failed miserably. On the other hand, Bill would often rate important meetings after the fact and critique our effectiveness, and I have emulated that practice with some success.

I had many opportunities to interact with President E. Gordon Gee. Gordon loves students and he has connected genuinely with students in every university where he has served as president. I lack his gift but share his passion for students and their success in life, and that became a strong bond between us. Lacking Gordon's affability, I have declared at every opportunity that our graduates are our most important contribution to the future and I am very proud of our students.

I quickly observed that President Gee was a very good listener, a very good judge of talent, and capable of revisiting a decision if presented compelling facts. Gordon helped me appreciate the importance of listening to all sides on an issue, surrounding myself with talented staff, and revisiting decisions when warranted. I persuaded Gordon to change course on decisions on several occasions, and we have maintained a strong trust and friendship over more than twenty-six years.

In 1994, President Gee had been left with the advice of departing provost Fred Hutchinson, who assumed the presidency at the University of Maine, to eliminate The Ohio State University Press. At the same time, I worked with the director of the press, Peter Givler, who later became president of the national association of university press directors, to develop a financial plan to keep the press alive until better times. Just before the president and I were scheduled to meet with Peter, Gordon called me into his office to ask if we should cancel the university press. I told him that if Harvard eliminated its press, the headlines in the *New York Times* would declare that Harvard was announcing the end of university presses, but if we made the announcement, the headline would be that the "corn people" had just eliminated their university press. He decided right there that the three of us would implement the austerity plan Peter and I devised to keep the press operating.

Gordon is famous for sending personal handwritten notes to people, a practice I have followed imperfectly, and despite my terrible handwriting, to let people know how much I appreciate their work and accomplishments. As I received notes from Gordon, I responded with typed messages because no one can read my handwriting. At a social event, Gordon came up to me and said: "I send you handwritten notes and you send me typed responses." I felt terrible, so I started sending handwritten responses. One day we had a surprise birthday gathering for him with cards, gag gifts, and cake. He started to open my present and I reminded him he had to read the card to understand the gift. He whispered that he could not read my handwriting, and I responded that I had typed the message.

Brit Kirwan became president at The Ohio State University in the summer of 1998, and he asked me to serve as executive vice president and provost. We became good friends in part because we shared a passion for diversity, inclusion, and social justice. Brit already had a national reputation for his efforts to advance those values at the University of Maryland, where he had served in many roles and completed his service as president of the university. Because of Brit's unwavering commitment, I found we could advance many initiatives. I argued that people study, teach, and do research on what they care about and used that approach to create a multicultural center; approve programs in Latino/Latina studies; provide offerings in Native American studies; establish language credit for American Sign Language; develop an office of disability services; provide matching funds to get the colleges of law, social and behavioral sciences, and humanities to develop what is now the Kirwan Institute for the Study of Race and Ethnicity in the Americas, housed in the college of law; and implement a number of other changes. In my role as president of Oregon State University, I understand how important it is to use my position to empower colleagues to accomplish goals that advance the university and improve our community.

Ohio State began its second university-wide fund-raising campaign in 1995 under the leadership of President Gee and the direction of the vice president for development, Jerry May. Bill Shkurti and I organized matters within the university. The original goal was set at $850 million. Shortly after Brit Kirwan arrived, we raised the goal to $1 billion, and the campaign closed in 2000 with $1.230 billion raised. This was a remarkably well-managed campaign and I learned a great deal. One disappointment for me was that we did not achieve much with regard to advancing diversity, inclusion, and community. I blame myself for that.

When I arrived at Oregon State, I learned that the university had never had a comprehensive fund-raising campaign and I made that a priority. The real work began when Mike Goodwin, Shawn Scoville, and the team they assembled at the Oregon State University Foundation were in place. We publicly launched our campaign in 2007 with a goal of $625 million, which we subsequently raised to $850 million and then $1 billion; we concluded the campaign in 2014 having raised $1.142 billion. Included in the Oregon State campaign was funding to rebuild four cultural centers, the Lonnie B. Harris Black Cultural Center, the Centro Cultural César Chávez, the Asian and Pacific Cultural Center, and the Native American Longhouse Eena Haws (Beaver House). This effort benefitted from funding by the Oregon State University Foundation, donors, the Associated Students of Oregon State University (ASOSU) student government, and the university. This initiative was informed by my failure to take appropriate action at Ohio State.

Starting in 1999–2000, Brit Kirwan and I initiated an effort with the deans to develop a strategic plan for the university. After several false starts, Brit, Chris Perry, a writer in communications, and I drafted what became the Academic Plan for Ohio State. When I arrived at Oregon State, there was no strategic plan. I enlisted colleagues here and remote help from Chris Perry to create a strategic plan for Oregon State in my first six months. We are now launching our fourth strategic plan document (SP4.0), and we are in the quiet phase of the next university-wide fund-raising campaign.

One important lesson I should have learned at The Ohio State did not take hold until I was here at Oregon State. In my last two years at the Ohio State University, I decided to move quickly on three major initiatives at once: grant an extended tenure and promotion process for tenure-track medical faculty from six to twelve years, a practice that already existed at thirty-seven of the fifty top-rated medical schools in the country; consolidate the five colleges of the arts and sciences into one college; and switch from quarters to semesters. I managed the first and started the second two, which were ultimately accomplished by Joe Alutto, Randy Smith, and other colleagues at Ohio State. I am reminded of one of Gordon Gee's sayings, that friends come and go but enemies accumulate. My ambitious goals garnered new enemies for me at an alarming rate.

Shortly after arriving at Oregon State University, I traveled two hours to Portland for a lunch at the Arlington Club with Orcilia Zuniga Forbes, who was soon to retire as vice president for advancement at the university. I enthusiastically shared my assessment of everything wrong at the university. When we parked, Orcilia observed that she could not disagree with any of my assessments, which meant I had a serious problem. I asked what she meant. Orcilia patiently explained that either I could prioritize and address the several most critical issues now and leave the rest to later, or I could try to fix everything at once and find people crossing the street to avoid having to talk to me. So, this was the lesson I was too dense to learn at Ohio State but finally got thanks to the assist from Orcilia.

The land-grant mission to bring learning, service, and innovation to the lives of all people in the state and now the nation and the world is reflected in the agricultural extension services, the agricultural research centers, and the forestry research labs that are part of every land-grant university. Oregon State has extension offices in all thirty-six counties of the state, and high school students throughout the state participate in our 4-H programs. At Oregon State University, we took that mission of going to where people live seriously, as did colleagues at Ohio State.

We now have a four-year regional campus in Bend, Oregon, the OSU-Cascades Campus, with 1,300 students in its fourth year of operation and a long-term goal of 3,000 to 5,000 students on our new, 126-acre campus. On the coast in Newport, where the National Oceanic and Atmospheric Administration docks its western research vessel fleet, we are building a state-of-the-art marine studies building that will provide a vertical evacuation site for all of those at the Hatfield Marine Science Center and other federal agencies if there is a major earthquake and associated tsunami. We are also leading the close to $300 million National Science Foundation grant to build three ships that will be part of the next generation of regional ocean-going research vessels. In short, we are everywhere in the state, making a difference in virtually every community, just as a land-grant university should.

When we were driving to the campus sixteen years ago for me to meet the Oregon University System Board of Trustees, I told Beth that by virtue of what I knew and what I learned at Ohio State, I thought I could really help some wonderful people accomplish amazing things. Only later did I come to appreciate how much my passion for the land-grant mission led us to accomplishments no one could have imagined.

33

Fostering Innovation and Collaboration within Land-Grant Universities

Joseph Steinmetz

I have been fortunate over the last thirty-two years to be a faculty member and administrator at four great US public universities: Indiana University, the University of Kansas, The Ohio State University and the University of Arkansas. Two of these institutions—Ohio State and Arkansas— share a special distinction: They are land-grant universities and their states' flagship institutions. At The Ohio State University, I served as executive dean and vice provost of the College of Arts and Sciences and later as executive vice president and provost. At the University of Arkansas, I serve as the chancellor of the land-grant, flagship campus in Fayetteville.

I was hired at Ohio State in 2009 by President Gordon Gee and Provost Joe Alutto with a specific task in mind: to unify the arts and sciences into a single, integrated college. The arts and sciences were separated into five stand-alone colleges in the late 1960s for reasons that are not altogether clear. President Gee and Provost Alutto recognized a number of disadvantages in maintaining five separate colleges that contained the arts and sciences disciplines. Three of these disadvantages stand out. First, the colleges seemed to be increasingly siloed and isolated, perhaps due in part to the responsibility-centered management system adopted by the university for allocating financial resources to academic units. Second, there were clear inefficiencies in operating five separate colleges and clear opportunities for cost savings with a more unified structure. Third, and perhaps most important, decreasing the barriers across colleges had the potential to create an environment that encouraged more collaboration and cooperation across disciplines, especially for teaching and research. This is a direction that higher education in general has headed over the last several years. To make a long story very short, a new unified arts and sciences college was designed and in operation on July 1, 2010.

I can argue that arts and science colleges are the foundation of almost all universities. It's where general education originates. They are comprehensive colleges where a variety of disciplines are taught and where a tremendously extensive range of research is conducted. Arts and sciences colleges are generally the home of the humanities and arts, most of the social sciences, and many of the science and computational disciplines. Further, and important for this volume, while the 1862 Morrill Land-Grant Act established colleges and universities that specialized in "agriculture and the mechanical arts," the language of the act also referenced classical studies and the importance of the working classes obtaining a liberal practical education, the very mission of most arts and sciences colleges. Thus, colleges of arts and sciences have always played major roles in the teaching, research, and outreach mission of our land-grant universities. The College of Arts and Sciences at Ohio State and the Fulbright College of Arts and Sciences at the University of Arkansas are great examples of this fact.

Arguably one of the biggest changes in higher education over the last several years is a move toward greater cooperation and collaboration at our institutions in the three mission areas that typically define land-grant universities—teaching, research, and service. There are several reasons for this movement. With regard to teaching, a number of interdisciplinary fields have emerged that require expertise from a number of disciplines to create a curriculum. The fields of neuroscience, cognitive science, and the data sciences are examples. These new programs require a much more collaborative-minded faculty than in the past. Also, business and industry have been emphasizing the need for our students to learn to work collaboratively with others on projects. This means that across the board, our curricula had to increasingly include these student experiences, and sometimes this has led to more courses that are team-taught, which sometimes requires faculty to collaborate more. On the research side, it has become increasingly apparent that the complexity of the research questions being asked has increased beyond the expertise of single investigators. Teams of researchers are now much more common, as are external funding opportunities for team-based research. Shared-equipment facilities are more common, in large part due to considerations of efficiency and cost-containment. I believe that the movement toward team-based teaching and learning as well as research and discovery has been good for our students and good for our faculty. Moreover, land-grant universities have been at the forefront of this shift in how we educate students and conduct research, perhaps because the breadth and depth of academic talent has traditionally been strong at these comprehensive institutions.

This more cooperative model of teaching and scholarship is certainly not new to me. My research field, behavioral neuroscience, has for many years been highly interdisciplinary. Further, I promoted a more collaborative model of teaching and scholarship in the mid-1990s when I chaired the Department of Psychology at Indiana University. There, we created a department administrative and governing structure that encouraged interdisciplinary pursuits and collaboration. We abandoned a more traditional structure that encouraged boundaries and promoted independence between the traditional areas of research and teaching common to experimental and clinical psychology. I also promoted this basic philosophy while dean of liberal arts and sciences at the University of Kansas.

My move to The Ohio State University afforded me a great opportunity to create a cooperative and collaborative environment for students, staff, and faculty from the ground up as I was tasked with creating a unified College of Arts and Sciences by combining five independent colleges that covered the arts, humanities, social sciences, biological sciences, and physical/mathematical sciences. The main challenges I saw were threefold: how to create a unified college administration, how to create a budget structure, and how to change a forty-year culture of faculty, students, and staff operating in smaller, independent colleges. Again, my fundamental goal was to promote collaboration wherever we could.

Before I arrived at Ohio State, a decision had been made to create a divisional structure by combining the arts and humanities into one unit, to create one science unit, and to maintain the social and behavioral sciences as a unit. It was clear at the outset that the size of a unified college would be too large to operate with a single dean to whom department chairs reported. With this fact in mind, we developed a divisional model with three divisional deans responsible for a number of units—Arts and Humanities, Social and Behavioral Sciences, and Natural and Mathematical Sciences. The divisional deans would report to the executive dean (who also had the title of vice provost for the arts and sciences). Prior to the restructuring, there were literally five of everything—five development offices, five financial offices, five student affairs offices, and so on. The restructuring provided an excellent opportunity to reduce the size of the administration by removing redundancy wherever possible. We created a college-wide shared services center by combining staff expertise from the legacy colleges who could develop skills in specific areas like human resources, travel, and procurement. This move allowed us to save dollars that were then redistributed to the departments and programs within the college. There was also a reduction in the number of administrators, such as associate deans, needed to operate the unified college. All these savings helped us deal with a rather deep recession that hit the economy, including higher education, hard around the time of the college restructuring. This economic downtown included a relatively large cut in state support. The savings realized by the restructuring in fact helped us deal with the 15 percent state support cut we saw as well as several years of minimal, if any, tuition increases.

The budget restructuring was challenging. The university operated under a responsibility center management (RCM) budget model where credit-hour production largely determined the distribution of resources. Each of the legacy colleges operated their RCM model differently, with models that varied from pushing RCM down to the level of individual departments to more central models for distributing funds from the dean to department chairs. The existing budget did not encourage collaboration but rather just the opposite because almost no dollars were available centrally to incentivize cooperation. There were distinct advantages to creating additional credit hours whenever possible, so there was competition between legacy colleges for students. And, because dollars recovered from federal indirect costs went directly to the colleges, research collaborations across colleges were often difficult to establish. To address these challenges, we created a more central budget model where distribution of dollars was based on more than credit-hour production. This affected many areas of operation, including the distribution of individual faculty lines, staffing, facilities, and financial commitments made to individual faculty as well as to departments and programs, to name a few. There was really only one fundamental principle for our budget restricting: We tried to encourage and reward collaboration wherever possible by thinking more about the contributions of individual faculty members across the college and less of contributions made more collectively by departments and programs.

I believe the biggest hurdle to overcome was to change the opinions and culture of the faculty and staff who made up the new unified arts and science college. Frankly, some of the faculty and staff did not believe the restructuring was a good idea. There were many reasons for this. Faculty and staff had established identities in the legacy colleges and feared the loss of their identities. The financial stabilities in the individual colleges varied—some were doing better than others under the RCM model. Some faculty didn't see the need for a collaborative environment and feared the loss of their individual identities as scholars. Indeed, the word *interdisciplinary* created angst in some even though we tried to stress whenever we could that our goal was to provide an opportunity for collaboration by removing barriers, not to force all to be collaborative. I don't know how many times I said that we fully realized that you could not have interdisciplinary opportunities without the foundation of disciplines. Finally, others simply didn't like change. I did sense a change in culture within the college when I left to become provost. For example, the shared service center was addressing the needs of the faculty and staff, which reduced some anxiety. And those faculty seeking to collaborate on their teaching and research now saw opportunities that were available. Perhaps more important, higher education in general has changed to a much more cooperative model and away from a model of solely independent scholarship. This is particularly evidenced in the new faculty we have hired in the last decade or so. They expect a collaborative environment. I believe the restructured College of Arts and Sciences offers this.

When I became executive vice president and provost at Ohio State, I looked for more opportunities to promote collaboration whenever possible to assist faculty, students, and staff in fulfilling our land-grant mission as a university. One example stands out in my mind: the university Discovery Themes. Over the years, Ohio State has made a number of large-scale investments in the research mission that also impacted the teaching and outreach missions of the university. The creation of the Discovery Themes was one of these investments. The opening statement on the university's discovery theme home page captures well the spirit of discovery important to these themes:

> Discovery at Ohio State is the way in which we connect diverse ideas and people across disciplines and communities. It's the way that our outstanding faculty, devoted university campuses, and engaged partners connect to form and scale teams that translate knowledge into solutions. It is a passion to ask questions yet to be asked and tackle problems yet to be solved.

It can be readily seen in this statement that collaboration across the university is the fundamental principle on which the Discovery Themes were based. It's the realization that solutions for the giant unsolved problems of our society will come when multiple disciplines and approaches are used to seek them. With this in mind, much of my time as provost was marked by creating the framework for the Discovery Themes.

The discovery areas framework emphasized principles that maximized opportunities for collaboration across the campus. First, the funding model created was outside the university's RCM system. Central funds were created mainly from an endowment that was created by a large one-time payment to the university when the parking concession was leased to a private company. And, investment in the Discovery Themes, such as new faculty lines, generally required a matching commitment from both the central administration and the academic colleges. Second, whenever possible, joint hires between colleges were promoted. Third, the selection of discovery theme areas to develop was made only after input from large, cross-disciplinary working groups was considered. These groups identified areas of strengths that existed in the university that with additional investment could lead to Ohio State establishing itself as a world leader in that area of discovery. Translational Data Analytics was the first area chosen for development. Since then other areas have been added, such as Chronic Brain Injury, Foods for Health, Food and Agricultural Transformation, Global Arts and Humanities, Infectious Diseases, Materials and Manufacturing for Sustainability, and Sustainable and Resilient Economy. All of these areas reflect the comprehensive nature of the talent at The Ohio State University as a land-grant university. Forth, and very important, leadership matters. Thus, the program leads for all the areas were chosen for their abilities to stress collaboration, team discovery, and integrative thinking. I believe this is an innovative and novel approach to investing in discovery that will pay off in years to come. Something like this is made possible by the fact that Ohio State is a comprehensive land-grant university with a great diversity of research and scholarship.

I left The Ohio State University and became chancellor of the University of Arkansas on January 1, 2016, and I have borrowed heavily on my experiences at Ohio State in leading this institution. Similar to my time at Ohio State, I have emphasized collaboration and team approaches to research, discovery, and outreach here at Arkansas. Though we are a much smaller institution that Ohio State, we still have the breadth and comprehensiveness one sees at a land-grant university and we try to exploit these characteristics whenever possible. Indeed, after a campus-wide planning effort, we created eight guiding priorities for the university. One of these is entitled "Building a Collaborative and Innovative Campus," recognizing that higher education has become increasingly more interdisciplinary and collaborative, like the world around. This priority reflects our desire to foster a university environment that embraces collaboration and interdisciplinary teaching and research pursuits.

We have launched several programs and initiatives here over the last three years to encourage collaboration, innovation, and entrepreneurship among our faculty and students. We created an annual $1 million Chancellors Collaboration and Innovation Fund and have received about seventy-five proposals annually for this fund from faculty groups. This fund provides support for collaborative research projects that bring groups of faculty members together in new ways in hopes of seeding external funding opportunities as well as the chance for our faculty to explore new ideas and new directions.

We have created new interdisciplinary programs for our students, including a new data science curriculum that has brought together our Fulbright College of Arts and Sciences, Sam M. Walton College of Business, and College of Engineering in truly cross-campus efforts. And, we are looking for new and innovative programs for our undergraduate and graduate students that will help them find great careers in a rapidly changing and unpredictable world.

With input from cross-cutting groups of our faculty, we have created three general research areas we believe will further bring our faculty and students together and flourish with additional investment—we refer to these as our signature research areas. These areas are Harnessing the Data Revolution, Promoting a Resilient and Sustainable Future, and Enriching Health and Communities. Similar to the Ohio State strategy, we believe that we have great existing strength in these areas, and with additional investment and encouragement, we can become world leaders in research and teaching in these areas.

Another area we are working on is how we integrate the arts more broadly across the University of Arkansas. This is not a new concept to me and is indeed related to building a collaborative and innovative campus. While executive dean and then as provost at Ohio State, I worked to more broadly define a role for the arts in the university and in the surrounding community. For me, the arts are not just for artists but rather an activity that should be accessed broadly by as many people as possible. The work of the Alliance for the Arts in Research Universities (a2ru), for example, has demonstrated the value that integrating arts with other disciplines has on creativity, research productivity, and problem solving. Collaborations between the arts and other disciplines will be greatly beneficial for all involved. Our new School of Art here, funded by a $110 million endowment from the Walton Family Charitable Support Foundation, includes a plan for a campus-wide integration and access to and collaborations with other disciplines.

Often institutions create significant roadblocks to student and faculty collaborations by maintaining policies that were written in an era when individual scholarship was the only form of discovery recognized as valuable. Times have changed, though, and it is important that institutions like ours make sure our policies allow (and reward) collaborative scholarship and recognize the value that this approach has. Administrative structuring policies, tenure and promotion policies, faculty evaluation policies, curriculum and program development policies, and faculty appointment policies are just a few examples of policies and processes we are currently examining to make sure they enable and promote a more collaborative and innovative campus.

One last point: The strong commitment to an outreach and engagement mission by land-grant universities remains a major distinguishing feature of the institutions. Historically, this mission typically centered around the strong presence of agricultural extension offices and research centers characteristic of land-grant institutions. This mission has broadened significantly over the years and includes much more, such as K–12 educational services, community design and consultation, and research expertise in just about every area represented in the land-grant university. I would also argue that there are many opportunities for collaboration in this area as well as we attempt to serve our communities better, which is the very basis for our existence. This can only help our institutions gain the confidence of our citizens as we improve the quality of lives in the states we serve in as many ways as possible.

In summary, it is my belief that one of the really great issues that can be tackled by land-grant and flagship universities is the promotion of innovative, collaborative models of research and teaching, which I believe are critical for the future of higher education and our society. Land-grant universities are by very design comprehensive. They therefore possess the variety of fields, disciplines, and scholars to work collectively in new and cross-cutting ways to answer the truly large research questions that are out there. Further, land-grant universities educate millions of students and thus are in the best position to influence the next generation of scholars who will work on these problems and the next generation of problems in business, engineering, the liberal arts, the sciences, the arts, and any other fields. And, land-grant universities can and should be in the business of improving lives through collaborative, broad-based outreach and engagement.

Conclusion

34

Parting Thoughts on Fulfilling the Twenty-First-Century Land-Grant Mission

Stephen M. Gavazzi and David J. Staley

As the editors of this collection, we promised to create a platform that would highlight the prominence and preeminence of work generated by faculty, staff, students, and stakeholders of The Ohio State University. The focus on prominence would generate support for the notion that there were people and activities that made Ohio State particularly visible among other universities. Attention to preeminence meant that these people and their activities placed this university at the very forefront of these institutions of higher learning. To fulfill this promise, our challenge to the contributors was threefold: focus on the difference between A and A+, discuss what it meant to be a land-grant university in the twenty-first century, and describe how Ohio State must innovate to remain relevant. In conclusion, then, we wish to ask: How well did we do collectively in terms of fulfilling our promise?

Looking over the collection of essays, we are gratified to close this effort out by noting that the authors certainly exceeded our personal expectations. We knew the leadoff essay for this book was going to be crucial. So, we were thrilled to witness how President Drake's contribution ignited a fire that would burn brightly throughout this collection by focusing so intensively on the land-grant legacy—access, affordability, and excellence—and its critical connection to the future of Ohio and the US. As editors, we worked to expand on this powerful opening essay, endeavoring to stoke these flames through our own written contributions.

Gavazzi focused on the *prima inter pares* (first among equals) status of our university that comes from a unique combination of resources: existing in an urban setting, running a premier medical center, being involved in Power 5 athletics, and having the great size of its student body and alumni base. In turn, Staley asked us to imagine—among other things—a "digital regional campus" that would crack open The Ohio State University to accommodate 100,000 students or more, perhaps at a potentially lower cost, to boot. Our exceptionality, combined with our continued advancement as an innovative institution, would seem to forecast continued relevance as a land-grant university far into the twenty-first century.

Next up were the three essays that laid out the foundation of our tripartite mission—teaching, research, and community engagement—and we believe they generated much food for thought. Halasek's discussion of the University Institute for Teaching and Learning underscored those activities aimed at creating a more robust and inclusive teaching culture at Ohio State. Weisenberger adroitly covered the strengths and challenges associated with cutting-edge empirical efforts within the university, not the least of which centered on how to continuously attract and support the brightest and most innovative faculty and student talent in the research realm. In turn, Myers rightly pointed out how well Ohio State has responded to the inevitability of change over the past century and a half, especially in its efforts to continually create meaningful partnerships that would engage communities on those issues and concerns that most demanded the attention of experts from various fields.

The "manifestation" section of this book—containing by far the largest number of contributions—is thought to have provided a wealth of insights regarding just exactly how land-grant universities in general and Ohio State more specifically are pushing the envelope across all three major activities related to its mission. For example, Kamp Dush and Gavazzi challenged us to recognize that no student—woman or man—will achieve their full potential until they understand how to balance work and family life. As well, through a focus on The Arts Initiative, Valarie Williams strongly asserted that a land-grant degree represents a well-rounded education, focusing as much on the arts and humanities as on the practical and vocational. And Jones reminded us we have six campuses that serve Ohio State's students, distributed across multiple geographic locations that serve a mix of urban, suburban, and smaller rural communities.

On the research front, we read numerous accounts of Ohio State people and programs leading the way. David Williams described how efforts within the College of Engineering have been aimed directly at reversing Ohio's population loss and associated economic decline by leading the way in such areas as transportation and new material development. Kress and Cochran reminded us both of Ohio State's cornerstone history as an agricultural school and its future as a cutting-edge research enterprise. Hoy and Snyder took this sentiment one step farther by focusing important attention on food insecurity and its association with poverty, racial disparity, and social support, all the while calling for interdisciplinary work within the academy and growing partnerships with public and private entities outside of the university. In turn, Moore provided us with a glimpse of how Ohio State's veterinary college protects animal well-being while simultaneously promoting biomedical research that advances both animal and human health.

There were many contributions to this collection that focused attention on community engagement activities. Bloir and Scheer highlighted how 4-H's humble roots, which began with the need for after-school programs, have been transformed into efforts that focus on science, technology, engineering, and math (STEM) in order to better meet the demand for workers in STEM-related fields. Gregoire provided an overview of efforts within the College of Social Work to overcome ideological differences that thwart social justice and oppress and divide people within our communities. The Ohio State response to the challenges of an urban world and the opportunities afforded by the new science of cities was discussed in detail by Miller. And Meadows reminded us of our 1890 land-grant partner—Central State University—and the importance of leveraging each other's strengths in service to the citizens of Ohio.

Within the student experience section, Mayhew and McChesney highlighted the university's 150-year-old pledge to mentally cultivate the ready student—no matter their background—in order to create a better world for all. And we witnessed just how broad that teaching mandate was in practice. Isaacs and colleagues brought into focus the newly developed Second-year Transformational Experience Program (STEP) and its efforts to contribute ever more significantly to the personal and professional growth of students. We learned from Ellison that our medical students are routinely exposed to leading work in organ transplants, burn and trauma care, and community efforts to reduce infant mortality. And former student athlete and board of trustee member Clark Kellogg summed up his own experiences at Ohio State by declaring his continued commitment to being more "fiercely land-grant" as both an alumnus and an advocate for the university.

The "insider observations" section of the book provided even more detail in terms of how Ohio State develops and maintains partnerships with community stakeholders. Brown discussed the university's efforts to train and prepare local elected and appointed officials. Rennekamp's discussion of the ethos of the engaged institution included an intensive focus on Cooperative Extension Services and the vital role their professionals play in connecting with cities and towns as well as the more rural parts of our state and nation. Stenta emphasized the importance of keeping Ohio State alumni engaged in activities that further develop knowledge and leadership skills over the life-span.

Essays from the insider observation section also provided readers with glimpses inside the inner workings of the university and what is being done to maintain Ohio State's edge. Martin and Switzer discussed how leadership development within the university must be comprehensive and systematic as it grounds itself in the foundation of what it means to be a land-grant institution. Schmiesing focused attention on the central role that departments play in the continued creation and dissemination of knowledge through teaching, research, and community engagement activities. Jaggars brought a unique perspective on what it meant to be a successful library within the land-grant context, measured in large part by how well it advances core land-grant values and missions. And Carpenter-Hubin helped readers understand how difficult it sometimes is to evaluate the success and value of our land-grant activities, especially in the realm of community engagement.

Our final section bought into the fore the "outsider observations" we had collected from four previous senior leaders of The Ohio State University. Former president Gee discussed his view that leading a land-grant university was a calling to a higher order, not merely a job that one sought. Former president Kirwan discussed the crisis all universities are facing in terms of not providing equal access to a quality education for nearly enough people to sustain our economy and to uphold our nation's founding values. Former provost Ray highlighted how his passion for the land-grant mission—first kindled here at Ohio State—would allow him to accomplish so much as president of Oregon State University. And former provost Steinmetz ended this section by underscoring how remarkably well his strong commitment to teaching excellence, research prowess, and meaningful engagement with communities while at Ohio State was immediately translatable to his chancellorship at the University of Arkansas.

In brief and in closing, we observed countless examples of Ohio State's prominence and preeminence throughout these essays. Time and again, we read examples that explained either directly or indirectly what the difference between an A versus an A+ effort looked like in the teaching, research, and engagement activities undertaken by faculty, staff, students, and community stakeholders. We witnessed an unrelenting discussion about what it meant to be a land-grant university in the twenty-first century. And last but certainly not least, we were privileged to behold the many viewpoints our contributors provided in terms of what Ohio State must do to innovate to remain relevant. Mission accomplished!

Contributors

JAVAUNE ADAMS-GASTON currently is the president of Norfolk State University in Virginia. In 2009, Dr. Adams-Gaston became Ohio State's first female African American vice president for student life. She arrived at Ohio State from the University of Maryland, where she served in a variety of administrative and faculty positions. Dr. Adams-Gaston is a scholar-practitioner with vast experience at Research 1 public institutions, including her senior administrative responsibilities in student affairs (senior vice president, executive director, psychologist), academic affairs (associate dean), intercollegiate athletics (assistant athletic director) and university-level administration (equity administrator).

KIRK BLOIR is an assistant professor of extension education in the College of Food, Agricultural, and Environmental Sciences at The Ohio State University. He currently serves as the interim assistant director for OSU Extension 4-H Youth Development. His leadership efforts focus on helping to create and increase county extension professionals' capacity, competence, and confidence in addressing human, fiscal, and liability-related issues associated with all aspects of extension program management in general, and risks specific to working with the complexities of 4-H programs and partnerships more specifically. His research explores organizational change management and volunteerism.

TREVOR BROWN serves as the dean of the John Glenn College of Public Affairs at The Ohio State University and executive director of the State of Ohio Leadership Institute, a resource for the next generation of Ohio state and local elected officials. He conducts research and teaches on public management and leadership, government contracting, public-private partnerships, and democracy and democratic transitions. He has worked with governments and public organizations to improve organizational and managerial performance. He has conducted applied research projects for the US Department of the Navy, the IBM Center for the Business of Government, the Pew Center on the States, the Eurasia Foundation, and the US Agency for International Development. He is also a fellow of the National Academy of Public Administration.

JULIE CARPENTER-HUBIN served The Ohio State University as the assistant vice president of institutional research and planning and the field of institutional research in various roles, including president of the Association for Institutional Research, a member of the US Department of Education's National Postsecondary Education Cooperative, and a member of the National Research Council's Data Panel. She is currently coediting a volume on ethics and data analytics.

GRAHAM R. COCHRAN serves as the associate dean for operations for the College of Food, Agricultural, and Environmental Sciences (CFAES) at The Ohio State University. He serves in a college-wide role, where he is responsible for providing leadership for strategy, including risk management, accountability, strategic planning, and associated resource allocation. He is an educator with over twenty-three years of experience at the local, state, national, and international levels in organizational development, leadership development, and workforce development, both with youth and adults in the workforce. He graduated from Marietta College with a certificate in leadership and bachelor of science in biology. He received his master of science in zoology with an emphasis on small mammal ecology from Miami of Ohio, and his PhD from The Ohio State University in human and community resource development focused on extension education and higher education administration.

MICHAEL V. DRAKE, MD, is the fifteenth president of The Ohio State University. His focus is on strengthening Ohio State's position as a leading public research university through excellence in five strategic areas: teaching and learning; access, affordability, and excellence; research and creative expression; academic health care; and operational excellence and resource stewardship. During his tenure, the university has seen record highs in applications, graduation rates, academic excellence, diversity, sponsored research awards, and donor support. An ophthalmologist by training, Dr. Drake is a leader in a number of national higher education organizations and is an elected member of the National Academy of Medicine and the American Academy of Arts & Sciences.

E. CHRISTOPHER ELLISON, MD, is an academy professor and the Robert M. Zollinger Professor of Surgery Emeritus at The Ohio State University College of Medicine. He was appointed in 2019 as the scholar-in-residence for the Medical Heritage Center in the OSU College of Medicine. He previously served as the president and CEO of the Ohio State University Physicians Practice Plan and was a founding member of that organization. He served as interim dean of the OSU College of Medicine from 2014 to 2016 and chair of surgery 2000 to 2013. He was previously recognized as the College of Medicine Distinguished Professor.

STEPHEN M. GAVAZZI is a professor in the human development and family science program in the College of Education and Human Ecology at The Ohio State University. He is the coauthor (with E. Gordon Gee) of *Land-Grant Universities for the Future: Higher Education for the Public Good*; *The Optimal Town-Gown Marriage: Taking Campus-Community Outreach and Engagement to the Next Level*; and *Families with Adolescents: Bridging the Gaps between Theory, Research, and Practice.* Known primarily for his expertise regarding the impact that families have on adolescent development and well-being, Gavazzi more recently has developed a line of scholarship that examines campus-community relationship health and leadership issues in higher education. He holds a bachelor's degree in psychology from Pennsylvania State University, and both a master's degree in marriage and family therapy and a doctoral degree in family studies from the University of Connecticut.

E. GORDON GEE is the president of West Virginia University. He is the coauthor of over a dozen books, including his two most recent, *Leading Colleges and Universities* and *Land-Grant Universities for the Future: Higher Education for the Public Good.* His research interests include education law, higher education administration, and the importance of land-grant universities.

TOM GREGOIRE was named acting dean of the College of Social Work in 2008 and appointed dean in 2010. Community engagement, social change, and innovation are hallmarks of the College of Social Work, and the college is known for its capacity to engage with constituents as partners toward the creation of a more just and equitable community.

KAY HALASEK serves as the director of the University Institute for Teaching and Learning at The Ohio State University, where she also holds an appointment as an associate professor of English. Her research spans a variety of areas within rhetorical theory and the teaching of writing, including feminist historiography, theories of writing, collaborative learning, writing program administration, portfolio assessment, and basic writing. Her current projects include a longitudinal study of student and expert responses to college writing assignments in massive open online courses.

CASEY HOY, professor and former associate chair of the Department of Entomology at The Ohio State University, has held the Kellogg Endowed Chair in Agricultural Ecosystems Management and provided leadership to the Agroecosystems Management Program of the Ohio Agricultural Research and Development Center since 2006. Hoy's past research has included systems analysis and its application to integrated pest management and applied agricultural ecology. His current work provides interdisciplinary leadership toward advancements in agroecosystem health and sustainable communities. He is the faculty director of the Ohio State University Discovery Themes initiative for Food and AgriCultural Transformation, InFACT, a significant investment in resilient and sustainable food security.

DAVID ISAACS handles news media inquiries to the Office of Student Life, along with other communications duties. He joined the university in 2012 after serving as communications director at the Ohio House of Representatives. Prior to that, he spent a number of years as a broadcast journalist, including news management positions at news radio stations in Columbus, Ohio; Grand Rapids and Detroit, Michigan; and Houston and Austin, Texas. Isaacs is a Columbus native, and received his BA from Denison University and an MA from the John Glenn College of Public Affairs at Ohio State.

DAMON E. JAGGARS serves as the vice provost and director of University Libraries at The Ohio State University. He previously worked for libraries at Columbia University, the University of Texas, and Iona College. His background includes service planning and assessment, collection development and management, facilities planning and design, and organizational development, as well as building distinctive and unique collections and developing information technology infrastructures within research libraries. His work has been published broadly in peer-reviewed journals and conference proceedings, and his editorial service includes board membership for *portal: Libraries and the Academy,* coeditorship of a special issue of *Evidence Based Library and Information Practice,* and a stint as editor-in chief of the *Journal of Library Administration.* He currently serves on advisory boards for OhioLINK, the Big Ten Academic Alliance, and TOME and on several committees for the Association of Research Libraries.

NORMAN W. JONES joined the Mansfield campus of The Ohio State University in 2004 as a member of the English Department. He earned his PhD from the

University of California, Los Angeles and his BA from Yale University. He teaches courses in twentieth- and twenty-first-century American literature, film, and the Bible. He has published four books and numerous essays exploring intersections among literature, sexuality, and religion. He now serves as the dean and director of the Mansfield campus, prior to which he served as faculty president, English program coordinator, associate dean, and interim dean and director.

CLAIRE KAMP DUSH is an associate professor of human development and family science in the Department of Human Sciences in the College of Education and Human Ecology. She is the principal investigator of two National Institutes of Health research grants. The National Couples' Health and Time Study is the first population-representative study of same- and different-gender couples in the US. The multimethod project will collect survey, time-diary, and biological data from over 2,500 couples. The Work and Family Life Study is a study of work and family life and their intersection with health over forty years in the US. A 2019 recipient of The Ohio State University Alumni Award for Distinguished Teaching, Kamp Dush is a passionate teacher and mentor.

CLARK KELLOGG has been a basketball commentator since 1987, having done radio and television broadcasting for the Indiana Pacers, Cleveland State University, the Atlantic 10 and Big East TV Networks, ESPN, Westwood One, and CBS Sports. Kellogg attended The Ohio State University and earned his marketing degree in 1996. He excelled as a three-year starter on the basketball team from 1980 to 1982, and as a junior he earned Big 10 MVP honors in 1982. After his junior season, Kellogg was the eighth player selected in the 1982 NBA draft. He spent his entire five-year playing career with the Indiana Pacers and was a unanimous 1st Team All-Rookie selection and had career averages of 19ppg and 9rpg before his retirement in 1987 due to chronic knee issues. He also has served on The Ohio State Alumni Association Board and The Ohio State Board of Trustees (2010–2019), and he is a director on First Merchants Bank Regional Board. A native of Cleveland, Ohio, he and his bride Rosy have three adult children and two granddaughters.

WILLIAM E. "BRIT" KIRWAN is a chancellor emeritus of the University System of Maryland (USM). He served as chancellor of USM for thirteen years (2002–2015), president of The Ohio State University for four years (1998–2002), and president of the University of Maryland, College Park for ten years (1988–1998). Prior to his presidency, he was a member of the University of Maryland mathematics faculty for twenty-four years. Among his many honors, Dr. Kirwan received the

2010 TIAA-CREF Theodore M. Hesburgh Award for Leadership Excellence and in 2009 the Carnegie Corporation Leadership Excellence Award. He was elected to the American Academy of Arts and Sciences in 2002.

DR. CATHANN A. KRESS has served as the vice president for agricultural administration and dean of the College of Food, Agricultural, and Environmental Sciences (CFAES) at The Ohio State University since May 2017. She has responsibility for leadership of the college, which also comprises OSU Extension, research centers including the Ohio Agricultural Research and Development Center, and the Agricultural Technical Institute in Wooster. She is also a full professor within the Department of Agricultural Communication, Education, and Leadership. Kress is a trustee of the W. K. Kellogg Foundation. She serves on the State of Ohio Livestock Care Standards Board, on the National 4-H Council Board, and as chair of the administrative heads section of the Board on Agriculture Assembly, Association of Public and Land-grant Universities. She graduated with distinction from Iowa State University, where she received her bachelor's degree. She received her master's and doctorate from the University of Iowa, where she was an American College Testing (ACT) Special Research Fellow.

RICK MARTIN has spent the past twenty-two years in progressively more responsible positions as a management consultant, project manager, and leadership coach, and has been at Ohio State since 2009. Prior to Ohio State, he worked with companies and nonprofits in a broad set of industries, including banking, manufacturing, real estate, and media. Martin has deep experience in leadership development, large-scale change, team effectiveness, and executive transition. Earlier in his career, he spent ten years in accounting and finance, including roles as a general accountant, financial analyst, financial consultant, public auditor, and CFO. He earned a master's degree in organization development from Bowling Green State University and his BSBA in accounting from The Ohio State University. He is married and lives in Columbus, Ohio, with his wife and dog.

MATTHEW J. MAYHEW is the William Ray and Marie Adamson Flesher Professor of Educational Administration and the director of the Higher Education and Student Affairs program at OSU, where he leads the College Impact Laboratory. Noted author of *How College Affects Students: 21st Century Evidence That Higher Education Works,* he researches the influence of college environments on student outcomes, with funded projects that examine innovation in higher education, interfaith learning and development, and graduate training in interdisciplinary sustainable energy programs.

ERIC McCHESNEY is a PhD student in higher education and student affairs at The Ohio State University. He earned his master of arts in education at the University of Florida and currently works as a researcher at the College Impact Laboratory (CoIL), where he studies the effects of humanistic education upon learning and social outcomes and the application of public intellectualism pedagogies to the liberal arts.

ANNE McDANIEL is the executive director in the Center for the Study of Student Life (CSSL). She joined the CSSL in 2013 as the associate director for research and data management. She earned a PhD in sociology at The Ohio State University and was a postdoctoral scholar at Columbia University's Institute for Social and Economic Research and Policy. Prior to joining CSSL, she was an assistant professor of education and sociology (by courtesy) at the University of California, Irvine. Dr. McDaniel's research interests include gender and racial inequalities in higher education, especially as they relate to student experiences and persistence. Her research has appeared in over twenty peer-reviewed journals and books, including recent publications in the *Journal of Student Affairs Research and Practice, Educational Researcher,* and *Sociology Compass.*

LAQUORE J. MEADOWS serves as the county extension director for Franklin County, Ohio. Prior to joining OSU Extension, she acquired nearly a decade of experience leading federally sponsored projects and college access programs. She has devoted much of her career and community work toward the enhancement of financial wellness and academic attainment for underserved populations. Meadows has served as an American Council on Education Fellow and is an active member of Delta Sigma Theta Sorority and a host of other professional organizations. She received her bachelor's degree from Tennessee State University, her master's in college student personnel from Miami University, and a doctorate in higher education administration from Ohio University.

HARVEY J. MILLER is the Bob and Mary Reusche Chair in Geographic Information Science, the director of the Center for Urban and Regional Analysis, and a professor of geography at The Ohio State University. He is also a courtesy professor in the Department of City and Regional Planning, a member of the Faculty Advisory Board of the Sustainability Institute, and an affiliated faculty of the Translation Data Analytics Institute at Ohio State. His research and teaching interests are at the intersection between geographic information science and transportation, in particular the analysis of human mobility within cities and regions. The main questions driving his research include sustainable transportation, livable cities, and the relationships between human mobility, health, and social equity.

RUSTIN M. MOORE is the dean of the College of Veterinary Medicine and the Ruth Stanton Chair in Veterinary Medicine at The Ohio State University. He has taught at all levels of the undergraduate, professional, and graduate curricula, both at Ohio State and at Louisiana State University over his twenty-five year faculty career. The college's work helps to benefit society and enhance the health and well-being of animals, people, and the ecosystem through excellence in education, research, patient care, outreach, and service, consistent with its land-grant mission. Currently he leads the effort for the college's ambition to Be the Model™ comprehensive college of veterinary medicine in the world, impacting animal and human health through innovation, collaboration, and excellence. Integrating the foundational principles of health and well-being, diversity and inclusion, advancing partnerships, and resource stewardship into the college's mission and activities is essential to reach this ambition.

STEPHEN C. MYERS was an associate vice provost at Ohio State who led a university-wide approach to engagement informed by the College Engagement Council, a university committee of thought leaders. He was a 2011–2012 Fellow in the American Council on Education. From 2005–12, Dr. Myers was the assistant director of the Ohio Agricultural Research and Development Center (OARDC), the research arm of OSU's College of Food, Agricultural, and Environmental Sciences. During that time he developed the Ohio Bioproducts Innovation Center (OBIC), a university-industry collaborative. He chaired Ohio State's Department of Horticulture and Crop Science from 1999 to 2005, with prior leadership as a department head at the University of Arkansas and a pomology teaching, extension, and research program at the University of Georgia. International activities include work with New Zealand industry and research collaborators. Dr. Myers received BS and MS degrees from Clemson and a PhD from Ohio State.

DR. EDWARD J. RAY became Oregon State University's president on July 31, 2003. He has led efforts to foster a more seamless P-20 system, working with area school superintendents and higher education leaders in Oregon to enhance the student experience. Dr. Ray helped to usher in a new era of partnership and cooperation among Oregon's public universities. On campuses in Corvallis and Bend, through online degree programs that are top ranked nationally, and through educational programs in Portland and communities across Oregon, Dr. Ray has led Oregon State in making remarkable impacts in teaching, research, and outreach and engagement. While a member of the economics faculty at Ohio State from 1970 to 2003, he served as the economics department chair from 1976 to 1992. He served as associate provost, then senior vice provost and chief information officer from 1992 to 1998, and as executive vice president and provost from 1998 to 2003.

Dr. Ray received his undergraduate degree in mathematics from Queens College (CUNY), graduating cum laude and Phi Beta Kappa. He earned his master's and PhD in economics from Stanford University.

ROGER RENNEKAMP is the recently retired director of The Ohio State University Extension. In that role, he provided administrative leadership to a statewide network of university faculty and staff charged with mobilizing the knowledge resources of the institution for the direct benefit of Ohioans. Prior to coming to Ohio, he served as the associate dean for outreach and engagement in the College of Public Health and Human Sciences at Oregon State University, where he led an effort to build the nation's first health-focused extension program within an accredited school of public health. He also led Oregon State's effort to achieve the Carnegie elective classification for community engagement. Rennekamp is a lifelong champion of land-grant outreach and community engagement. He is a graduate of the Engagement Academy and has written broadly about outreach and engagement throughout his career. He is a founding fellow of the Academy of Community Engaged Scholarship.

SCOTT D. SCHEER is a professor of extension education and the interim chair for the Department of Agricultural Communication, Education, and Leadership in the College of Food, Agricultural, and Environmental Sciences at The Ohio State University. His research focus is on outreach education and theoretical modeling for program development. He also studies youth development in an ecological systems perspective. He has been recognized with awards including a National Communicator Award, Distinguished Service Award, and Extension Outstanding Teaching Award.

RYAN J. SCHMIESING is the vice provost for outreach and engagement and an associate professor in the Department of Agricultural Communication, Education, and Leadership at The Ohio State University. As vice provost, he provides leadership for Ohio State's outreach and engagement portfolio, including serving as the liaison to the university's regional campuses. His research and published work in peer-reviewed journals has focused on volunteer leadership and management, particularly related to university extension education.

BRIAN SNYDER is the executive director of the Initiative for Food and AgriCultural Transformation (InFACT) at The Ohio State University. Previously, he served as the executive director of the Pennsylvania Association for Sustainable Agriculture (PASA), and The William J. Gould Associates, which operates Gould Farm, a 700-acre sustainable farm and mental health treatment facility in Western Massachusetts. He sits on the advisory board of the Resnick Center for Food Law and Policy at UCLA School of Law, has served as president of the Pennsylvania State Council of Farm Organizations, and was the founding cochair of the Food System Integrity Committee of the National Sustainable Agriculture Coalition. He holds two master's degrees, from Harvard University in theological studies and from the University of Massachusetts in business administration.

DAVID J. STALEY is the director of the Humanities Institute at The Ohio State University. He is an associate professor in the Department of History, where he teaches courses in digital history and historical methods. He also holds courtesy appointments in the department of design, where he has taught courses in design history and design futures, and in educational studies, where he has led the "Forum on the University." He is the author most recently of *Alternative Universities: Speculative Design for Innovation in Higher Education* (2019). His other books include *Brain, Mind and Internet: A Deep History and Future* (2014); *Computers, Visualization and History* (2nd ed., 2013); and *History and Future: Using Historical Thinking to Imagine the Future* (2007). He is the lead instructor of the Buckeye Biography, a open online course that explores the 150-year history of The Ohio State University. He serves as host of the *Voices of Excellence in the Arts and Sciences* podcast.

JOSEPH STEINMETZ is the chancellor of the University of Arkansas. Prior to this position, he was the executive vice president and provost and executive dean of the College of Arts and Sciences, both positions at The Ohio State University, as well as the dean of the College of Liberal Arts and Sciences at the University of Kansas. Prior to moving to Kansas, he spent nineteen years on the faculty at Indiana University in the Department of Psychology, including several years as department chair. A behavioral neuroscientist, Steinmetz studied the neurobiology of learning and memory as well as brain correlates of behavioral and cognitive function.

DON STENTA serves The Ohio State University Alumni Association as the assistant vice president for alumni experiences. In this role, he supervises outreach and engagement programs that connect to over 570,000 living alums. He earned his PhD in educational policy and leadership in 2001 from The Ohio State University and also has degrees from Binghamton University and the University of Vermont. Stenta has worked at Ohio State since 1992 in a number of roles with Student Life (Residence Life, Student Activities, Ohio Union, Recreational Sports) and in student services roles at the John Glenn College of Public Affairs. In addition to his role with the Alumni Association, he serves as a distinguished adjunct professor at the Glenn College and as a faculty mentor with the Second-year Transformational Experience Program (STEP).

TAYO SWITZER is an executive coach and consultant working with senior organizational leaders since 2001. He has worked for two Fortune 500 companies as an organization development consultant and from 2008 to 2019 as a leadership coach and consultant at The Ohio State University. Switzer recently joined the business management consulting firm Centric Consulting as a member of their national team focused on leadership, culture and team effectiveness, enterprise-wide change, and organization design. His scholarship focuses on the relationship of leadership and workplace disruption. He is a chapter author in Donna Ladkin's forthcoming second edition of *Rethinking Leadership,* where his practitioner experience is applied to her ontological model of leadership. He received his bachelor of arts in advertising, his master's degree in organization development, and his PhD in leadership and change. He lives in Columbus, Ohio, with his wife and two sons.

JANET WEISENBERGER is the senior associate vice president for research at The Ohio State University, responsible for helping to guide the university's wide range of research activities and to develop and implement new strategic directions for Ohio State's research enterprise. She has maintained an active research program focused on human perception in virtual and augmented reality, most recently in driving simulation. Over the years, her research has been funded from the National Institutes of Health, National Science Foundation, Air Force Office of Scientific Research, Department of Education, Department of Transportation, state of Ohio, industry, and private foundations. Weisenberger is also a professor of speech and hearing science at Ohio State. She received her doctorate in psychology in 1981 from Indiana University, and following ten years as a research scientist and professor of speech and hearing science at Washington University in St. Louis, joined Ohio State's faculty in 1991.

M. SUSIE WHITTINGTON directs the research on *Improving the Cognitive Capacity of Students by Engaging Professors in the Teaching/Learning Process* and has been awarded the Author of the Year and the Distinguished Researcher Award from her professional organizations. She is the junior author of *Methods of Teaching Agriculture* and *Toward Cultural Proficiency.* For nearly thirty years she taught methods of teaching for preservice teachers. Currently she teaches a university-wide general education course, Toward Cultural Proficiency and Advanced Methods of Teaching. Her teaching was awarded the USDA National Teaching Excellence Award and the North American Colleges and Teachers of Agriculture's Teaching Award of Excellence. She was awarded The Ohio State University Alumni Association's Josephine Sitterle Failer Award for Outstanding Service to Students and served on the provost's task force to propose the University Institute for Teaching and Learning. Dr. Whittington directs and mentors the university's Second-year Transformational Experience Program.

DAVID B. WILLIAMS is the dean of the College of Engineering at The Ohio State University. A leader in helping universities drive economic development, he represents Ohio State on the US Business Higher Education Forum, the US (and Global) Council on Competitiveness, and the boards of Lightweight Innovations for Tomorrow, One Columbus, and the Transportation Research Center. Williams was the president of the University of Alabama, Huntsville (2007– 2011). There he served on the boards of the Tennessee Valley Corridor, The US Space and Rocket Center, the Huntsville Chamber of Commerce and the Alabama Business Council. Before Huntsville, Williams was the vice president of research at Lehigh University, where he was on the boards of the NE Pennsylvania Ben Franklin Technology Partnership and The Pennsylvania Life Sciences Greenhouse.

VALARIE WILLIAMS served as the associate dean for outreach and engagement for arts and sciences (2017–2018); as the associate dean for arts (2006–2009) and arts and humanities (2009–2017); and as the executive director of The Arts Initiative (2012–2017), where she led the award-winning Urban Arts Space, the OSU–Royal Shakespeare Company partnership, and the Town and Gown Advisory Committee, promoting collaborations highlighting arts faculty and student scholarship. She is the recipient of grants from the National Endowment for the Arts, Ohio Arts Council, and Greater Columbus Arts Council and has served on the boards of the Dance Notation Bureau, International Council of Kinetography Laban/Labanotation, Alliance for Arts in Research Universities, Opera Columbus, and Columbus Cultural Leadership Consortium. A 1987 Presidential Scholars in the Arts honorable mention recipient in ballet, Williams holds a BFA from The Juilliard School and an MFA and PhD from Texas Woman's University.